Humanitarianism,
Communications
and Change

Simon Cottle
General Editor

Vol. 19

The Global Crises and the Media series is part
of the Peter Lang Media and Communication list.
Every volume is peer reviewed and meets
the highest quality standards for content and production.

PETER LANG
New York • Bern • Frankfurt • Berlin
Brussels • Vienna • Oxford • Warsaw

Humanitarianism, Communications and Change

Simon Cottle & Glenda Cooper, EDITORS

PETER LANG
New York • Bern • Frankfurt • Berlin
Brussels • Vienna • Oxford • Warsaw

Library of Congress Cataloging-in-Publication Data

Humanitarianism, communications and change /
edited by Simon Cottle, Glenda Cooper.
pages cm. — (Global crises and the media; v. 19)
Includes bibliographical references and index.
1. Humanitarianism. 2. Communication. 3. Non-governmental organizations.
I. Cottle, Simon. II. Cooper, Glenda.
BJ1475.3.H865   361.2'6—dc23   2015003306
ISBN 978-1-4331-2527-0 (hardcover)
ISBN 978-1-4331-2526-3 (paperback)
ISBN 978-1-4539-1531-8 (e-book)
ISSN 1947-2587

Bibliographic information published by **Die Deutsche Nationalbibliothek**.
Die Deutsche Nationalbibliothek lists this publication in the "Deutsche
Nationalbibliografie"; detailed bibliographic data are available
on the Internet at http://dnb.d-nb.de/.

The paper in this book meets the guidelines for permanence and durability
of the Committee on Production Guidelines for Book Longevity
of the Council of Library Resources.

Table of Contents

Part Five: Changing Communications and Communication Power

Conclusion

Global Crises and the Media

We live in a global age. We inhabit a world that has become radically interconnected, interdependent, and communicated in the formations and flows of the media. This same world also spawns proliferating, often interpenetrating, 'global crises'.

From climate change to the War on Terror, financial meltdowns to forced migrations, pandemics to world poverty, and humanitarian disasters to the denial of human rights, such crises represent the dark side of the globalisation of our planet. Their origins and outcomes are not confined behind national borders, and they are not best conceived through national prisms of understanding. The impacts of global crises often register across 'sovereign' national territories, surrounding regions and beyond, and they can also become subject to systems of governance and forms of civil society response that are no less encompassing or transnational in scope. In today's interdependent world, global crises cannot be regarded as exceptional or aberrant events only, erupting without rhyme or reason or dislocated from the contemporary world (dis)order. They are endemic to the contemporary global world, deeply enmeshed within it. And so, too, are they highly dependent on the world's media and communication networks.

The series Global Crises and the Media sets out to examine not only the media's role in the *communication* of global threats and crises but also how they can variously enter into their *constitution*, enacting them on the public stage, and helping to shape their future trajectory around the world. More specifically, the volumes in this series seek to: (1) contextualise the study of global crisis reporting in relation to wider debates about the changing flows and formations of world media communication; (2) address how global crises become variously communicated and contested in both so-called 'old' and 'new' media around the world; (3) consider the possible impacts of global crisis reporting on public awareness, political action, and policy responses; (4) showcase the very latest research findings and discussion from leading authorities in their respective fields of inquiry; and (5) contribute to the development of positions of theory and debate that deliberately move beyond national parochialisms and/or geographically disaggregated research agendas. In these ways the specially commissioned books in the Global Crises and the Media series will provide a sophisticated and empirically engaged understanding of the media's changing roles in global crises and thereby contribute to academic and public debate about some of the most significant global threats, conflicts, and contentions in the world today.

In *Humanitarianism, Communications and Change* edited by Simon Cottle and Glenda Cooper, as the editors elaborate in their Introduction, the collection sets out to examine today's rapidly changing media and communications environment against the backdrop of an increasingly globalised and threat-filled world. The collection explicitly examines 'how media and communications, both old and new, and often in complex interaction, enter into humanitarian disasters from the outside in, and inside out, changing humanitarian capabilities and challenging as they do traditional relations of communication power.' The recent explosion of social media, growth in mobile telephony, deployment of remote satellite surveillance, development of crisis mapping and crowd sourcing, SMS (short message service) texting, and new digitalised appeals and donation transfers are all, amongst others, now making their mark on the contemporary field of humanitarianism. The opportunities that these and other technologies afford, as well as their associated risks and the sometimes less than progressive uses to which they can be put, warrant careful scrutiny. But new communications are only one dimension of today's changing global field of humanitarianism.

The nature and forms of humanitarian disasters in a globalising world are also fast changing—and becoming increasingly more complex. The crises of ecology, economy, energy shortages and ideological enmity, for example, often converge in compound conflicts that extend across space, encompassing diverse peoples and places, and can unfold over extended periods of time or even become institutionalised and routinised into 'permanent crises'. The challenges they pose to humanitarian organisations are often acute, sometimes next to intractable. And, disturbingly, they have recently included the direct threat of violence and deliberate killing of humanitarian workers—sometimes malevolently choreographed in front of cameras. These new challenges warrant no less serious recognition—and concerted world responses. New forms of global crises and today's communications ecology it seems have become deeply, sometimes disturbingly, intertwined. And this in a time when the very principles, philosophy, and practices of humanitarianism have become subject to increased external criticism as well as internal reflexivity and critique. Discourses of humanitarianism now increasingly rub up against contending and/or politically augmenting discourses of human rights and human security—not always comfortably.

This collection, then, aims to better understand how contemporary media and communications enter into fields of conflict and humanitarian crises and how they can variously contribute to, condition, or challenge the humanly destructive processes that unfold within them. In an overview introduction and nineteen authoritative and complementary chapters, *Humanitarianism, Communications and Change* examines how humanitarian communications both advance and condition humanitarian practices in the twenty-first century at a time when the nature of humanitarian threats and humanitarianism itself are fast changing. The editors have deliberately included a wide range of reflective accounts and short case studies from experienced humanitarian communications practitioners and journalists as well as more theoretically driven and research-based pieces from academics. These different constituencies have much to offer and much to learn from each other. Both are absolutely necessary, suggest Cottle and Cooper, if we are to arrive at a deeper understanding of the problems and possibilities of humanitarian communications in the decades ahead. It is essential, they say, that expert communication practitioners, who engage at the sharp end of media and communication practices and struggle with real-world problems and dilemmas, and academics privileged with the time and opportunity to gather evidence and reflect on how things could be better conceptualised and theorised, listen attentively to each other. This book aims to both contribute to and facilitate such productive engagement. And, in this way, it aims to render explicit and accessible the latest communication practices and thinking in these practitioner and academic fields and thereby help to leverage improved understanding in the face of pressing global threats and humanitarian needs.

—Simon Cottle, Series Editor

Humanitarianism, Communications, and Change

SIMON COTTLE AND GLENDA COOPER

The world of humanitarian communications is changing fast. From geo-stationary satellites charting disasters from space to social media uploading raw emotions and scenes of devastation on the ground. From 24/7 news channels broadcasting crisis reports live from distant locations to crowd-sourcing and crisis-mapping visualizing local hotspots and sources of relief. From new volunteer technical communities mobilized at their desktop computers anywhere in the world to diasporic communities settled in distant countries donating funds 'back home' via their mobile phones. And from choreographed, videoed acts of inhumanity targeting humanitarian workers to calls for help from disaster survivors and potential atrocity victims fearing for their lives—all uploaded to the world's media via a networked inter-linkage of mobile telephony, social media, Internet, satellites, and overlapping national and international news ecology. These and a host of other communication developments are posing new challenges and new opportunities for those who variously work in, are concerned about, are subject to, or who seek to mobilize humanitarian communications.

Humanitarianism, Communications, and Change sets out to explore today's rapidly changing media and communications environment against the backdrop of an increasingly globalized and threat-filled world. The volume explores how media and communications, both old and new, and often in complex interaction, enter into humanitarian disasters from the outside in, and inside out, changing humanitarian capabilities and challenging as they do traditional relations of communication power. Today the field of humanitarianism also exhibits complexity and change. Across recent decades humanitarianism has become buffeted by real-world processes, challenged by new political discourses and insider critiques, and conditioned by international frameworks of law and human rights (Reiff, 2002; Barnett & Weiss, 2008; Wilson & Brown, 2009; Hannigan, 2012; Oxfam, 2012).

Humanitarianism, it seems, has become not only a contested terrain but also something of a 'sticky signifier', capable of holding on simultaneously to multiple discourses and meanings. These include the relatively elastic, bland, and politically all-encompassing: 'We're all humanitarians now'—individual charity givers, welfare agencies, even democratic states pursuing liberal interventionism and military forces violently securing the same through so-called military humanism. But humanitarianism today also continues to signal and register the historically fixed, prescriptive, and apolitically sealed. Under this humanitarian guise, 'humanitarians' are those who 'voluntarily seek to protect humanity', and they are committed to do so, for example, in the founding terms of the International Committee of the Red Cross (ICRC), through practical actions based strictly on impartiality, neutrality, and independence. This encompassing and elastic quality of humanitarianism has stretched further since its organisational effervescence in the nineteenth century that gave institutional form to Enlightenment sentiments for humanity and compassionate, often religiously inspired, motivations to help others (Wilson & Brown, 2009). Which is not to suggest, of course, that such organised and outwardly directed sentiments did not have their antecedents in the earlier formation of ethical values and just-war principles evolved across millennia (Walzer, 2006; Robertson, 2012; Johnston, 2011).

Most recently humanitarianism, alongside organised churches and other sacral institutions, has lost something of its inviolate institutional standing, becoming subject to public scrutiny, accountability, and media scandals and criticism (Cottle & Nolan, 2007). And yet, at the same time, we also witness the increased propensity of individuals and societies to commit to humanitarianism, to become actively involved in compassionate causes, to give generously, to protest and demonstrate, and to demand action from governments in the face of human suffering around the globe (Cottle & Lester, 2011). Michael Barnett and Thomas G. Weiss (2008), in their scholarly disquisition on humanitarianism, observe two fundamental trends defining its contemporary standing. The first is an observable tendency of increased awareness of and preparedness to respond to those in need around the world.

Radical improvements in information technology and logistical capacity, growing international support for a duty to aid and a responsibility to protect victims, multiplying numbers of relief organisations, and spikes in available resources offer the promise of an enhanced collective capacity to provide war victims with relief, rescue and reconstruction. Although the slow-motion genocide in Darfur and other tragedies are stark reminders that good thoughts and solemn proclamations are never enough, there now exists an international network that can act when and if called. Although these pledges serve as a bitter-sweet reminder of unkept promises, they at least represent the possibility of a more just world order. (Barnett & Weiss, 2008, p. 2)

They also observe a counter-trend at work in the increased dangers and risks posed to civilians in contemporary humanitarian crises as well as to humanitarians seeking to intervene.

Although willing to answer the call, humanitarian organisations have been generally ill-equipped for what they have found: war zones where civilian populations are the intended victims, where access is difficult, where aid workers are in danger of being received as a threat or as a resource to be captured, and where their own physical safety is in doubt. (Barnett & Weiss, 2008, p. 2)

These two trends have prompted a degree of professional introspection within the humanitarian community worldwide, as well as fuelling contradicting celebratory claims for the new humanitarianism and its international capacity to alleviate suffering and right wrongs on the one hand, and more sceptical if not cynical claims on the other about the political hijacking of humanitarianism, its selective recognition of needs around the world and subservience to Western governments, geo-political interests, and funding coffers. Barnett and Weiss, rightly in our view, signal the importance of radical improvements in information technology as a prominent spur in the contemporary flourishing of humanitarianism, though here we would also want to explore further and drill down into the rapidly changing communications environment more widely—and, with the help of our contributors, will do so.

This book also confines its analytical sights on the contemporary, though at the outset we may want to consider how communications have historically been implicated in the development of human societies throughout the ages and, specifically, in relation to the growing recognition of distant others as not so different from ourselves—a fundamental prerequisite in the development of a humanitarian sensibility. This 'expanding human circle' (Ignatieff, 1998; Rifkin, 2009; Singer, 2011) or 'circle of concern' (Nussbaum, 2013) can be traced in respect of a number of historical trajectories; some imposed through the 'leading edge' of Western military conquest and unassailable commerce (Ferguson, 2003; Mann, 2012), others more generic to the history of humankind (Harari, 2014). Notable amongst them are the rise of the first axial age (monotheistic, universalizing) religions (Bellah, 2011; Bellah & Joas, 2012) helping to open up a religio-normative space for critique and social challenge; the origins and formalization of justice and law, both on and off the battlefield (Walzer, 2006; Robertson, 2009; Johnston, 2011; Crowe, 2014); the expansion of city-states, trade, and commerce encouraging associational contacts, mobility, and mutual understanding (Gellner, 1990; Mann, 2012); state formation, war, and the (internal) pacification of violence (Giddens, 1985; Elias, 1994; Pinker, 2012; Goldstein, 2011; Morris, 2014); the Enlightenment—both of science and, importantly, the philosophy of sentiments and sympathy (Pagden, 2013; Mazlish, 2014); and the advances of individualism, democracy, and, of course, humanitarianism, and more recently human rights (Tilly, 2007; Keane, 2009; Hunt, 2007; Ishay, 2008; Robertson, 2012).

To be clear, these developments are not separate from the all-together more historically brutal and violent processes and past struggles that helped spawn them—whether state formation (Elias, 1994; Tilly, 1990), endemic European wars (Morris, 2014), slavery and colonialism (Blackburn, 2011), or the early frontier 'dark side of democracy' (Mann, 2005). There is no comforting teleology or cunning hand of reason gently unfolding through history (Bauman, 1989; Maleševic, 2010). Still, these same destructive forces have simultaneously also contributed to historically expanding ideas and outlooks of a more inclusive 'human circle', both spatially and morally conceived. They are also at work in the historical formation and continuing evolution of ideas of humanitarianism, including the latest debates centering on cosmopolitanism in globalizing media context (Beck, 2006; Robertson, 2010).

Throughout these historical trajectories, the changing forms of media and communications have performed their part, progressively collapsing time and space (Thompson, 1995; Poe, 2011), documenting and representing humanitarian tragedies and atrocities and, more recently, bearing witness to many of them (Zelizer, 2007; Sambrook, 2010; Batchen, Gidley, Miller, & Prosser, 2012; Allan, 2013; Cottle, 2013). It is important to note that media and communications have increasingly given expressive, narrative, and visual form to human suffering as well as humanitarian and human rights responses (Hunt, 2007; Linfield, 2010; Laquer, 2011; Borer, 2012; Balabanova, 2014; Cottle & Hughes, 2015). Increased recognition of distant others, as not so dissimilar to ourselves, and perceived through an increasingly empathetic and compassionate lens (Rifkin, 2009), suggests that contemporary trends in humanitarianism have long historical antecedents and that these are considerably more deeply embedded within the ebb and flow of human societies than any easy idea of technological or communications determinism can accommodate. Nonetheless, media and communications, we suggest, have entered increasingly and sometimes profoundly into the contemporary field of humanitarianism and this warrants sustained, critical attention.

Barnett and Weiss's observation on the second fundamental trend in contemporary humanitarianism, namely, the increased risks and dangers for targeted civilian populations and humanitarians themselves, also, we think, demands serious consideration in respect of the contemporary media and communications environment (Price & Thompson, 2002; Thompson, 2007; Soderlund, Briggs, Hildebrandt, & Sidahmed, 2008). We need to better understand how contemporary media and communications enter into fields of conflict and humanitarian crises and how these can variously contribute to, condition, or challenge the humanly destructive processes that unfold within them. Is it possible that media and communications are sometimes deployed in ways that become complicit with, as much as shine a spotlight on, humanitarian crises and denied humanity? (Cottle, 2009, 2011). When we ask such questions, especially within globalising contexts of interdependency and extensive communication surveillance, the historically elastic nature of humanitarianism again begins to stretch, overlapping with but also rubbing up against more politically inflected notions of human rights (and communication entitlements) and contemporary conditions of 'precarious life' (Butler, 2009) and human insecurity more widely conceived (Duffield, 2001, 2007; Kaldor, 2007).

This book takes its departure from these wider debates. *Humanitarianism, Communications, and Change* first contextualises its key concerns in respect of the changing and historically unprecedented global threats and crises currently gathering momentum in the present and that can be extrapolated into the foreseeable future with profound consequences for humanitarians worldwide. Second, the volume and its contributors focus in on the changing forms, current performance, and future potentials of communications when deployed principally within the field of humanitarianism as well as overlapping fields of human rights and human insecurity. More specifically the book and its contributing authors traverse a range of critical themes. These include the changing nature of communications and human insecurity in a globalised world; the often vexed relationships among charities, communications, and donations; the politics of pity and the poverty of media representations of human suffering; the nexus between humanitarian NGOs and mainstream journalism and the impacts of humanitarian communications on policymaking and publics; as well as expert accounts and reflections on the opportunities and challenges posed by diverse media and communication developments in recent years including, inter alia, video advocacy, 'Big Data', crowd-sourcing, social media, mobile telephony, and new news aggregation and verification practices.

This volume comprises authoritative, cutting-edge reflections and analyses of contemporary humanitarian communications and how these both advance and condition humanitarian practices in the twenty-first century. To this end the editors have deliberately included a wide range of reflective accounts and short case studies from both humanitarian communications practitioners and journalists as well as more theoretically driven and research-based pieces from academics. These different constituencies, we suggest, have much to learn from each other and only together can we arrive at an informed and deeper understanding of the problems and possibilities of humanitarian communications in the years ahead. It is essential, we think, that expert communication practitioners who daily engage with the sharp-end of media and communication practices and encounter real-world problems and dilemmas on the ground, as well as academics privileged with the time and opportunity to gather evidence and reflect on how things could be better conceptualised and theorised, listen attentively to each other. This book aims to both contribute to and facilitate such engagement. To this end it aims to render explicit and accessible the latest practices and thinking in these fields and is directed at understanding today's changing communications environment and leveraging, possibly, its advantages in the face of pressing global threats and humanitarian needs. The remainder of this chapter provides an overview of the book structuration, introducing its five substantive sections and 19 individual chapters.

BOOK STRUCTURE

One of the fundamental premises of the Global Crises and Media Series, of which this volume is part, is that the world today is confronted by a range of unprecedented challenges and threats and that many of these are endemic to, entrenched within, and potentially encompassing of today's globalizing world. Whether climate change, food and water shortages, energy depletion, population movements, and rampant pandemics or new wars and terrorism, these and other issues become played out in and through today's complex media and overlapping communications ecology—an ecology that is itself increasingly globalised and encompassing (Cottle, 2009, 2011). These same global challenges frequently result in humanitarian crises, exacerbate the abuse of human rights, and contribute to the general condition of human insecurity around the globe (Duffield, 2001; 2007; Kaldor, 2007; Beck, 2009; Oxfam, 2012). Part 1, Humanitarianism and Communications in a Changing World, comprises four chapters each of which reflects on these wider changes and the roles and responsibilities of media and communications within them. These themes are then taken up and pursued in more empirically detailed and/or communicatively focused ways across the chapters that follow.

In chapter 1, 'Humanitarianism, Human Insecurity, and Communications: What's Changing in a Globalised World?' Simon Cottle provides an opening overview of how processes of globalisation are contributing to endemic world threats and producing new forms of complex, often overlapping, humanitarian disasters. The chapter also seeks to clearly set out what is distinctive and new about today's reconfiguring communications ecology in the opening decades of the twenty-first century. Both the extensity and intensity of media and communications under conditions of globalization enter into humanitarian crises, he suggests, and do so in six analytically distinct ways: scale, speed, saturation, social relations enfranchisement, surveillance, and the sensory privileging of seeing. Cottle then considers some of the profound ways in which media and communications have become deeply etched into situations of human (in)security broadly conceived, including new forms of war and conflict that threaten civilian populations with extreme violence and generate new forms of humanitarian crises. Finally the chapter turns to the disturbing and malevolent aims that new communications have been put to when deliberately targeting humanitarian workers in callous acts of videoed inhumanity disseminated around the globe. These too are part of the changing humanitarian and communications environment and serve to remind us of the diverse ways in which new communications can become enacted and deployed, from the potentially democratising and enfranchising to the tyrannical and egregiously inhumane.

Chapter 2, 'Media Futures and Humanitarian Perspectives in an Age of Uncertainty and Complexity', by Randolph Kent of the Humanitarian Futures Project, also addresses processes of unprecedented global change and how these, based on current world trajectories, are anticipated to pose new challenges and opportunities for humanitarianism in the future. Developing on a critique of the contemporary media that discerns how there is 'no consistent media attention given to engaging with the public about longer-term threats and opportunities' or the ways in which 'the media, governments, international and non-governmental organisations should be prepared', Kent makes the case for 'media futures' and in ways that can progressively and beneficially engage publics in the global challenges and expected humanitarian crises ahead.

The two chapters that follow, written by two experienced and accomplished communication practitioners, succinctly reflect on the changing nature of humanitarian communications over recent decades. Chapter 3, 'From Buerk to Ushahidi: Changes in TV Reporting of Humanitarian Crises', by Richard Sambrook, charts the changing nature of humanitarian reporting from one of the most iconic moments of humanitarian broadcasting to one of the most exciting online developments in recent times. Written by a former director of BBC Global News, the piece describes the professional impacts of the changing news ecology and new communication technologies from Michael Buerk's seminal news reporting of the 'biblical' Ethiopian famine (filmed by Mohammed Amin) in 1984 to the latest developments of open-access, crowd-sourcing, and mapping such as Ushahidi (Swahili for *testimony* or *witness*) since 2007.

Chapter 4, 'Digital Humanitarianism', by Paul Conneally, also provides an authoritative overview and critical insights and here from the vantage point of Conneally's experience as a public communications manager working for the International Federation of the Red Cross and Red Crescent Societies. In this reflective piece he eloquently discerns the game-changing nature of new digital communications when inserted into the emergency field of competing humanitarian organisations and pressing humanitarian needs. He argues in a challenging but ultimately upbeat mode, stating: "It has always been the elusive ideal to ensure full participation of people affected by disasters in the humanitarian effort." And he concludes, "We now have the tools. We now have the possibilities. There are no more reasons not to do it."

The three chapters that comprise part 2, Cash, Charity and Communication, provide perhaps a slightly less optimistic appraisal when focusing on the humanitarianism field's dependency on the pursuit of donations and charitable giving. Chapter 5, "Give Us Your ****ing Money': A Critical Appraisal of TV and the Cash Nexus', by Glenda Cooper, provides an incisive account of the critical dilemmas and seemingly inescapable compromises that have coloured past emergency relief campaigns and that continue to structure many of those in the present. Not that this underpinning political economy of charitable giving and communications should be conceived in ahistorical or relatively staid and static ways. In chapter 6, 'NGOs, Media, and Public Understanding 25 Years On', Glenda Cooper engages in interview Paddy Coulter, former Head of Media Oxfam, inviting him to analytically reflect on the changing, sometimes vexed, relationships and aims characterising mediated NGO campaigns and appeals.

Finally in this section, chapter 7, '3000 Words that Explain How to Build a Powerful Fanbase, Make Your Message Go Viral, and Raise Millions for Your Cause', written by Liz Scarff from Fieldcraft. Cognisant of and experienced in deploying new media, Scarff reflects on the practicalities and multiple media opportunities that now present themselves when humanitarian organisations seek to win increased public recognition, support, and funding and can do so in and through new social media and aligned modes of communication.

Possibly one of the most contentious and developed areas of academic criticism in respect of the world of humanitarianism is found in its critical analyses of the representations of distant suffering, especially when such images are deployed to appeal to Western publics, arouse sympathies, and/or open purse strings (Cohen, 2001; Sontag, 2003; Chouliaraki, 2006, 2013; Mody, 2010; Borer, 2012; Dogra, 2012; Orgad, 2012; Kennedy & Patrick, 2014). Material inequalities all too often become symbolically replicated in and through such media representations and the latter, so it is often lamented, provide little by way of resources with which to better understand much less challenge prevailing international and structural conditions of oppression and disadvantage. Perhaps it is historically the time to shift from a prevalent 'politics of pity', formed earlier alongside the rise of religiously inspired and compassion-filled humanitarian organisations to a 'politics of recognition' based more on human rights and entitlements—including communication entitlements?

Part 3, The Politics of Pity and the Poverty of Representation, explores the contemporary nature of humanitarian appeals and representations in three distinct critical analyses. Chapter 8, 'International NGOs, Global Poverty, and the Representations of Children', by Nandita Dogra, offers an analysis of INGOs' messages and how these are based on a double representational logic of 'difference' and 'oneness' and does so by focusing specifically on portrayals of children. Her analysis and critique based on systematic empirical analysis concludes that INGOs in and through their representations 'symbolically infantilise the majority world', that the connotations of 'overpopulation' and 'irrationality' associated with the majority world assigns 'blame' to them for their plight, and that these and other myths negate the aims of those INGOs aimed at 'root causes of poverty.'

Chapter 9, 'Underline, Celebrate, Mitigate, Erase: Humanitarian NGOs' Strategies of Communicating Difference', by Shani Orgad, explores how NGO practitioners' frames of thinking and understanding shape their portrayals of difference and otherness—and in varied ways. In particular she identifies four strategies employed by NGOs in their planning and production of communications of international development, humanitarian aid, and human rights abuses. These are 'underlining', 'celebrating', 'mitigating', and 'erasing difference' and they often feature in overlapping and contradictory ways. Her analysis, based on in-depth interviews with NGO professionals as well as communication materials, identifies continuing representational deficits and unresolved tensions in the organisational aims and practices of many humanitarian NGOs.

Finally in this part, chapter 10, 'Solidarity in the Age of Post-humanitarianism', by Lilie Chouliaraki, provides a sophisticated disquisition on the changing politics of solidarity encapsulated in the notion of 'post-humanitarianism'. She argues that solidarity today replaces "common humanity" with "the self" as the privileged morality of solidarity, a wider cultural disposition or orientation that tends toward the narcissistic and which thereby displaces or diminishes the central subject of distant suffering. Her argument is grounded in the interrogation of contemporary humanitarian appeals, celebrity advocacy, and disaster news and in the recognition of the shortfalls of solidarity when conceived in terms of private choice and self-fulfilment.

While the study of media communications and representations has secured sustained, often incisive commentary and critique, the relatively invisible world of NGOs and their impact upon processes of government policymaking, audience reception, and involvement within today's fast-changing media ecology has, with few exceptions, received relatively little in-depth empirical study (Höijer, 2004; Cooper, 2007; Cottle & Nolan, 2007; Fenton, 2009; Waisbord, 2011; Powers, 2014). This is not to say, however, that sometimes-inflated claims based on little if any serious evidence do not also circulate widely, and often go unquestioned. Oft-heard assertions about the "CNN effect", for example, abound both within (self-aggrandising) media and beyond. This easy claim both proposes and presumes strong media causality propelled into the realm of government policy intervention via images of human suffering circulated by 24/7 news media and subsequent public calls that 'something must be done' (Gilboa, 2005; Robinson, 2005; Cottle, 2009, pp. 127–145). It is also heard in the conceptual inverse of the CNN effect, namely the idea of 'compassion fatigue' (Moeller, 1999). In the latter it is precisely the surfeit of media images of human suffering that denudes them of their moral claims upon us, it is said, with such scenes becoming so much wallpaper with little if any resonance for, much less moral compulsion on, ratings-driven news producers (Moeller, 1999) and easily distracted audiences (Tester, 1994). The chapters that follow, each in its own way, secure increased empirical and conceptual traction on these generalising debates and speculative claims.

In part 4, NGO Communications: Impacts, Audiences, and Media Ecology, three chapters examine from their own distinct perspectives some of the complex ways in which humanitarian communications enter into the wider fields of government policymaking, processes of audience reception, and changing media ecology. Chapter 11, 'From Pictures to Policy: How Does Humanitarian Reporting Have an Influence?,' by Suzanne Franks, tackles head-on the arguments of the CNN effect clearly outlaying the arguments for and against advanced by advocates and critics before proceeding to provide unique and critical insights into the case of the 1984 Ethiopian famine. Here the alleged role of news broadcasting at this time in influencing government humanitarian relief policies is critically scrutinized on the basis of insider accounts from the time and marshalled in Franks's insightful analysis.

In chapter 12, 'Learning from the Public: UK Audiences' Responses to Humanitarian Communications', Irene Bruna Seu provides fascinating insights into how audiences actually understand and respond—cognitively, emotionally, and through actions—to communications from humanitarian and international development NGOs. Based on a significant sample of participants taking part in 20 nationwide focus-group discussions who commented on communications from a range of major NGOs, Seu discerns which communications manage to break through the seeming obstacle of 'denial' (Cohen, 2001) and how and why exactly they manage to do so. She explicitly asks and addresses by what mechanisms NGO communications manage to persuade, or not, members of the public to engage with, donate to, or become actively involved in humanitarian causes. This, surely, is a timely and critical concern of interest to us all.

Chapter 13, 'NGO Communications in the New Media Ecology: How NGOs Became the "New(s) Reporters"', by Kimberly Abbott, formerly of the International Crisis Group and now vice president of Communications for World Learning, provides an insider's NGO perspective on the changing nature of NGO communications and practices in respect of the transforming new media ecology. Today, she argues, 'NGO communications experts are posted around the world, tweeting, photographing, producing video documentaries, creating mapping tools, blogging, and supplementing news coverage in parts of the globe from which foreign reporters have retreated.' The chapter describes how 'NGOs have adapted to and become part of the new media ecology' and how they have invented and reinvented their communications strategies, increasingly positioning them as central to their mission. Her chapter reflects in this context on the changing relationships between NGOs and journalists and how, specifically, these formerly distinct worlds have become blurred.

In part 5, Changing Communications and Communication Power, five chapters explore in focused discussions some of the ways in which different communication mediums and practices are transforming communications and relations of communication power. Humanitarian NGOs have themselves become intensely interested in new communications and how, with each subsequent major disaster, these seem to play a more innovative and game-changing role (Nelson, Sigal, & Zambrano, 2011; United Nations Foundation, 2011; Office for the Coordination of Humanitarian Affairs, 2013). The chapters that follow provide close-up observations and reflections on these diverse, frequently interconnecting, communication developments.

Chapter 14, 'Visualizing Human Rights: The Video Advocacy of WITNESS', by Stuart Allan, explores the emergence, associated practices, and hopes and dilemmas of video advocacy in the field of human rights abuses. Specifically he focuses on WITNESS, an NGO launched in 1992 that 'empowers human rights defenders to use video to fight injustice, and to transform personal stories of abuse into powerful tools that can pressure those in power or with power to act'. Through this case-study approach Allan authoritatively reflects on how one of the most vital of human rights, the right to bear witness, has become a site of struggle amongst diverse communities of interest mobilising across globalising communicative networks.

In chapter 15, 'Big Data and Humanitarian Response', by Patrick Meier, former leading member of Ushahidi, considers how the massive outpouring of communicated information during disasters can be as paralyzing to humanitarian response as the absence of information. This "Big Data" (or Big Crisis Data) is being generated, he observes, by the massive volume of user-generated content shared on such social media platforms as Facebook, Twitter, Instagram, and YouTube. Social media, he suggests, 'can accelerate the assessment of disaster damage and needs during disasters', but he also cautions that today the challenge is to make better use of this outpouring of user-generated content, unlocking its relevance for enhanced disaster situational awareness. Meier proposes that microtasking—an example of human computing—can be better deployed to make sense of Big Data during disasters in tandem with machine computing (artificial intelligence) both supporting and accelerating such processes.

Chapter 16, "'Power in my Pocket": How Mobile Citizen Reporting Challenges Digital Elitism', by Alice Klein, underlines how some of the most transformative and democratizing forms of communication are not high-spec, expensive tech but are in fact, and understandably so given the under-resourced contexts in which they become deployed, relatively low-spec, low-cost technologies. Based on her practice and experiences of Radar, an organization committed to working in under-resourced countries and facilitating citizen journalism training, Klein considers the benefits of mobile telephony, including short message servicing (SMS), in contrast to more conventional modes of journalist writing. Careful not to position mobile technology as a simple panacea for all problems relating to decades of inequality in developing countries, her reflections nonetheless support the claim that 'it *can* facilitate participation and in so doing, flip the power dynamic so that citizens become active creators and curators of news, not merely consumers or passive subjects in a correspondence that is carried out around them.'

The focus of news continues in chapter 17, 'New Approaches to Aggregation and Verification in Humanitarian Newsgathering and Coverage', by Claire Wardle. She considers the rapidly transforming and increasingly complex communications environment of news production and how NGOs may now seek to leverage this. Notwithstanding the proliferation of exciting new social media and complex communication environments, she argues that the mass media continue to exercise an important and traditional agenda-setting role, shaping the conversations and priorities of the political and cultural elite. Press officers at humanitarian organisations, as anywhere else, she argues, still crave column inches, airtime, and opportunities for spokespeople to be interviewed. However, for Wardle it is unhelpful to see this as a situation of social media versus mainstream media. Rather she identifies the increasingly important role performed by social media in terms of connecting organisations with mainstream media and allowing content created by NGOs to be used by the media.

Chapter 18, 'Mobile Emergencies, Mobile Phones: The Hidden Revolution', by Imogen Wall and Kyla Reid, provides an expert view on the importance of phones and connectivity for survivors in disasters. It does so against the backdrop of the exponential growth of mobile telephony subscriptions in the developing world. This rarely commented on but remarkable fact is reconfiguring communications in Africa, Asia, and many other parts of the less-developed world. As the authors observe, more people in developing countries now have access to a mobile phone than to basic sanitation or reliable electricity. And 130 million people in the developing world are becoming mobile service users every year, a trend that is expected to continue until at least 2017. We have yet to fully understand the implications of this exponential growth in mobile telephony say Wall and Reid. Specifically, 'Learning how to apply humanitarian principles in this emerging sector, especially the importance of meeting the needs of the most marginalised (in this instance those with no or limited access to services)', they argue, 'is critical for mobile phone companies and humanitarians alike'.

To conclude, chapter 19, 'Humanitarianism, Communications, and Change: Final Reflections', by Glenda Cooper and Simon Cottle, draws together some of the principal themes and debates that have surfaced across the preceding chapters. Here some concluding thoughts on the field of humanitarianism are offered as well as its inevitable and increasing dependency on changing communication networks and technologies in the foreseeable future.

REFERENCES

Allan, S. (2013). *Citizen witnessing*. Cambridge, MA: Polity.

Balabanova, E. (2014). *The media and human rights*. London: Routledge.

Barnett, M., & Weiss, T. (Eds.). (2008). *Humanitarianism in question: Politics, power, ethics*. Ithaca & London: Cornell University Press.

Batchen, G., Gidley, M., Miller, N., & Prosser, J. (Eds.). (2012). *Picturing atrocity: Photography in crisis*. London: Reaktion.

Bauman, Z. (1989). *Modernity and the Holocaust*. Cambridge, MA: Polity.

Beck, U. (2006). *Cosmopolitan vision*. Cambridge, MA: Polity.

Beck, U. (2009). *World at risk*. Cambridge, MA: Polity.

Bellah, R. (2011). *Religion in human evolution: From the Paleolithic to the Axial Age*. Cambridge, MA: Harvard University Press.

Bellah, R., & Joas, H. (Eds.). (2012). *The Axial age and its consequences*. Cambridge, MA: Harvard University Press.

Blackburn, R. (2011). *The American crucible: Slavery, emancipation and human rights*. London: Verso.

Borer, T. A. (Ed.). (2012). *Media, mobilization, and human rights*. London: Zed.

Butler, J. (2009). *Frames of war: When is life grievable?* London: Verso.

Cairns, E. (2012). *Crisis in a New World Order: Challenging the Humanitarian Project*. Oxfam Briefing Paper 158. Retrieved from http://policy-practice.oxfam.org.uk/publications/crises- in-a-new-world-order-challenging-the-humanitarian-project-204749

Chouliaraki, L. (2006). *The spectatorship of suffering*. London: Sage.

Chouliaraki, L. (2013). *The ironic spectator*. Cambridge, MA: Polity.

Cohen, S. (2001). *States of denial*. Cambridge, MA: Polity.

Cooper, G. (2007). *From their own correspondent? New media and the changes in disaster coverage: Lessons to be learnt*. Oxford: Oxford University, Reuters Institute for the Study of Journalism.

Cottle, S. (2009). *Global crisis reporting: Journalism in the global age*. Berkshire, UK: Open University.

Cottle, S. (2011). Taking global crises in the news seriously: Notes from the dark side of globalization. *Global Media and Communication, 7*(2), 77–95.

Cottle, S. (2013). Journalists witnessing disasters: From the calculus of death to the injunction to care. *Journalism Studies, 14*(2), 232–248.

Cottle, S., & Hughes, C. (2015). "The responsibility to protect" and the world's press: Establishing a new humanitarian norm? In J. Hoffmann & V. Hawkins (Eds.), *Communication for peace* (pp. 76–91). London: Routledge.

Cottle, S., & Lester, L. (Eds.). (2011). *Transnational protests and the media*. London: Peter Lang.

Cottle, S., & Nolan, D. (2007). Global humanitarianism and the changing aid-media field: "Everyone was dying for footage." *Journalism Studies, 8*(6), 862–878.

Crowe, D. (2014). *War crimes, genocide, and justice*. New York: Palgrave.

Dogra, N. (2012). *Representations of global poverty*. London: I. B. Tauris.

Duffield, M. (2001). *Global governance and the new wars: The merger of development and security*. London: Zed.

Duffield, M. (2007). *Development, security and unending war*. Cambridge, MA: Polity.

Elias, N. (1994). *The civilizing process*. Oxford: Blackwell.

Fenton, N. (2009). NGOs, New Media and the Mainstream News: News from Everywhere. In N. Fenton (Ed.), *New media, old news: Journalism and democracy in the digital age* (pp. 153–168). London: Sage.

Ferguson, N. (2003). *Empire: How Britain made the modern world*. London: Penguin.

Gellner, E. (1990). *Plough, sword and book*. Chicago: University of Chicago.

Giddens, A. (1985). *The nation-state and violence*. Cambridge, MA: Polity.

Gilboa, E. (2005). The CNN effect: The search for a communication theory of international relations. *Political Communication, 22*, 27–44.

Goldstein, J. (2011). *Winning the war on war*. New York: Dutton, Penguin.

Hannigan, J. (2012). *Disasters without borders*. Cambridge, MA: Polity.

Harari, Y. (2014). *Sapiens: A brief history*. London: Harvill Secker.

Höijer, B. (2004). The discourse of global compassion: The audience and media reporting of human suffering. *Media, Culture and Society, 26*(4), 513–531.

Hunt, L. (2007). *Inventing human rights*. New York: W.W. Norton.

Ignatieff, M. (1998). *The warrior's honour: Ethnic war and the modern conscience*. London: Chatto & Windus.

Ishay, M. (2008). *The history of human rights*. Berkeley: University of California Press.

Johnston, D. (2011). *A brief history of justice*. London: Wiley-Blackwell.

Kaldor, M. (2007). *Human security*. Cambridge, MA: Polity.

Keane, J. (2009). *The life and death of democracy*. London: Simon & Schuster.

Kennedy, L., & Patrick, C. (Eds.). (2014). *The violence of the image: Photography and international conflict*. London: I. B. Tauris.

Laquer, T. (2011). Mourning, pity, and the work of narrative in the making of "humanity." In R. Wilson & R. Brown (Eds.), *Humanitarianism and suffering* (pp. 31–57). Cambridge: Cambridge University Press.

Linfield, S. (2010). *The cruel radiance: Photography and political violence*. Chicago: Chicago University.

Malešević, S. (2010). *The sociology of war and violence*. Cambridge: Cambridge University Press.

Mann, M. (2005). *The dark side of democracy*. Cambridge: Cambridge University Press.

Mann, M. (2012). *The sources of social power. Vol. 1: A history of power from the beginning to AD 1760*. Cambridge: Cambridge University Press.

Mazlish, B. (2014). *Reflections on the modern and the global*. London: Transaction.

Mody, B. (2010). *The geopolitics of representation in foreign news: Explaining Darfur*. Lanham, MD: Lexington.

Moeller, S. (1999). *Compassion fatigue: How the media sell disease, famine, war and death*. New York: Routledge.

Morris, I. (2014). *War: What is it good for?* London: Profile.

Nelson, A., Sigal, L., & Zambrano, D. (2011). *Media information systems and communities: Lessons from Haiti*. Miami, FL: Knight Foundation.

Nussbaum, M. (2013). *Political emotions: Why love matters for justice*. Cambridge, MA: Belknap Harvard.

Office for the Coordination of Humanitarian Affairs (OCHA). (2013). *Humanitarianism in the network age*. United Nations: (OCHA).

Orgad, S. (2012). *Media representation and the global imagination*. Cambridge, MA: Polity.

Pagden, A. (2013). *The Enlightenment: And why it still matters*. Oxford: Oxford University Press.

Pinker, S. (2012). *The better angels of our nature*. London: Penguin.

Poe, M. (2011). *A history of communications*. Cambridge: Cambridge University.

Powers, M. (2014). The structural organization of NGO publicity work: Explaining divergent publicity strategies at humanitarian and human rights organizations. *International Journal of Communication, 8*, 90–107.

Price, M., & Thompson, M. (Eds.). (2002). *Forging peace: Intervention, human rights and the management of media space*. Edinburgh: Edinburgh University Press.

Reiff, D. (2002). *A bed for the night: Humanitarianism in crisis*. London: Vintage.

Rifkin, J. (2009). *The empathic civilization*. Cambridge, MA: Polity.

Robertson, A. (2010). *Mediated cosmopolitanism: The world of television news*. Cambridge, MA: Polity.

Robertson, G. (2012). *Crimes against humanity*. London: Penguin.

Robinson, P. (2005). The CNN effect revisited. *Critical Studies in Media Communication, 22*(4), 344–349.

Sambrook, R. (2010). *Are foreign correspondents redundant?* Oxford: Reuters Institute for Journalism.

Singer, P. (2011). *The expanding circle*. Princeton, NJ: Princeton.

Soderlund, W., Briggs, E., Hildebrandt, K., & Sidahmed, A. (2008). *Humanitarian crises and intervention*. Sterling, VA: Kumarian.

Sontag, S. (2003). *Regarding the pain of others*. New York: Farrar, Straus & Giroux.

Tester, K. (1994). *Media, culture and morality*. London: Routledge.

Thompson, A. (Ed.). (2007). *The media and the Rwanda genocide*. London: Pluto.

Thompson, J. (1995). *The media and modernity*. Cambridge, MA: Polity.

Tilly, C. (1990). *Coercion, capital, and European states, AD 900–1990*. Malden, MA: Blackwell.

Tilly, C. (2007). *Democracy*. Cambridge: Cambridge University Press.

United Nations Foundation. (2011). *Disaster Relief 2.0. Information Sharing in Humanitarian Emergencies*. Retrieved from http://hhi.harvard.edu/sites/default/files/publications/publications%20-%20crisis%20mapping%20-%20disaster%202.0.pdf

Waisbord, S. (2011). Can NGOs change the news? *International Journal of Communication, 5*, 142–165.

Walzer, M. (2006). *Just and unjust wars*. New York: Basic.

Wilson, R., & Brown, R. (Eds.). (2009). *Humanitarianism and suffering: The mobilization of empathy*. Cambridge: Cambridge University Press.

Zelizer, B. (2007). On 'having been there': "Eyewitnessing" as a journalistic key word. *Critical Studies in Media Communication, 24*(5), 408–428.

PART ONE

Humanitarianism and Communications in a Changing World

CHAPTER ONE

Humanitarianism, Human Insecurity, and Communications

What's Changing in a Globalised World?

SIMON COTTLE

The recent explosion of social media alongside the exponential growth in mobile telephony around the world, as well as remote satellite surveillance, crisis mapping and crowd sourcing, SMS (short message service) texting, and new digitalised appeals and donation transfers are just some of the communication developments now making their mark on the contemporary field of humanitarianism.[1] To borrow a phrase from social theorist John Thompson, they are contributing to the 'transformation of visibility' (1995, pp. 119–148) and, as they do so, they are helping to shift traditional relations of communication power (Pantti, Wahl-Jorgensen, & Cottle, 2012). The opportunities that these technologies afford, as well as their associated risks and the less-than-progressive uses to which they can sometimes be put, demand careful attention. But this is only one half of a globally spinning coin. On its other side, the nature and forms of humanitarian disasters in a globalising world are also fast changing, and these warrant no less serious recognition—and concerted world responses. And, as we shall consider, new forms of global crises and today's communications ecology have become deeply, sometimes disturbingly, intertwined.

This chapter sets out first to briefly situate the changing nature of humanitarian disasters in globalised context before, second, offering some general observations on what exactly is distinctive about today's reconfiguring communications ecology in the opening decades of the twenty-first century and how it matters within the field of humanitarianism. Third, we then consider some of the new ways in which media and communications are becoming deeply etched into situations of human (in)security more broadly conceived, including new forms of war and conflict that threaten civilian populations with extreme violence. Here the discussion turns to how situations of globally produced human (in)security and violation of human rights are not only *mediated* or reported but increasingly *mediatized*, that is, shaped or enacted in and through media and communications. In today's globally expansive and encompassing media and communications ecology this can assume different forms, some of them in sympathy with humanitarian and democratizing impulses, others malign and dehumanizing—including the deliberate targeting of humanitarian workers and journalists.

My principal argument throughout is that it is imperative that we keep both the changing nature of humanitarian disasters and their interconnection with deep-seated processes of global change clearly in view alongside today's rapidly transforming communication ecology. This is no time for lop-sided media-centrism, much less technological (communications) determinism, but it is a propitious moment to address how today's communication ecology, incorporating both 'old' and 'new' media, enters into the course of globally endemic humanitarian disasters and contexts of human (in)security and affects them from the inside out and outside in.

HUMANITARIAN CRISES AND DISASTERS...
IN A GLOBALIZED WORLD

Humanitarian crises and major disasters around the world are on the increase and infused by a number of global 'mega-trends'. These include environmental despoliation and climate change, world poverty and enforced migration, economic interdependency and financial crises, and new forms of conflict and war—including new wars in failed and failing states, transnational terrorism and Western (militarised) interventionism (Global Humanitarian Forum, 2009; Cairns, 2012; UNISDR, 2012). Many so-called natural disasters today can be more accurately described as "unnatural disasters" given their determination by complex, systemic social forces now shaping human habitats and human life chances, ecology, and climate around the globe. Disasters can also be seen as unequally distributed hazards. "Natural disasters" have long hidden their "socialized nature" (Giddens, 1990) and unequal impacts around the globe (poorly constructed buildings, not earthquakes, for example, kill people, and elaborate risk-reduction strategies invariably cost money). In this sense natural "hazards only become disasters when they exceed a community's ability to cope" (Holmes & Niskala, 2007, p. 2; see also United Nations Environmental Program, 2007).

The outbreak of the deadly Ebola Virus Disease (EVD) in West Africa is a case in point. At the time of writing (November 2014) the World Health Organization

(WHO) estimates there have been more than 10,000 suspected cases and nearly 5,000 deaths, with hospitals in Guinea, where the outbreak first began, as well as those in neighbouring Liberia, Sierra Leone, and Nigeria struggling to cope with this highly contagious disease. U.S and British medical workers who contracted the disease have been speedily airlifted home in specially charted, carefully quarantined, flights to receive the best possible medical attention including the very latest drugs. They have fared considerably better than their West African counterparts. Moreover, not all disasters, whether natural or unnatural, automatically find prominent news exposure, and thereby encourage donor funds for specific disaster relief operations.

The vast majority of "uninsured lives" in the South, it seems, are not only cheap (Duffield, 2007) but also un-newsworthy. This is often explained in terms of impinging geo-political interests, national cultural outlooks, and the operation of foreign news values (Benthall, 1993; Galtung & Ruge, 1981; Hawkins, 2008; Moeller, 1999; Seaton, 2005)—factors institutionalised and professionally routinised in today's journalistic "calculus of death" (Cottle, 2009a, 2013). The latter provides an institutionally sanctioned and professionally accepted disposition to humanitarian situations around the world. One where correspondents and other news workers select and differentially report disasters according to historical factors, cultural proximity, and geo-political and national interests alongside the crude operation of body count thresholds and availability of dramatic visuals (Cottle, 2013).

Today humanitarian disasters around the world need to be situated within a broader conceptualization of global crises (Cottle, 2011) and what Ulrich Beck refers to as global "manufactured uncertainty" (1992) and, in a post–9/11 world, "manufactured insecurity" (Beck, 2009). In addition to anthropogenic climate change and global market meltdowns, the threats now confronting human populations include exacerbating crises of water, food, and energy shortages; pandemics; forced migrations; intensified ethnic conflicts; state human rights violations, as well as the global insecurity of transnational terrorism and new forms of Western "risk-transfer" warfare (Abbott, Rogers, & Sloboda, 2006; Bauman, 2007; Amnesty International, 2009; Mousseau, F., & Bailey, 2009; Taylor & Shuemer-Cross, 2009; Cairns, 2012; Rifkin, 2009; Shaw, 2005)—the latter increasingly positioning humanitarian workers in harm's way.

In a globalised world we need to develop concepts of humanitarian disasters that accurately map onto the endemic and encompassing nature of many of today's global crises (Cottle, 2011). Evidence for globally produced disasters and catastrophes is not difficult to find. It is documented, for example, in the International Panel on Climate Change (IPCC) (2007, 2013) reports, Kofi Annan's Global Humanitarian Forum's (2009) calculations of 300 million people now being seriously affected by climate change each year, including 300,000 deaths; the precariousness of interlocking global financial systems, periodic melt-downs, and their devastating impacts on developing countries (United Nations, 2009); the alarming rise of weather-borne (Magrath, 2007) and vector-borne diseases (World Health Organization, 2007); and the world audits of human rights abuses and their interlinkage with these and other forms of world crises (Amnesty International, 2009).

To add to this global complexity, disasters and crises are not necessarily self-contained but often interlock with and/or mutate into related crises and humanitarianism (Ahmed, 2010; Held, Kaldor, & Quah, 2010; Cottle, 2011). Changing climate, we know, can exacerbate competition for land, water, and food; it can create conditions for civil strife and political instability and thereby produce issues of national and international security, including forced migrations of eco- and political refugees (International Institute of Strategic Studies, 2007) and human security more widely (Kaldor, 2007).

A complex of factors contributed to the global food crisis of 2008. These included increased demand for grain-intensive meat production in developing economies such as China and India; poor harvests exacerbated by climate change in others; the production of biofuels displacing food production in the South to support climate change policies in the North; and rising world energy costs. Together these contributed to a marked increase in world food prices and a global food crisis that impacted the world's poor and led to food riots in scores of cities around the world (Taylor, & Shuemer-Cross, 2009).

In a fast-moving, interconnected, and globalized world, the spread of influenza and deadly diseases such as Ebola have also become more difficult to contain and control. More people now live in cities than at any other time in history (more than 50%, and by 2050 this is expected to grow to 70%). In crowded and squalid urban conditions diseases can easily become incubated and spread rapidly. More people are also on the move than at any previous time in human history—for security, for work or for leisure. They move within and across national borders and continents. Increasingly many of them have become internally displaced through war, conflicts, and the environmental impacts of climate change, forcing them to inhabit places that render them vulnerable to increased dangers and risks including outbreaks of disease and epidemics. And the speed and volume of contemporary transport systems, principally aviation, now facilitates this mobility of vast numbers of people around the planet—and in hours not days. The International Air Transport Association (IATA), for example, estimates that in 2013 more than 8 million people flew on average every day with more than 3 billion passenger flights across the year (IATA, 2013). Not only does this massive volume of air traffic contribute to the world's unsustainable carbon footprint, it also deposits passengers around the world in major, crowded cities and before any of them may be aware they're carriers of possibly lethal contagious disease. The threats posed by new global pandemics today are all too real and, according to the World Health Organization (WHO), pose one of the principal threats to global health security. It is important, therefore, to keep the multidimensional and mutating character of global crises and their humanitarian disasters clearly in view if we are to avoid dissimulating the complex global interconnections and inequalities involved (Calhoun, 2004). And so too, of course, we must also aim to better understand and make use of the increasing centrality and capability of media and communications within their unfolding course and conduct, discussed next.

COMMUNICATING HUMANITARIAN DISASTERS: WHAT'S NEW?

It is worth remembering given the current buzz about 'new' communications that the involvement of media communications in disasters is far from new. Throughout history we know that communication technologies have been used to convey information and accounts of disaster events and their impacts, progressively collapsing both space and time. The rise of printing and news sheets in England in the middle of the fifteenth century and the development of public postal services in Europe in the seventeenth century, the construction of rail networks, then telegraph systems in the United States in the 1840s, followed by the laying of underwater telegraphic cables linking Britain and India in the 1860s, and Marconi's experiments with radio transmission in the late 1890s that led to radio broadcasting in the 1920s, all, for example, progressively extended the range and speed by which calamitous events could be communicated to others (Flichy, 1995; Thompson, 1995; Rifkin, 2009; Briggs & Burke, 2002). And before these modern means of communication, foreign envoys, travelling merchants, and seafarers would have imparted by word-of-mouth accounts of the same, rhetorically embellished no doubt to enthral listeners and draw a crowd. More than 300 years ago Daniel Defoe (1704) published his journalistic account of the Great Storm of 1703 and the loss of more than 8,000 souls in Britain, and based this on first-hand accounts of eyewitnesses. Reports of disasters, including those based on personal testimonies and graphic accounts, are also, it seems, not entirely new.

Nonetheless there is something new in today's communication environment and how this enters into contemporary humanitarian disasters. Earlier historical communication trends have progressively collapsed both time and space but these trends have now reached a point where communications can reach deep inside disasters, shaping their subsequent unfolding and forms of local-global response as they do so. The *extensity* and *intensity* of media and communications in disasters, I suggest, is unparalleled and in at least six analytically distinguishable ways, each impacts the field of humanitarianism. Many could hardly have been imagined only a decade or so ago.

1. **Scale.** Significant parts of today's media and communications ecology now exhibit extensive scale in terms of their encompassing global reach, which, since the advent of geo-stationary satellites and the Internet, can communicate images and information about humanitarian disasters and catastrophes simultaneously to vast swathes of the world's population (Allan & Thorsen, 2009; Thorsen & Allan, 2014; Rai & Cottle, 2010). It is estimated, for example, that more than a billion people tuned in around the world to watch live on their television screens the rescue efforts of the Chilean authorities to save 33 miners trapped beneath ground in the 2010 San Jose copper mine disaster (Jiménez-Martínez, 2014).

2. **Speed.** The accelerated speed of media and communications around the globe has now also reached a point in which time has effectively become collapsed when transmitting 'live' or in near real-time images, speech, and text to globally dispersed audiences and potential relief organisations. Indeed, virtual time in the context of impending disasters may even be reversed with new means of predictive visualisation, charting the anticipated course of hurricanes or the consequences of melting ice caps, and so on before they happen. Inevitably the rapid speed of communications when reporting unfolding events also grants emphasis to immediacy and experience over analysis and deliberation which, in turn, can contribute to the undermining of traditional practices of information management (see Cottle & Nolan, 2007; Gowing, 2009).

3. **Saturation.** The increasing saturation of human society with universalising means of communication such as mobile phones (see below) contributes to the establishment of normative expectations about communications access and availability and the preparedness of everyone concerned to use them in disaster situations, including the survivors of disasters, the formerly communications disenfranchised (see Nelson, Sigal, & Zambrano, 2011; United Nations Foundation, 2011; Cairns, 2012; OCHA, 2013).

4. **Social relations enfranchisement.** These same universalising technologies also communicatively expand and enfranchise disaster social relations, increasingly incorporating survivors as well as relief workers and those responsible for averting disasters or ameliorating their effects, and reconfiguring the communications field as they do so. The development of voluntary technical communities (VTCs), monitoring and detailing for free and from afar destroyed infrastructure via remote-sensing satellite images overlaid on pre-disaster maps, for example, rapidly compiles composite pictures of where resources are still available within disaster areas and directing both NGOs on the ground and victims in need of where to go (United Nations Foundation, 2011).

5. **Surveillance.** The increasing availability of new 'bottom-up', 'many-to-many', 'interactive' communications alongside established 'top-down', 'few to many', 'one way' communications, with both now facilitating communications beyond as well as within national borders, all significantly enhance the surveillance capacity of contemporary media as does, important to note, satellite monitoring sponsored by civil society actors and governments. This renders attempts by states to keep major disasters 'out of sight' and 'out of political mind' much more difficult than in the recent past, as was demonstrated, for example, by the haemorrhage of video images and eyewitness accounts from Burma following Hurricane Nargis in 2008, in comparison, say, to the news blackout imposed by the Chinese authorities following the Tangshan earthquake in 1976, one of the deadliest in human history.

6. **Seeing.** It is important to realize that contemporary media and communications also provide unprecedented opportunities for us to not only read and to hear about but also to see disasters, sometimes as they unfold 'live' on screens in front of us. This enhanced capacity for the communication of dramatic visuals, both moving and still also provides enhanced opportunities to 'bear witness' to disasters around the world and their human consequences—a prerequisite it seems for empathetically informed humanitarian response (Chouliaraki, 2006; Laqueur, 2009; Rifkin, 2009; Cottle, 2013).

In these six analytically distinct albeit often condensed characteristics of *scale, speed, saturation, social relations' enfranchisement, surveillance,* and *seeing,* earlier historical spatial-temporal trends of media and communication have reached new global heights of extensity and intensity. In such ways today's media and communication environment is not only deeply entwined within wider society but, inevitably, becomes infused inside many contemporary disasters and shapes their unfolding trajectory and global responses. As these six characteristics begin to suggest, however, it is not helpful to view communication technologies simply as external technologies or as communication adjuncts to society. From the printing press to the Internet and beyond, they are in fact profoundly entwined within the fabric of social life and constitutive of processes of societal change—features no less relevant, as we shall discuss, in the context of humanitarian disasters and in contexts of human (in)security more broadly.

To take media and communications seriously and to explore their involvement in humanitarian disasters, therefore, is not to presume a simple media causality or technological determinism, but rather to propose that we begin to see how today's media ecology is interwoven within social relations and the conduct of society more generally. As John Thompson argues, 'In a fundamental way the use of communication media transforms the spatial and temporal organization of social life, creating new forms of action and interaction, and new modes of exercising power, which are no longer linked to the sharing of a common locale' (1995, p. 4). Crucially, this re-ordering of time and space by media and communications contributes to the 'transformation of visibility' that in turn unsettles traditional social relations and the exercise of hierarchical political power (Thompson, 1995, pp. 119–148). This more socially embedded, less technologically fixated view of media and communications and the 'transformation of visibility' as constitutive rather than simply causative in social life, has particular relevance I think for understanding humanitarian disaster communications today and may even contribute to the wider care for distant others and the 'democratization of responsibility' (Thompson, 1995, p. 263).

Consider, for example, how the following contribute to the 'transformation of visibility' of disasters today. Geospatial remote-sensing satellites now document and help to verify humanitarian disasters and human rights abuses in different conflict zones, whether Darfur (2004–2005), Sri Lanka (2009), South Sudan (2012), or Syria (2013) and Iraq (2014), and routinely map the shifting progress and severity of droughts, hurricanes, forest fires, and melting glaciers.

The recent proliferation of 24/7 television news channels around the world (Rai & Cottle, 2010) has expanded the capacity to circulate images of disasters and human suffering from distant locations, and global news providers such as CNNI and BBC World now frequently commission or produce their own film reports on distant disasters (Volkmer, 1999; Cottle & Rai, 2010; Robertson, 2010). National broadcasters, for their part, have access to significant resources and the latest technologies which enabled, for example, Japan's NHK to put helicopters into the air and film and broadcast live the 2011 tsunami that brought a wave of death and destruction to communities along the country's Pacific coast.

Ordinary people and citizen journalists around the world now routinely use videophones and social media, recording images of the drama and despair of cataclysmic events and uploading them to the Internet and YouTube (Allan, 2006; Allan & Thorsen, 2009; Pantti et al., 2012; Thorsen & Allan, 2014) or forwarding them directly to the world's news media for wider circulation. Open access crowdsourcing technologies such as Ushahidi (Swahili for 'testimony') dynamically map and visualise the moving hotspots of disaster.

And, on a planet of 7.1 billion people with an estimated 6.8 billion mobile phone subscriptions, more than 4.5 billion are now in the disaster-prone developing world (ITU, 2011, 2013). This relatively unremarked but profound revolution in communications facilitates early disaster warnings as well as the communication of public health messages and survivors' needs, as was so evidently documented, for example, in the Haiti earthquake of 2010 (Nelson et al., 2011; United Nations Foundation, 2011; Cairns, 2012; OCHA, 2013).

In all these and other ways, today's media and communications are undoubtedly contributing to Thompson's 'transformation of visibility' and, as they do so, they are complexly entering into the course and conduct of disasters (Pantti et al., 2012). There is also a seventh analytically distinguishable way in which media and communications are entering into the humanitarian field however, and this develops on both the new forms of media and communications surveillance and seeing capacity afforded by these new technologies and ongoing processes of globalization. It centres on issues of *human (in)security*. 'Human security' says Mary Kaldor, 'is about the security of individuals and communities rather than the security of states, and it combines both human rights and human development' (2007, p. 182). This, as we shall hear, exhibits both benign as well as malign communications dimensions when confronting the extreme threats and mortal violence that confront population groups in the twenty-first century—including, increasingly, humanitarian workers. This warrants recognition and further discussion.

HUMAN (IN)SECURITY AND MEDIATIZED VIOLENCE

The human insecurity and humanitarian catastrophes that result from new forms of violent conflicts and warfare cannot be seen as aberrations only, as simply a result of excess violence. According to Kaldor they are endemic to the nature of new wars, their goals, methods, and means of funding (2006, pp. 95–118). New wars take place in failed and failing states and are usually defined by their extreme violence: the deliberate targeting of non-combatants, use of systematic terror, and forced expulsions ('ethnic cleansing'). They can be situated and theorized in global context (SIPRI, 2004; Duffield, 2001; Kaldor, 2006; Project Ploughshares, 2007) where their global entanglement 'challenges the distinction between the "internal" and the "external"' (SIPRI, 2004, p. 1). When global economic forces exacerbate processes of state failure and dissolution and prompt shadow economies, illicit global transactions, criminal and terrorist networks, and new forms of social violence (Duffield, 2001, 2007; Kaldor, 2006; UN, 2009), these are forms of global enmeshing and response—from the inside out. When military intervention, under the guise of humanitarian motives ('military humanism') and humanitarian interests allied to military and state objectives ('humanitarian war'), come to characterize Western forms of intervention, as they have in recent decades (Macrae, 2002; Rieff, 2002; Duffield, 2007; de Waal, 2007; Weiss, 2007; Barnett & Weiss, 2008), those on the receiving end become enmeshed within the surrounding regime of global power—from the outside in.

But new wars are not only globally enmeshed in the ways noted. When subject to global media surveillance, their violence can reverberate vicariously beyond the killing zone. Global media surveillance has become, I suggest, more than simply monitoring and information conveyance—more than a matter of cognition. In a world in which the capacity to bear witness to human suffering anywhere in the world has become technologically feasible, the potential for global surveillance can itself become implicated within those very same events, in profound but sometimes disturbing ways. Four principal ways are identified below, each of which enters into the contemporary field of human insecurity and humanitarianism.

First, in a world progressively sensitized to human rights now upheld by international institutions and frameworks of law (Hunt, 2007; Robertson, 2012), the imperative to report atrocities and collective human rights abuses around the world finds wide normative support (Weiss, 2007; Kaldor, 2003, 2007; Balabanova, 2014). This has been deepened and sometimes even advanced by the historical formations of journalism that manage to index the expanding ethical horizons of civil societies, including the rise of humanitarianism and human rights and that position journalists and correspondents inside the 'eye of the storm'. With an institutionalised, professional commitment to the 'public's right to know' growing numbers of staffers and freelancers in recent years have sought to report from the killing zone of conflicts around the world. And far too many of them have paid with their lives (Cottle, Mosdell, & Sambrook, forthcoming). The Committee to Protect Journalists (CPJ) documents 70 cases of journalists killed (motive confirmed) and a further 25 (motive unconfirmed) and 4 related media worker deaths in 2013 alone, the majority covering news beats of politics, war, and human rights (CPJ, 2014).

Ideas of inviolable national sovereignty historically embedded since the Treaty of Westphalia in 1648 have also become qualified in this *longue durée* of history and alongside the (faltering) march of humanitarianism and human rights. Both the United Nations General Assembly and the UN World Summit of 2005, for example, endorsed the 'Responsibility to Protect' (R2P) doctrine (Weiss, 2007; Barnett & Weiss, 2008; Evans, 2008). With its injunction to all nation-states to intervene, and with military force if expedient, to protect populations from the four atrocity crimes of genocide, war crimes, ethnic cleansing, and crimes against humanity, the R2P doctrine is fundamentally about securing human security.

In the recent post–Cold War era this 'new humanitarianism' (Reiff, 2002; Barnett & Weiss, 2008) recognizes human insecurity and human rights abuses as global concerns. They can be construed as 'global crises' even when the direct political-economic interests of major state powers are not directly involved, because there is now 'a worldwide *perception* of large-scale violations of life and globally legitimate principles' (Shaw, 1996, p. 156; Ignatieff, 1998). Media surveillance of human rights abuses around the globe has thereby become historically infused with a moral imperative 'to do something', registering both institutionalized norms and a wider civic culture of humanitarianism. This is not a rehashed 'CNN effect' claim based on the dubious causality too easily assumed to run directly from scenes of human suffering to public outrage to foreign policy response and military intervention (Gilboa, 2005; Robinson, 2005). But it does point to the more complex and constitutive role of global media surveillance within an increasingly human rights–aware world. Here global news media can potentially perform important roles in representing the three principal aspects of the UN's fledgling commitment to the 'responsibility to protect': the responsibility to prevent, the responsibility to react, and the responsibility to rebuild (Weiss, 2007, p. 101; see also Price & Thompson, 2002; Cottle & Hughes, 2015).

Second, global media surveillance is not only confined to new wars and the new humanitarianism, it also conditions the 'new Western way of war' (Shaw, 2005). In modern Western wars, argues Martin Shaw, the physical risks of war are transferred from governments to the military, and, because of the political damage incurred by news reports of military casualities and returning body bags, military risks become transferred to civilian non-combatants (via high-altitude bombing, in contrast to boots on the ground, for example) (see also Tumber & Webster, 2006). This helps to explain the increased incidence of civilian casualties, so-called collateral damage, in contemporary Western wars in contrast to the deliberate use of violence targeting non-combatants in new wars—though important in both, civilians are exposed to increased deadly violence. Shaw's thesis of risk-transfer war thus recognizes the enhanced importance of the news media in managing public perceptions of war as well as the added risks to the political legitimacy of states, politicians, and military when war is subject to global news surveillance.

The significance of global news surveillance is not exhausted, however, with reference to the global spotlighting of human rights abuses, humanitarian actions, or even the conditioning impacts exerted in the "new Western way of war"— important as these are. Third, some wars and conflicts remain largely invisible within the world's news media, notwithstanding the advanced development of the technological means of recording and disseminating news images around the world (AlertNet, 2009; Hawkins, 2008). But even here when lack of media visibility renders some wars and conflicts into "hidden wars" and "forgotten disasters," the latter are not necessarily untouched by the technological capability for global media surveillance—such is the universalizing impact of today's potential media surveillance. If new wars are characterized by endemic, extreme violence targeting non-combatants in contravention of international humanitarian law and universal human rights, those who seek to commit such acts will generally (though not always, as discussed below) seek to do so out of sight of the world's news cameras (Rwanda, Srebrenica, Aceh, DRC, Darfur).

It is for this reason, in part, that the deliberate targeting of journalists and humanitarian workers by insurgents and combatants has increased over recent years with perpetrators seeking the cloak of invisibility for their inhumane acts including atrocity. In globally mediated times, the news media, as paradoxical as it may sound, can thereby influence the field of violence when both reporting it as well as when they do not. In today's mediated world, the absence of the world's media and news cameras unwittingly becomes complicit with the murderous practices of contemporary warfare and, by its collective silence—its 'silent moral scream'—facilitates war's most inhumane expressions. In today's news environment of potential global surveillance, 'proper distance' (Silverstone, 2007) shrinks necessarily, if repugnantly, to the killing zone. The rise of social media, citizen journalists, and combatants equipped and capable of recording scenes of impending and unfolding atrocity and quickly disseminating them via the Internet to the 'outside' world fundamentally renders any future claim that 'we did not know' implausible. Regrettably, such communications though necessary cannot in themselves be taken as sufficient to guarantee, post-Holocaust, post-Rwanda, post-Srebrenica, that the world's repeated pledge to 'never again' finally comes true (Sri Lanka, Syria, South Sudan).

Fourth, there is one further, morally repugnant, way in which contemporary media have entered into the field of humanitarianism (and journalism) practice. This deliberately turns the spotlight onto the humanitarians and journalists themselves, forcing them to become both spectacle and story. Two dreadful incidents, ten years apart, underline what's at stake. On October 19, 2004, Margaret Hassan, director of Care International based in Bagdad, was kidnapped. Her captors, calling themselves 'an armed Islamic group', soon released a video of her in which she was visibly distressed. A further video was then released to Al-Jazeera. This video was so distressing the global broadcaster refused to screen much of it. According to those who have seen it, the first part showed Margaret Hassan pleading for her life before suddenly fainting. A bucket of water was then poured over her as she lay on the floor. She was then forced to stand and, crying, again pleaded for her life. Her captors threatened to hand her over to Abu Musab al-Zarqawi, (the leader of Al-Qaeda Iraq), who had earlier beheaded Kenneth Bigley on October 7, a British civil engineer working in Iraq. (His colleagues Jack Hensley and Eugene Armstrong had also been kidnapped, and earlier brutally murdered. Videos of their killings had been posted on websites and blogs and before that videos recording their pleas for help and scripted criticisms of the British and U.S governments' intervention.) Margaret Hassan's sister also made an emotional media plea for her release following her sister's distressed video that was broadcast and publicised widely. She emphasised how her Irish-born sister was now an Iraqi, having married an Iraqi man, and how she had selflessly dedicated her life to helping the Iraqi people. Her appeal evidently fell on deaf ears and dead hearts. A further video was passed to Al-Jazeera, this time of her execution. She had been blindfolded and shot in the back of the head and died on the second attempt as she slumped onto a plastic sheet (Burke, 2004; Fisk, 2008).

Ten years on, in August 2014, the Islamic State of Iraq and Al-Sham (ISIS) captured U.S. journalist James Foley. In a chilling video he was beheaded in the desert in an orange jump suit in front of a camera, terrible images that were subsequently posted to the world via the Internet, though quickly censored by most websites. The video was preceded by the words of a British jihadist extolling the virtues of the Islamic State and challenging both the U.S. and Western governments and condemning their interventionist actions. Over the following two months Steven Sotloff, another U.S. journalist, was also paraded on video by the same group and similarly killed. Two British aid workers, David Haines, and then later Alan Henning, former taxi driver and volunteer aid worker, followed. Video appeals by friends and families and condemnatory statements by politicians and religious leaders have become an established part of the visual iconography surrounding these staged, choreographed, videoed killings. Across the ten-year period since the killing of Margaret Hassan it is not only high-profile Westerners who have been targeted for publicity purposes however; scores of local NGO workers and journalists have been targeted, kidnapped, and killed, a wider and disturbing trend considered further below.

In these crude DIY 'shock and awe' video productions, the iconic and symbolic become merged in an inhumane spectacle designed to augment their chilling effects. These repugnant images are produced to shock and assault most, though clearly not all, moral sensibilities and they communicate a dreadful message to aid workers, foreign nationals, and their countries of origin. Such calculating 'violent symbolism'—staged, choreographed, and disseminated around the world—functions as both weapon and tactic in the new warfare. As Michael Ignatieff observes: 'Terrorists have been quick to understand that the camera has the power to frame a single atrocity and turn it into an image that sends shivers down the spine of an entire planet. This gives them a vital new weapon' (2004, p. 2).

This is 'image wars', where violence and war is enacted and conducted in and through media and communications as well as being communicated and represented by them. In so far as this both prompts and shapes the practices of violence, as it most certainly does, so this becomes an example of *mediatized conflict* (Cottle, 2006, pp. 143–166). In mediatized war and conflicts, then, the involvement of media and communications becomes actively and performatively heightened, becoming disturbingly implicated in the acts of violence themselves. It appears that the historical 'transformation of visibility' (Thompson, 1995) facilitated by new media and communications has thus taken a new and discernibly malevolent turn in the field of mediated human (in)security and conflict.

Such violent, inhumane, mediatized productions are constructed in a global context of political and religiously inspired enmity and hatred and often for local-global audiences. They are part of asymmetric warfare. They cannot simply be taken in technologically determinist fashion as manifestations of the latest new communication technologies but as expressive of a dangerous turn in world affairs where humanitarians (as well as journalists) have become increasingly perceived as working at the behest of Western governments and/or colluding with them. Humanitarian-aid spending by Western donor governments, according to the Global Humanitarian Assistance Report (2014) has risen to nearly 75% over the past ten years. Aid has also become increasingly militarised. When the U.S military and other coalition forces distributed aid in Afghanistan as a means of encouraging local support they also thereby compromised the claimed independence and political neutrality of NGOs working there. The proposed benign use of surveillance drones by humanitarians has also similarly become compromised by their preceding deadly military use. Above all perhaps, the U.S-led 'War on Terror' has precipitated the world's political tectonic plates to shift dangerously and injuriously for populations living in Afghanistan and Iraq and, following the Arab Spring, Libya and Syria, but also more widely in neighbouring countries and surrounding regions. This political ferment has seen the opening up of the traditional schism between Sunni and Shia Muslims and the rise of fundamentalist Islam pitted against the West and all those who are thought to represent or collude with its interests, including humanitarian workers. The Director of Operations for the UN's Office for the Coordination of Humanitarian Affairs (OCHA), John Ging, sums up well the changed global context of human insecurity confronting humanitarians: "More and more we're seeing parties to conflicts around the world ignore the rules of war to achieve a political end—directly targeting civilians, carrying out collective punishment, inciting ethnic violence, impeding the delivery of lifesaving humanitarian supplies to affected people and attacking humanitarian actors themselves" (Ging, cited in Whiting, 2014, p. 1).

Humanitarian Outcomes (2014) documents 460 aid workers deliberately subjected to violence in 2013 (155 killed, 171 seriously wounded, 134 kidnapped). As I write, 79 aid workers have died in the first eight months of 2014, more than the whole of 2012. A total of 251 separate attacks involving 460 humanitarian workers occurred in 30 countries in 2013, but three quarters of these took place in five countries: Afghanistan, Syria, South Sudan, Pakistan, and Sudan. Shootings and kidnappings remain the most prevalent types of major violence seen in these attacks, followed by assaults with non-firearm weapons or no weapons. The majority of aid workers attacked were staffers working for national NGOs and Red Cross/Crescent societies, often working to implement international aid in their own countries. The number of aid workers killed relative to the estimated total number of aid workers (the attack rate) continues to rise. It is in this global context that humanitarian workers and journalists find themselves on the receiving end of targeted violence, and it is in this same context that new communication technologies, as we have seen, are increasingly put to work in mediatized acts of inhumane violence.

The new forms of media surveillance and involvement in the context of human (in)security can prove, as we have heard, both humanly solidaristic and democratizing or inhumanely particularistic and tyrannical. The extended gaze of the contemporary media and communications ecology can be taken as solidaristic and democratizing in so far as the availability of new digital technologies, ease of visual recording, and access to communication systems seemingly enfranchises everyone, from ordinary citizens and human rights activists to foot soldiers and even torturers who can bear witness to their own and others' acts of inhumanity anywhere in the world, and thereby encourage appropriate humanitarian and political responses. But so too can it also prove inhumanely tyrannical in so far as these same communication technologies and developments have also led to a new 'amoral economy' in which the production and circulation of acts of violence have increasingly become staged and produced deliberately for the media in support of particularistic identities and tactical aims—whether building public support and legitimacy for war through distancing or aestheticized spectacles of war and other forms of 'symbolic violence' or the production and dissemination of public fears through mediatized acts of terror based on 'violent symbolism' as we have seen (Cottle, 2006, pp. 155–162).[2]

CONCLUSION

The discussion above has deliberately sought to position both the changing nature of humanitarian disasters and human security as well as today's rapidly changing media and communications ecology in global context. Humanitarian disasters are increasingly bound up in endemic global forces that unequally shape life chances and for some the very chance of life itself on an economically driven, ecologically threatened, and politically conflicted planet. Global interdependencies of economics, energy, and environment look set to converge into complex and enduring global crises in the future. Today's extensity and intensity of media and communications under such conditions of globalization enters into humanitarian crises in diverse ways as we have seen. They do so from *the outside in*, and *inside out* and whether in respect of their *scale, speed, saturation, social relations enfranchisement, surveillance*, and sensory privileging of *seeing*.

Media and communications can monitor and document acts of inhumanity and atrocity around the globe via satellites in the sky and social media on the ground alongside and often in interaction with mainstream media including telephony, 24/7 new broadcasters, and the Internet. Today's global communication ecology can thereby play its part in the international community's 'responsibility to protect', alerting the UN and the world's nations to their obligation to safeguard populations from war crimes, genocide, ethnic cleansing, and crimes against humanity in new wars and other situations of human insecurity as well as enter into the public deliberation of humanitarian interventions (or imposition of Western "liberal peace"). Contemporary media can also shape the "new Western way of war," where democratic governments sensitive to Western public opinion and the scenes circulated by national and global news media seek to transfer risks and thereby increase so-called collateral damage. And so too can the media's 'silent moral scream' unwittingly help facilitate the deliberate killing of civilians under the cover of news media invisibility in hidden wars and forgotten—conflict-based—humanitarian disasters. They can also be put to more visceral and morally repugnant ends when deployed in image wars involving the deliberate staging and enactment of atrocious acts of 'violent symbolism'.

Together, these and other forms of communications within the field of humanitarianism and human insecurity are now transforming the visibility of humanitarian disasters and the plight of human populations around our rapidly globalizing world. They pose new challenges, benign opportunities, and malign threats. This demands increased recognition, extensive analysis, and improved understanding in the years ahead.

NOTES

1. This chapter draws on and augments a working paper Humanitarian Disasters and Communications in a Globalized World, first prepared for The Future of Humanitarian Reporting conference organised by City University's Centre for Law, Justice and Journalism in partnership with the Red Cross in April 2013, as well as earlier publications (Cottle, 2006, 2009a, 2009b, 2011, 2013, 2014).
2. The late French sociologist, Pierre Bourdieu, defined symbolic violence as the ways by which institutions and language encode and enact a 'gentle, invisible form of violence' that informs relations of communication which are also relations of power and domination (cited in Thompson, 1984, p. 43). When applied to images specifically, various features and artifices such as selection and omission, juxtaposition and framing, focus and perspective, cropping and digital manipulation, can all enact forms of 'symbolic violence'. They may do so, for example, by symbolically occluding or symbolically annihilating the presence, interests, and identities of the Other (most conflicts tend to produce and *mis*recognize 'Others'), or by valorizing, affirming, and mobilizing group identities and allegiances premised on ideas of dominance, right, or legitimacy again premised on a silent Other. Here I contrast 'violent symbolism' with Bourdieu's linguistically subtle 'symbolic violence' and do so to highlight the far-from-gentle or invisible use of actual, atrocious violence that is deliberately staged, choreographed, and enacted on people and bodies to both shock and send a message—one that is morally repugnant to all but the (a)morally self-righteous and fanatically deluded.

BIBLIOGRAPHY

Abbott, C., Rogers, P., & Sloboda, J. (2006). *Global responses to global threats: Sustainable security for the 21st century.* Oxford: Oxford Research Group. Retrieved from www.oxfordresearchgroup.org.uk.
Ahmed, N. M. (2010). *A user's guide to the crisis of civilization.* London: Pluto.

AlertNet. (2009). AlertNet: Alerting Humanitarians to Emergencies. Retrieved from http://www.alertnet.org/.

Allan, S. (2006). *Online news*. Maidenhead, UK: Open University.

Allan, S., & Thorsen, E. (Eds.). (2009). *Citizen journalism: Global perspectives*. London: Peter Lang.

Amnesty International. (2009). *The state of the world's human rights: Amnesty International Report 2009*. London: Amnesty International.

Balabanova, E. (2014). *The media and human rights*. London: Routledge.

Barnett, M., & Weiss, T. (Eds.). (2008). *Humanitarianism in question: Politics, power, ethics*. Ithaca & London: Cornell University Press.

Bauman, Z. (2007). *Liquid times*. Cambridge, MA: Polity.

Beck, U. (1992). *Risk society*. London: Sage.

Beck, U. (2009). *World at risk*. Cambridge, MA: Polity.

Benthall, J. (1993). *Disasters, relief and the media*. London: I. B. Tauris.

Briggs, A., & Burke, P. (2002). *A social history of the media: From Gutenberg to the internet*. Cambridge, MA: Polity.

Burke, J. (2004, 17 November). Margaret Hassan: Obituary. *The Guardian*, Wednesday.

Cairns, E. (2012). *Crisis in a New World Order: Challenging the Humanitarian Project*. Oxfam Briefing Paper 158. Retrieved from http://policy-practice.oxfam.org.uk/publications/crises-in-a-new-world-order-challenging-the-humanitarian-project-204749.

Calhoun, C. (2004). A world of emergencies: Fear, intervention, and the limits of cosmopolitan order. *The Canadian Review of Sociology and Anthropology, 41*(4), 373–395.

Chouliaraki, L. (2006). *The spectatorship of suffering*. London: Sage.

Committee to Protect Journalists (CCPJ). (2014). International journalists killed at high rate in 2014; Middle East deadliest region. Retrieved from http://www.cpj.org/.

Cottle, S. (2006). *Mediatized conflicts: New developments in media and conflict studies*. Maidenhead, UK: Open University.

Cottle, S. (2009a). *Global crisis reporting: Journalism in the global age*. Maidenhead, UK: Open University.

Cottle, S. (2009b). Global crises in the news: Staging new wars, disasters and climate change. *International Journal of Communication, 3*, 494–516.

Cottle, S. (2011). Taking global crises in the news seriously: Notes from the dark side of globalization. *Global Media and Communication, 7*(2), 77–95.

Cottle, S. (2013). Journalists witnessing disasters: From the calculus of death to the injunction to care. *Journalism Studies, 14*(2), 232–248.

Cottle, S. (2014). Rethinking media and disasters in a global age: What's changed and why it matters. *Media, War & Conflict, 7*(1), 3–22.

Cottle, S., & Hughes, M. (2015). The United Nations' responsibility to protect and the world's press: Establishing a new humanitarian norm? In J. Hoffmann & V. Hawkins (Eds.), *Communication for peace: Charting an emerging field* (pp. 76–91). London: Routledge.

Cottle, S., & Nolan, D. (2007). Global humanitarianism and the changing aid field: "Everyone was dying for footage." *Journalism Studies, 8*(6), 862–878.

Cottle, S., & Rai, M. (2010). Global 24/7 news providers: Emissaries of global dominance or global public sphere? In J. Gripsrud, G. Murdock, & A. Molander (Eds.), *The public sphere* (pp. 1565–1582). London: Sage.

Cottle, S., Sambrook, R., & Mosdell, N. (forthcoming). *Reporting dangerously: Journalist killings, intimidation and security*. Houndmill, UK: Palgrave.

Defoe, D. (1704/2005). *The storm*. London: Penguin.

De Waal, A. (2007). No such thing as humanitarian intervention: Why we need to rethink the "responsibility to protect" in wartime. *Harvard International Review*. Retrieved March 21, 2009, from http://www.harvardir.org/articles/print.php?article=1482.

Duffield, M. (2001). *Global governance and the new wars*. London: Zed.

Duffield, M. (2007). *Development, security and unending war*. Cambridge, MA: Polity.

Evans, G. (2008). *The responsibility to protect*. Washington, DC: Brookings Institute.

Fisk, R. (2008, 7 August). The tragic last moments of Margaret Hassan. *The Independent*.

Flichy, P. (1995). *Dynamics of modern communication*. London: Sage.

Galtung, J., & Ruge, M. (Eds.). (1981). The structure of foreign news. In S. Cohen & J. Young (Eds.), *The manufacture of news: Deviance, social problems and the mass media* (pp. 52–63). London: Constable.

Giddens, A. (1990). *The consequences of modernity*. Cambridge, MA: Polity.

Gilboa, E. (2005). The CNN effect: The search for a communication theory of international relations. *Political Communication, 22*, 27–44.

Global Humanitarian Assistance (GHA). (2014). *Emerging Findings from the Forthcoming 2014 Global Humanitarian Assistance (GHA) Report Highlights*. Retrieved from http://www.globalhumanitarianassistance.org/wp-content/uploads/2014/06/GHA-2014-highlights-summary-1.pdf.

Global Humanitarian Forum (GHF). (2009). *Human Impact Report: Climate Change—The Anatomy of a Silent Crisis*. Geneva: Global Humanitarian Forum.

Gowing, N. (2009). *"Skyful of lies and black swans": The new tyranny of shifting information power in crises*. Oxford: University of Oxford, Reuters Institute for the Study of Journalism.

Hawkins, V. (2008). *Stealth conflicts: How the world's worst violence is ignored*. Houndmill, UK: Palgrave.

Held, D., Kaldor, M., & Quah, D. (2010). *The hydra-headed crisis*. London: London School of Economics.

Holmes, J., & Niskala, M. (2007). *Reducing the Humanitarian Consequences of Climate Change*. International Federation of Red Cross and Red Crescent Societies. Retrieved from http://www.ifrc.org/en/news-and-media/opinions-and-positions/opinion-pieces/2007/reducing-the-humanitarian-consequences-of-climate-change/.

Humanitarian Outcomes (2014) *Aid Worker Security Report 2014*. Humanitarian Outcomes, London: Canalot Studios.

Hunt, L. (2007). *Inventing human rights: A history*. London: Norton.

Ignatieff, M. (1998). *The warrior's honor: Ethnic war and the modern conscience*. London: Chatto & Windus.

Ignatieff, M. (2004, November 20). The terrorist as film director. *The Age* (Melbourne), p. 2.

International Air Transport Association (IATA). (2013, December 31). New Year's Day 2014 Marks One Hundred Years of Aviation. Press Release No.72. Retrieved from http://www.iata.org/pressroom/pr/Pages/2013-12-30-01.aspx.

International Federation of Red Cross and Red Crescent Societies. (2013). *World Disasters Report: Focus on Technology and the Future of Humanitarian Action*. Retrieved from http://www.ifrc.org/PageFiles/134658/WDR%202013%20complete.pdf.

International Institute of Strategic Studies (IISS). (2007). *Strategic Survey 2007: The Annual Review of World Affairs*. London: IISS.

International Panel on Climate Change (IPCC). (2007). *Climate Change 2007: The Physical Science Basis. Summary for Policy Makers*. Geneva: IPCC Secretariat. Retrieved from http://www.ipcc.ch/publications_and_data/ar4/wg1/en/spm.html.

International Panel on Climate Change (IPCC). (2013). *Climate Change 2014: Fifth Assessment Synthesis Report.* Geneva: IPCC Secretariat. Retrieved from http://www.ipcc.ch/report/ar5/syr/.

International Telecommunications Union (ITU). (2011). *The World in 2011: Facts and Figures.* Retrieved from http://www.itu.int/ITU-D/ict/facts/2011/.

International Telecommunications Union (ITU). (2013). *The World in 2013: Facts and Figures.* Retrieved from http://www.itu.int/en/ITU-D/Statistics/Documents/facts/ICTFactsFigures2013-e.pdf.

Jiménez-Martínez, C. (2014). Disasters as media events: The rescue of the Chilean miners on national and global television. *International Journal of Communication* (8), 1807–1830.

Kaldor, M. (2006). *New and old wars: Organized violence in a global era.* Cambridge, MA: Polity.

Kaldor, M. (2007). *Human security.* Cambridge, MA: Polity.

Laqueur, T. (2009). *Mourning, pity, and the work of narrative in the making of "humanity."* In R. Wilson & R. Brown (Eds.), *Humanitarianism and suffering: The mobilization of empathy* (pp. 31–57). Cambridge: Cambridge University Press.

Macrae, J. (Ed.). (2002). *The new humanitarianism: A review of trends in global humanitarian action.* HPG Report 11. London: Overseas Development Institute.

Magrath, J. (2007). *Climate alarm.* Oxfam Briefing Paper 108. Retrieved from http://policy-practice.oxfam.org.uk/publications/climate-alarm-disasters-increase-as-climate-change-bites-114103.

Moeller, S. (1999). *Compassion fatigue: How the media sell war, famine, war and death.* London: Routledge.

Mousseau, F., & Bailey, M. (2009). *A Billion Hungry People.* Oxfam Briefing Paper 127. Retrieved from http://www.oxfam.org/sites/www.oxfam.org/files/bp127-billion-hungry-people-0901.pdf.

Nelson, A., Sigal, L., & Zambrano, D. (2011). *Media information systems and communities: Lessons from Haiti.* Miami, FL: Knight Foundation.

Office for the Coordination of Humanitarian Affairs (OCHA). (2013). *Humanitarianism in the Network Age.* United Nations: OCHA.

Pantti, M., Wahl-Jorgensen, K., & Cottle, S. (2012). *Disasters and the media.* New York: Peter Lang.

Price, M., & Thompson, M. (Eds.). (2002). *Forging peace: Intervention, human rights and the management of media space.* Edinburgh: Edinburgh University Press.

Project Ploughshares. (2007). *Armed Conflict Report 2007 Summary.* Ontario: Project Ploughshares.

Rai, M., & Cottle, S. (2010). Global news revisited: Mapping the contemporary landscape of satellite television news. In S. Cushion & J. Lewis (Eds.), *The rise of 24-hour news television: Global perspectives* (pp. 51–79). New York: Peter Lang.

Rieff, D. (2002). *A bed for the night: Humanitarianism in crisis.* London: Vintage.

Rifkin, J. (2009). *The empathic civilization: The race to global consciousness in a world of crisis.* New York: Penguin.

Robertson, A. (2010). *Mediated cosmopolitanism: The world of television news.* Cambridge, MA: Polity.

Robertson, G. (2012). *Crimes against humanity: The struggle for human justice.* London: Penguin.

Robinson, P. (2005). The CNN effect revisited. *Critical Studies in Media Communication, 22*(4), 344–349.

Seaton, J. (2005) *Carnage and the media: The making and breaking of news about violence.* London: Penguin.

Shaw, M. (1996). *Civil society and media in global crises.* London: St Martin's.

Shaw, M. (2005). *The new Western way of war: Risk-transfer war and its crisis in Iraq.* Cambridge, MA: Polity.

Silverstone, R. (2007). *Media and morality: On the rise of the mediapolis.* Cambridge, MA: Polity.

Stockholm International Peace Research Institute (SIPRI). (2004). *SIPRI yearbook 2004: Armaments, disarmament and international security.* Oxford: Oxford University Press.

Taylor, B. H., & Shuemer-Cross, T. (2009). *The Right to Survive: The Humanitarian Challenge for the Twenty-First Century.* Oxfam International. Retrieved from http://policy-practice.oxfam. org.uk/publications/the-right-to-survive-the-humanitarian-challenge-for-the-twenty-first-cen tury-112372.

Thompson, J. (1984). *Studies in the theory of ideology.* Cambridge, MA: Polity.

Thompson, J. (1995). *The media and modernity.* Cambridge, MA: Polity.

Thorsen, E., & Allan, S. (Eds.). (2014). *Citizen journalism: Global perspectives, Vol. 2.* New York: Peter Lang.

Tumber, H., & Webster, F. (2006). *Journalists under fire: Information war and journalistic practices.* London: Sage.

United Nations. (2009). *United Nations Conference on the World Financial and Economic Crisis and Its Impacts on Development.* Retrieved from http://www.un.org/ga/president/63/interactive/financialcrisis/PreliminaryReport210509.pdf.

United Nations Environmental Programme (UNEP). (2007). Vulnerable in a World of Plenty. *Global Environment Outlook 4,* Fact Sheet 14. Retrieved from www.unep.org/geo/geo4/.

United Nations Environmental Programme (UNEP). (2009). *From conflict to peacebuilding: The role of natural resources and the environment.* New York: UNEP.

United Nations Foundation. (2011). *Disaster Relief 2.0. Information Sharing in Humanitarian Emergencies.* Retrieved from http://hhi.harvard.edu/sites/default/files/publications/publications %20-%20crisis%20mapping%20-%20disaster%202.0.pdf.

United Nations International Strategy for Disaster Reduction (UNISDR). (2012). *Disasters through a different lens: Behind every effect there is a cause.* New York: UNISDR.

Volkmer, I. (1999). *News in the global sphere: A study of CNN and its impact on global communication.* Luton: University of Luton Press.

Weiss, T. (2007). *Humanitarian intervention.* Cambridge, MA: Polity.

Whiting, A. (2014). Attacks on Aid Workers Worldwide Hit Worst Levels on Record. *Reuters.* Retrieved from http://uk.reuters.com/article/2014/08/19/uk-foundation-aid-attacks-idUKKB N0GJ05820140819.

World Health Organization (WHO). (2007). *A Safer Future: Global Public Health Security.* Geneva: WHO. Retrieved from http://www.who.int/whr/2007.

CHAPTER TWO

Media Futures and Humanitarian Perspectives in an Age of Uncertainty and Complexity

RANDOLPH KENT

Media have increasingly become a driving force in human development not only a Fourth Estate reporting on the activities of the government and society, but a dynamic and determinative force that shapes our politics, economics, culture and history. The information revolution increasingly puts the destiny of humanity in our own hands. (Hoffman, 2013, p. 234)

And, it is with this underlying assumption about transformations in the media noted by the eminent media analyst that this chapter suggests that the media's importance needs to become ever more so as the impact of future humanitarian threats become increasingly more global, interactive, and complex.

For those with humanitarian roles and responsibilities, the increasingly complex and seemingly random nature of humanitarian crises and the contexts in which they occur require new ways of preparing for the challenges of the future. New approaches to innovation and innovative practices, new understandings about the nature of risks and crisis drivers, and new types of partnerships will be essential to meet such challenges. Casting his eyes around participants from the military, the private sector, and international governmental and non-governmental organisations in a recent workshop on humanitarian action, a senior representative of the International Committee of the Red Cross remarked, 'I guess we're all humanitarians now'.

In retrospect one group that was absent were representatives from the media. Historically the aid sector has not always recognised that information and communication are a form of aid, and the media has also not sufficiently recognised its importance at the humanitarian table. In certain ways, as this discussion will suggest, its absence is not consistent. The media as a humanitarian participant pops in and out. In an ever more vulnerable world, however, this inconsistency should end, and the media ought to recognise that it needs to be a fully committed participant; and the humanitarian sector will need to welcome it.

In so saying, this discussion raises four concerns. The first focuses on the sorts of issues that will make media an increasingly critical factor in humanitarian action. The second and third—closely interrelated—suggest ways that the media will have to engage to enhance its credibility over the next decade, or, in what might be described as a 'futures context', and also to recognise transformations in the very concept of media that will have particular relevance to humanitarian futures. Finally, even for the increasingly disparate and diverse sector called 'media', might there be lessons common to all that should be taken on board now in anticipation of media futures?

MEDIA FUTURES IN A HUMANITARIAN CONTEXT

The types of humanitarian crisis drivers, their dimensions, and dynamics will rapidly increase, in some instances exponentially. The interface between natural hazards and technology may well lead to ever more deadly and disruptive crises; and, here, the 2011 Fukushima tsunami-triggered nuclear reactor crisis is a case in point. The interrelationship between disasters, normally reflecting the effects of natural hazards, and emergencies, triggered by internal and international conflict, will most likely be more prevalent. The potential threat arising from melting snows in the Himalayas, and the disputes which those 'waters of the Third Pole' could trigger in countries of South Asia is a well-documented case of such potential interrelated crises (China Dialogue et al., 2010).

The possibility that cybernetic failures could bring down systems to which human survival has become dependent is increasing, as the spectrum of applications—from remittance transfers and mobile phones to financial transactions, warehouse codes, petrol pumps, government departments, and the media—all become cyber dependent around the world. One highly respected analyst even warns that the threat of 'synchronous failures' is increasingly plausible, where complete collapse of social, economic, and biophysical systems will 'arise from simultaneous, interacting stresses acting powerfully at multiple levels of these global systems' (Homer Dixon, 2002). Such speculation is not an isolated phenomenon, but rather is increasing amongst a growing number of distinguished scientists who are seeking to give some guidance about 'the what might be's' when it comes to humanitarian crises of the future.[1]

All such analyses implicitly or explicitly take into account demographic factors—population increases, major population shifts, and the growth of denser, ever more vulnerable urban and peri-urban populations. On top of all of this are the ubiquitous consequences of climate change, and those of pandemics that will spill over borders, in many instances regionally and increasingly globally, and in so doing create political as well as social challenges well beyond their source.

In a geo-political context, since disasters and emergencies began to gain media prominence in the 1970s, there had been an implicit assumption that those in the so-called third world or developing world were comparatively hapless and vulnerable in the face of humanitarian threats, while the 'developed world' was inherently resilient. Even when it came to the former, however, governments of disaster-prone countries normally regarded humanitarian crises as unfortunate but aberrant phenomena on the periphery of governmental concerns.

Yet, whether in the developed or the developing worlds, governments, and in most instances the media, failed until the 1990s to recognise that such crises were not aberrant phenomena or 'Acts of God', but rather reflections of the ways that societies are structured and governments allocate their resources. Today there is increased acceptance that vulnerability, development, and economic growth are interrelated, and that the ways governments not only respond to such crises, but also promote disaster prevention and preparedness will very often determine governments' very survival. This in no small part explains, for example, the reluctance of the government of Myanmar in the aftermath of the 2008 Cyclone Nargis initially to accept international assistance, or, similarly Turkey's hesitation to open up to international aid following a magnitude 7.2 earthquake in 2011 and the U.S. government's determination to bring BP to account for the 2010 Deepwater Horizon oil spill.

Such potential political implications also have to be seen in the context of social impact and in some instances social transformations. Disasters more and more will rarely be incidents that have finite ends. Their fallout will most likely have enduring effects upon afflicted populations and beyond that will last for several years, if not decades. This has become evident in such recent crises as Hurricane Katrina in 2005, Colombia's continuing internal displacement crisis, and China's 2008 Sichuan earthquake. Each of these cases also suggest the interactive nature of crisis drivers, and each demonstrate how one crisis can at the same time trigger others that ultimately have compound impacts—all in various ways falling upon the shoulders of government.

Understanding about their causes, impacts, and ways to mitigate them will have to confront their ever-increasing complexity, and here the importance of that 'funny mix of being really substantive on really big, complicated topics, but presented in a really approachable way' will become increasingly valued by those whom the media seeks to engage (Donovan, 2014).

To date the sources of such longer-term threats, their consequences, and ways to mitigate them are issues rarely given much media attention. There is, of course, the occasional focus on catastrophic and in some instances existential threats, and there, too, is occasional media interest in innovations that might address such serious longer-term humanitarian-crisis drivers. A number of specialist media outlets such as the Earth Journalism Network, the Professional Society of Drone Journalists, and the Society of Environmental Journalists are examples of myriad specialist media groups that do confront the complex and that do point to ways to mitigate and prevent looming crises. Nevertheless, there is no consistent media attention given to engaging with the public about longer-term threats and opportunities to deal with them for which the media, governments, and international and non-governmental organisations should be prepared.

THE MEDIA FUTURES PROPOSITION

When this Media Futures proposition was put to a range of media representatives during the course of 2012–2013, there were generally four types of responses.[2] There was a relatively consistent theme that 'the longer-term does not sell newspapers.' Whatever aspect of conventional media to which one turned, for example, newspapers, television, radio, there was a clear perception that the public just would not 'buy' news that was presented as being beyond the immediate. A second response was that the media already paid attention to such longer-term issues, but they were necessarily a small portion of a more complicated news nexus. By no means could issues about longer-term crisis threats be a dominant feature in media offerings.

Respondents, too, felt that there was an issue of integrity involved in making longer-term crisis drivers a media feature. Beyond the world of science fiction, it was difficult to offer news when, in all likelihood, a degree of certainty and 'the facts' were not available. This was not to say that the media did not have what was called 'a speculative role', but to generate concerns about crisis threats that had societal-wide implications without adequate proof was seen as too close to the margins. A final and consistent theme that arose in these rounds of media discussion groups was the challenge posed by the need to identify and prioritise such risks. Even if there were decisions made to focus more consistently and systematically on the sorts of longer-term threats that were plausible, to what extent could one say with any certitude that a particular risk or set of risks deserved attention instead of others?

That said, emerging out of the changing nature of humanitarian crisis drivers are direct challenges to the media. One of these is that, despite the responses to the media futures proposition, it is increasingly apparent that longer-term perspectives not only can make a good story, but increasingly such perspectives will be expected by a growing number of media users. The concern that longer-term crisis drivers reflect speculation bordering on science fiction is also an increasingly questionable proposition. This is not to say that predicting the longer-term future has become an exact science, though it does suggest that a range of "tools"—from "big data" to new forms of cross-sectoral partnerships—are making an understanding of the longer-term more accessible.

Perhaps one of the most important assumptions underpinning respondents' attitudes to the media futures proposition is that information receivers cannot cope with ambiguity, that recipients cannot deal with the 'what might be's'. Of course, those who responded to the media future proposition made certain assumptions about the media itself. One was that there was a hierarchy of products: Internet, television, radio, newspapers—each used in ways that predominantly reflect demographic, educational, and economic criteria. Yet, there is growing evidence that increasingly in times of crises and most likely in anticipating future crises, there will be a medley, if not cacophony, of media instruments that will become sources at the same time. The challenge that this plausible reality will bring is to what extent to which information from these myriad sources will be relatively consistent and in different ways carry the same overarching message?

LONGER-TERM PERSPECTIVES CAN MAKE A GOOD STORY

'Why can't you use your wordsmithing skills to make longer-term crisis threats a compelling story?' A question that was never directly answered in the research undertaken for the Media Futures project, the question, itself, opens up the prospect that longer-term risk identification and reduction can be turned into a compelling story. The answer lies in for whom and why.

In the aftermath of severe flooding in England's Somerset Levels in early 2014, a growing crescendo from many of the flood-affected accused the government of failing to have anticipated the crisis. Anticipation was perceived to be a role that increasingly had to be seen as part of normal life, and certainly an obligation of government. And while the extent to which one can draw more general implications from this vignette remains uncertain, there are potential directions to be considered when it comes to media futures. There is in this context a plausible correlation between changing concerns of media audiences, accessibility to data that reflects longer-term patterns with greater predictability, the search for more sustainable media roles and the very nature of media, itself.

The Future as a Media Focus

When it comes to potential threats, there should be far greater attention given to plausible hazards and ways to deal with them. And yet the problem is that governments on the whole are not consistently adequate communicators, and all too often 'warnings' as well as recommended actions are greeted with degrees of suspicion or indifference. Nevertheless, governments might value the sensitisation that comes from a more active media focusing in a consistent manner on potential hazards and ways to address them, 'translating' and disseminating relevant information. Conversely, the fact that the media may increasingly see an emerging role in the Somerset Levels sense might in turn compel governments to be more open about information about longer-term threats and opportunities.

The potential for both can be surmised from a March 2014 discussion with a media-savvy former senior civil servant, who greeted the Somerset Levels disaster as a major accomplishment. When asked why, the official noted that because of plans not to attempt to stem the floods in Somerset, the Thames barriers only needed to be raised twice throughout the whole incident—suggesting that densely populated London was protected by allowing waters to accumulate in sparsely populated areas of the West Country. The official then noted that this success would never get the publicity it deserved because the political uproar that would be generated by the affected populations would be more than a calculated political risk.[3]

Yet, fundamental to this irony is that the public has rarely been introduced to the dilemmas surrounding longer-term risks and ways that they can be mitigated. There are few incentives or little encouragement to use the wordsmithing capacities of trained journalists to inform the wider public about longer-term future threats and their inherent complexities. Part of the reason is that, as noted earlier, response to the media futures proposition suggests that those who were interviewed were reluctant to generate concerns about crisis threats that had societal-wide implications without adequate proof. Information recipients would not be able to deal with the ambiguity.

This is not to say that the media is insensitive to new types of crises. It has clearly dealt with ambiguous situations. As has been pointed out, the media has picked up on new types of crises such as global warming, forced migration, and war on terrorism—all laden in various ways with ambiguity—and despite this have in some instances actively supported efforts to increase global awareness about such risks and also promoted a sense of global responsibility (Cottle, 2009). Others, too, have suggested that the power of the media is increasing as never before—resulting in outcomes both good and bad—and that the media in many ways can take the lead in transforming public attitudes at a level never before imagined, again overcoming the ambivalence arising out of uncertainty (Hoffman, 2013).

Focusing on the uncertainties that might stem from increasingly complex and unclear longer-term threats may, however, be an assignment too far. If the World Economic Forum's Global Agenda Council on the Future of Media is right when it suggests that the most pressing challenges facing the media in the longer term are trust and accuracy, (World Economic Forum, 2014), then to what extent might either result from dealing with what could be seen as distant and speculative reportage? The answer might be seen from two interrelated perspectives, namely, the role of dialogue in media futures and the transformations of the very concept of media.

Media Futures as Dialogue

The position of the majority of those participating in the media futures discussion groups was more than understandable. They were concerned that in dealing with longer-term crisis threats, speculative analysis would be dismissed or greeted with fear and hostility. The very nature of ambiguity in the futures context seems to go against some of the most challenging aspects of communication. It can be described as reflecting completely new situations with no familiar cues or precedents, a complex situation in which there are a great number of cues and stakeholder interests to be taken into account or a situation that is apparently insoluble or one that cannot be solved in usual ways.

However, there is a significant body of research that suggests that speculation and dealing with ambiguity become acceptable to the extent that information recipients regard themselves as part of an information dialogue. This was evident in recent work undertaken about communities' reactions to emerging consequences of climate change. In this instance, researchers had initially assumed that information about the potential longer-term consequences would either be ignored, seen as irrelevant or as unwarranted 'scare mongering'. The contrary was the case. Information—no matter how potentially disruptive—was regarded as acceptable by communities, for example, in Senegal and Kenya when they received warnings through a variety of media and governmental channels about climate change predictions.

The reason for this reaction was the realisation that communications that allowed dialogue between the supposed receivers and providers of information not only enhanced its acceptability but also its credibility. More important, 'reasoned uncertainty' was deemed to be acceptable by information recipients, and the critical factor was dialogue. In the Senegal and Kenya cases, the focus was on meteorological information about climate change that would affect lives, crop production, and related livelihoods. Media outputs, radio, newspaper, and local authority communications had hitherto reflected the one-way flow of meteorological 'experts'—experts that transmitted information that lacked local experience and relevant understanding.

However, once those who prepared such broadcasts made efforts to have more interactive dialogues with information recipients, and incorporated local knowledge into their broadcasts, there was a greater inclination by those in the community to accept media information—no matter how disconcerting or potentially disrupting. They recognised their 'voices', and according to researchers, this dialogue also reflected those communities' relative willingness to accept ambiguity. Interestingly, too, an unanticipated feedback-loop was that the source of information—the meteorological experts—found that the intended users' information clearly enhanced the substance of the former.

In the world of the media, it might well be argued that this emphasis on dialogue is merely another description of what is a fundamental part of journalists' toolkits, namely, interviews and engagement with those who are part of the story. And, indeed, that view is correct, but with one important distinction, the dialogue's perspective. The short-termism that marks so many of the stories about hazards was not ex post facto analyses about events and responses to them, but about a dialogue concerned with longer-term prospects redolent with uncertainty.

In that sense, there is an analogue between this latter perspective and the strictures of humanitarian accountability. Traditionally, humanitarian workers were held accountable for the ways that they provided assistance for past humanitarian action (Obrecht, 2014). More and more, however, they will be held accountable for anticipating what they should be doing. Accountability futures and media futures may increasingly share a common perspective—that focusing upon the future may be as valuable as attempting to explain the past. Responsibility for focusing on the needs of the future may, in other words, eventually be as expected as explaining and justifying actions that relate to the past.

MULTIDIMENSIONALITY OF MEDIA FUTURES

Researchers from Columbia University's Tow Center for Digital Journalism suggest:

> The news ecosystem of 2020 will be a study in expansion, with heightened contrasts between extremes. More people will consume more news from more sources.... Readers, viewers and listeners will disassemble it and distribute the parts that interest them to their various networks. An increasing amount of news will arrive via these ad hoc networks than via audiences loyal to any particular publication. (Anderson, Bell, & Shirky, 2012, p. 2.)

In the aftermath of the 2011 Fukushima nuclear accident the role of the media was placed under severe scrutiny. The assumptions that were made about the use of the Internet as a communications provider were severely challenged. The all-pervasive and accessible nature of information and communications technology (ICT) was proven false. Radio came into its own, as victims of the floods and indirect impacts of the nuclear meltdown provided a source of communications that were instantly available to the elderly and to those uncomfortable with 'new media'. Even newspapers and handwritten posters were regarded as useful alternatives (Appleby, 2013).

Within that context, the Fukushima crisis clearly demonstrated that the very term 'media' has to be seen as a multifaceted means of communications, particularly when it comes to dealing with communications in the midst of crises. This by no means suggests that throwbacks to earlier forms of communications, for example, the radio and newspapers, circumscribe the nature of media in times of humanitarian crises. It does, on the other hand, suggest that media in all its forms—formal and informal—need to be adopted to communicate the threat of hazards, their impacts, and evolution and sources of assistance. In that sense, Fukushima symbolises the fact that no single form of communication is sufficient to rely upon for effective crisis prevention, preparedness, and response. A full panoply of media instruments and techniques—sensitive to types of recipients and to the conditions affected by the crisis itself—is essential to convey the message, and will probably continue to be so in the foreseeable future.

MIT's Civic Media Lab's definition of 'civic media' as 'any form of communication that strengthens the social bonds within a community or creates a strong sense of civic engagement' reflects the interactive nature of media—what earlier had been called 'dialogue'—and reconfirms that the tools and the boundaries of media are expanding, and so, too, are the objectives.

The challenge for this ever-widening spectrum of media is to have some broad element of consistency. This naturally presents a profound dilemma for those who see the diversity of views as fundamental to the media's role. While in no sense proposing to curtail 'freedom of the press', there is nevertheless a growing need to help communities—be they in cities or in rural areas—to be prepared for the implications of paradigmatically different types of humanitarian threats. Nevertheless, the plethora of media systems will in the future generate inconsistencies and contradictions about what receivers understand as humanitarian solutions as well as threats. A foretaste of what this might look like was recounted by a senior UN official when explaining the dilemma that aid workers had to face in dealing with contending media information in the immediate aftermath of the 2010 Haitian earthquake.

In this instance, according to the UN official, a search and rescue team was confronted with two sets of media information. The first was radio broadcasts confirming that a highly impacted zone was clear of earthquake victims; the second was a 'blazing tweet campaign' begging the search and rescue team 'to save our daughter' from that same zone. In light of the latter, the team returned to the site that had been cleared to find that the daughter had been dead for two days. The parents who had pursued this call for help knew that she had been dead, but explained that—dead or alive—they wanted to have their daughter back. The UN official, though sympathetic to the plight of the daughter's family, explained that this contending information meant that the valuable time of the search and rescue team to rescue the living had been diverted to deal with the dead.[4]

The challenge is how media so diverse and ever more so can come together to reflect common parameters of information if not common agreement on the implications of such information. In posing this challenge, the answer cannot come from the hope that it would be possible to create a universally accepted framework that would promote an agreed-upon discourse. Yet, given the threats that are increasingly centre stage across regions and the globe, are there means to sensitise such a diverse community of players to issues that should be of common concern?

PREPARING FOR MEDIA FUTURES: SEVEN STEPS

Media futures so vast, unpredictable, and so replete with unknowns cannot be controlled nor can they be treated as an entity with any clear or consistent underpinnings—other than communications with a force-multiplier effect. And yet, it would be irresponsible in light of the types of humanitarian crises that may well be part of the longer-term future to dismiss efforts to promote greater understanding about potential threats and opportunities to mitigate or prevent them.

In so saying, there is a series of steps that might be considered for dealing with the 'what might be's':

1. **Clarity of the message.** Global-climate change is an obvious example of the difficulties of developing messages that are futures-oriented and that reflect consensus. In this sense, the message of media futures is not that one knows what will be, but rather one needs to be sensitive to plausible threats and prepared to adjust and adapt accordingly. As noted earlier, specialist media do this in terms of shorter-term threats. The objective of the media futures' message is to promote discourse around a particular proposition about being sensitive to plausible future threats. Governments and international organisations have, on the whole, consistently opted for the immediate or the relatively short-term, and in many ways this perspective has been re-enforced by their perceptions of what 'the public' would accept or at least tolerate. The proposition therefore is to get a wider public to think in terms of longer term perspectives, to recognise the practical consequences of this sort of thinking, and that is the message that very difficult message needs to be clear.
2. **Foster dialogues.** The ambivalence or disinterest of information recipients about such issues as longer-term humanitarian threats can be lessened if both providers and recipients are willing and able to create means of exchanging views about future threats. The provider can sort through the glut of information for the recipient about possible futures. However, the receptivity of the recipient to the message will equate to that person's sense of engagement with the issue and with the provider. Realistically speaking

the opportunities for promoting such dialogues are relatively few, though there are growing number of examples about how this is being undertaken at community levels. The importance of recognising their value for fostering new ways of thinking can be reflected not only in what the information provider can learn from the recipient but also how that message is spread through informal media by the recipient.

3. **Formal and informal networking.** The interaction between the formal and informal media is well established and reflected in many guises. It is more than likely that this sort of interaction will intensify and that the overlap between one and the other will increase exponentially. For the media futures proposition, the importance of promoting such networking when it comes to fostering consistent and systematic discourse on longer-term humanitarian threats and opportunities is fundamental. Once again, the issue of dialogue is a critical factor—moving away from the presumption of the 'expert' dispensing knowledge and towards a discourse in which opinions and views are to be shared. That said, it is more than likely that much of the impetus will have to come from more formal media, and that interactive dynamics will ensue. The key is to engage, to raise the discourse on longer-term futures to be part of an acceptable norm and not as an aberrant happenstance.

4. **Reputation for concern.** It would be a mistake to pursue the media futures proposition as an activist campaign, intended to establish a particular point of view at the expense of others. And while the media futures proposition does seek to promote a particular perspective, it does so without intentionally seeking to diminish others. It is, in that sense, a 'do-no-harm' humanitarian proposition. In other words, the media futures proposition should establish a reputation based on the need for the global community to reflect more on the consequences of longer-term humanitarian threats than it does, and that to do so, does not directly detract from other concerns. Inevitably the longer-term consequences of sensitizing the public as well as decision and policymakers to plausible futures may well result in different approaches for anticipating and dealing with longer-term threats. Well before such action, however, is fostering the perception that the objective is to foster positive concern about the longer term, and beyond that the media futures proposition is not prescriptive.

5. **Cross-sectoral websites.** Websites have become commonplace as sources of information. In a recent study on ways to promote more effective partnerships between the private and humanitarian sectors, it was proposed that two key UN agencies and the World Economic Forum could establish an interactive portal that would be updated by all who wished to contribute. It would not necessarily attract all who represented either sector, but was seen as a way of beginning the process of bringing others into the fold,

and in turn generating spinoffs though other social media. In this sense, interested parties from the world of science, the academic communities, governmental, inter- and non-governmental organizations should consider means for promoting longer-term disaster-related discourse through websites and related forms of social media.

6. **Sensitization initiatives.** While those groups of media specialists that discussed the media futures proposition in 2012 and 2013 raised a number of concerns, they consistently—perhaps paradoxically—suggested that the proposition would be worth introducing in media training courses. There are various courses in journalism where the proposition could fit, and it would inevitably raise issues that go in some senses to the very core of journalism, its parameters, roles, and responsibilities over time. Equally as important are to use established media foundations and academic institutions to facilitate discussions and fora on the media proposition with established journalists and media experts. The importance of not only exploring and debating the proposition but also focusing on how its core message can be improved and developed further should reflect the potential dynamism of the media futures proposition.

7. **Media futures incentives.** An incentive programme should be developed for those in the world of formal and informal media to highlight the importance of longer-term strategic thinking about new types of humanitarian threats. Its purpose would be to establish an annual event of global awards for those who have explored, revealed, and tested ways in which organisations with humanitarian roles and responsibilities are developing the core capacities that will equip them to deal with new types of humanitarian emergencies.

The sheer complexity of attempting to adjust the media's narrative to include—in ways consistent and systematic—the longer-term humanitarian future can be seen as overwhelming and outside the scope of media roles and responsibilities. And yet, in an increasingly vulnerable world where threats over time will be more and more complex and their consequences ever more devastating, will the media be at the humanitarian table to help re-enforce the importance of preparing for the 'what might be's'?

NOTES

1. A recent example of very prominent scientists engaged in anticipating longer-term crisis threats includes the University of Cambridge's Centre for the Study of Existential Risk.
2. In addition to a series of interviews with media specialists from China, Japan, Spain, Iraq, the United Kingdom, and the United States during the course of 2013, there were two Media

Futures Conferences. The first was facilitated by the Thomson Reuters Foundation on 11 January 2013, and the second by the Humanitarian Futures Programme at King's College, London, 5 March 2013.

3. Confidential discussion with a former senior official at the UK's DEFRA, London, 18 March 2014.

4. Personal communication, PAGER meeting, Ottawa, 26 October 2011.

REFERENCES

Anderson, C. W., Bell, E., & Shirky, C. (2013). *Post-industrial journalism: Adapting to the present.* New York: Columbia University's School of Journalism, Tow Center for Digital Journalism.

Appleby, L. (2013). *Connecting the last mile: The role of communications in the Great East Japan Earthquake.* Internews Europe, London.

China Dialogue, Humanitarian Futures Programme & University College, London. (2010). *Waters of the Third Pole: Sources of Threat; Sources of Survival.* HFP, King's College, London.

Cottle, S. (2009). *Global crisis reporting; Journalism in the global age.* Maidenhead & Berkshire, UK: Open University.

Donovan, C. (2014, 23 April). Q&A: David Leonhardt says The Upshot won't replace Nate Silver at The New York Times. Nieman Journalism Lab, 23 April. Retrieved from www.niemanlab.org

Hoffman, D. (2013). *Citizens rising: Independent journalism and the spread of democracy.* New York: CUNY Journalism.

Homer Dixon, T. (2002, 4 December). *Synchronous Failure: The Real Danger of the 21st Century.* The Robert J. Pelosky Jr. Distinguished Speaker Series, The Elliott School of International Affairs, George Washington University, Washington, DC.

Obrecht, A. (2014). *Accountability in a Humanitarian Futures Context.* Paper delivered at the Humanitarian Futures Programme, King's College, London, Stakeholders Forum, 2014.

World Economic Forum. (2012). Global Agenda Council on the Future of Media, 2012–2014. Retrieved from www.weforum.org/content/global-agenda-council-future-agenda-media, 2012–2014.

CHAPTER THREE

From Buerk to Ushahidi

Changes in TV Reporting
of Humanitarian Crises

RICHARD SAMBROOK

Thirty years on, Michael Buerk's 1984 report of famine in Ethiopia is still seen as an iconic example of TV journalism. For a while, it was the "biggest" story ever broadcast in terms of global audience and impact—and Buerk and his cameraman Mo Amin, who was later killed in an aircraft hijacking, became the most famous TV news team in the world.

It led, of course, to the Live Aid benefit concert and a huge global relief effort. But what were the factors that led to its success—and what has changed in the way TV news, still the most powerful medium in the world, reports humanitarian crises?

Buerk was pointed towards Ethiopia by his friend Paddy Coulter who worked for Oxfam. The NGO's intelligence was crucial in facilitating him reaching the right place at the right time. The BBC decided, largely for competitive reasons, to make a landmark report and flew Buerk and his material back to London to assemble the report rather than filing from Kenya or South Africa. This allowed time and space to assess the material and put together a powerful script and edit. It was a script designed for maximum impact.

> Dawn, and as the sun breaks through the piercing chill of night on the plain outside Korem it lights up a biblical famine, now, in the twentieth century.

The BBC decided to lead with an extended report on its tea-time news at six o'clock—an unusual move—and the report was subsequently picked up by broadcasters around the world. As a consequence half a billion people saw the report—many times more than had ever viewed a single news report before.

However, with hindsight there have also been criticisms.[1] It is a report of its time, featuring white aid workers helping black famine victims and observing events from a journalistic distance. Some believe the origins of the famine, including civil war and mismanagement of aid, were inadequately reported. There has been a subsequent debate about whether stimulating a tide of Western aid is really the most effective response to famine.

In the thirty years since, much has changed in the way media approaches reporting humanitarian crises—but much also remains the same.

The media landscape has transformed. There are now multiple global channels, broadcasting twenty-four hours a day. In 1984, there were none. And of course there is the Internet and mobile technology which dictate how many people throughout the world consume news and information. All of these outlets are seeking the attention of a public who have more choices than ever. Paradoxically, as the media sector has grown over the last thirty years, the influence of any individual outlet has decreased. The power of the evening newscast is denuded.

Within this change we have seen a decline in international reporting and the numbers of Western foreign correspondents as budgets have been slashed to maintain corporate profits or to fund new digital services (Sambrook, 2010). As a consequence, more freelancers and local journalists are now reporting for major international news organisations. The BBC now has bilingual African reporters in Kenya, Nigeria, South Africa, and elsewhere. This brings advantages—in local knowledge and contacts—and some disadvantages. Local journalists can be more vulnerable to social and political pressures and can sometimes fail to bridge the cultural gap between international audiences. However, onscreen representation has certainly improved. The notion of a white correspondent interviewing white aid workers about a crisis affecting black Africans would be unacceptable today.

As subsequent journalists sought to match Buerk's original report, there was a sharp rise in "empathy" reporting from developing countries and in extended reports. The crises in Sudan, Somalia, Rwanda, and the Democratic Republic of the Congo (DRC) all attracted coverage designed to shock the public and engage them with a sympathetic response. In doing so, famine too often was seen as a natural disaster rather than one with possible political origins.

Another BBC correspondent, George Alagiah, acknowledges that in hindsight issues appear more complex than they did to him at the time. He reported the refugee exodus from Rwanda during the genocide in the 1990s. A million refugees moved to Goma in DRC during a period of just three or four days. It was, he says, a nation in exile. As cholera set in he reported on the suffering of the victims.

But I forgot to remind the audience that a cholera victim may well have been wielding a machete a few days earlier... The longer I have done it (crisis reporting) the less convinced I've become of my role in the process. I think you have to be ready to look critically at refugee status—in some places (for example Sudan) they are second or third generation refugees. (personal communication, January 2014)

He believes today it is important to ensure a full political context is provided to reporting refugee crises—whatever the cause. In other words, empathy is not sufficient. In some sense this reflects the inbuilt nature of TV news, which is a powerful communicator of events—but less effective at reporting process. The dramatic nature of pictures means the moment makes a stronger impression than analysis of what led up to it.

The growth in media—broadcast and online—has seen the further erosion of traditional objective reporting. Al Jazeera, with a highly ethnically diverse staff, promotes reporting "the south" to "the north". Channels like TeleSur in Venezuela, Press TV from Iran, Russia Today, or France24 were all launched to offer a national perspective on global events. Today, new digital services go further. Vice News reports news with an attitude deliberately designed to appeal to younger viewers (Ellis, 2014). In the struggle to engage global audiences we have moved from objectivity, to empathy, to national voice, to "attitude". The distanced observational reporting style of 1984 seems increasingly anachronistic.

Charities recognise more than ever the importance of media coverage to stimulating a public response and have invested in their own media operations, producing video, and other material for use by the media or on their own websites. News editors suggest charities have become more sophisticated at PR and marketing of crises to stimulate response. This can lead to tension.

Both constituencies are working in a far more competitive environment—media for attention, NGO's for funds—than was the case in 1984. And both are struggling with the well-documented notion of "famine-fatigue" on the part of a public tiring of distressing images and feeling relatively helpless in response to them.

A study by the Fritz Institute and the Reuters Foundation in 2004 found that NGO press officers were critical of the journalists they encountered, saying the overall quality of reporters had declined. In parallel, for the same study, the journalists said criticism and scepticism in the press about relief organisations had increased (Fritz Institute, 2004, pp. 7–9).

Jonathan Munro, head of newsgathering at the BBC, says the aid agencies have become more media savvy and professional in working with journalists. "We liaise over how to bring issues and stories to air with impact. The agencies are full of very professional PR people—they are more competitive than ever from attention and funds" (personal communication, January 2014). For example, he suggests that if the UN's strict definition of a famine is not met, agencies will refer instead to "famine conditions" in an attempt to drive attention.

He also points up the strong role played by the Disasters Emergencies Committee (DEC), which co-ordinates the leading aid agencies to speak with one voice—including asking for TV airtime for appeals. "If DEC say they want to do something there is an expectation the broadcasters will respond. It's almost like a right to airtime." (When in 2009 the BBC refused to broadcast an appeal for refugees in Gaza, saying it meant adopting a political position, there was a backlash and campaign to try to get them to comply with the DEC request.) Munro says the broadcasters value aid agency–produced video—but always subject it to verification and don't broadcast it unchecked or unattributed—although such checks may not be true of all broadcasters at all times.

The agencies perhaps see less change than the broadcasters. Ian Bray is the senior humanitarian press officer for Oxfam. "News values are the same," he says. "It's the impact, the change in technology, the logistics which has changed." He refers to the use of smartphone pictures, instant live coverage, and the way social media has allowed more voices into crisis coverage. "But the major broadcasters still dominate. We need to get them on board. Our own coverage is incremental—our importance is in facilitating major news coverage." He points to one other crucial difference between media and aid agencies. "The number of deaths still skews the news value. For us, it's the living which are most important" (personal communication, January 2014).

It points up that media and aid agencies have different objectives. For the agencies, it is to relieve suffering, for the media it is to inform their audiences. The two aims can be mutually supportive, but they are not the same. Both parties have had to become more sophisticated to engage in a mutually beneficial way—and for both the risks of failing have grown in a more competitive environment. The risk, as Glenda Cooper (2011) has pointed out, is that these pressures lead to a blurring of the lines between agencies and media.

In the end, both constituencies need pictures to serve their ends and technology is perhaps the single biggest change to how crises are reported, in particular, the ability to report live from anywhere in the world. The growth of live channels and portable technology means "going live" is now a significant factor in news coverage. For Ian Bray of Oxfam the benefit is clear. "Live coverage keeps the story going and means more coverage for longer. 'Live' says to the audience the story is important and happening now." As a result, Oxfam has invested in its own live technology to enable live interviews and reporting from locations of its choice.

Jonathan Munro of the BBC says live coverage is crucial for broadcasters. "It just has more impact," he says. In 1984, extended coverage was a ten-minute report which was allowed to play out around the world over subsequent days. Technology has changed that. Munro points to the Haiti earthquake in 2010 (when he worked for ITN). "We all went there and covered the story non-stop 24 hours a day for several days—and appetite sated quickly. Within a few days we had covered most of the island, the infrastructure, aid stories, human stories and then we pulled out. We were there for a shorter period of time because technology allowed us to do all that more quickly than in the past."

But if the duration of each deployment may be shorter, the number may be growing. Nik Gowing, a presenter on BBC World News, believes that live technology has increased the overall volume of crisis coverage. "Look at Alastair Leithead reporting live from South Sudan as a military ambush took place, or at the live reporting from civil conflicts in Mali or Abidjan. These are stories that might not have got on before" (personal communication, January 2014).

He also believes that technology, social media, and mobile phones, as much as live satellites, are changing the definition of humanitarian crises. "We used to think of such crises as essentially rural. Now look at the material coming from cities in Syria. That is an urban humanitarian crisis."

It's a view shared by the American network NBC that recently ran a special series of reports as a forty-eight-hour documentary "Inside the Humanitarian Crisis of the Syrian War" (Ariens, 2014). Reports were streamed live over the Internet from inside refugee camps and hospitals and across all the networks main news programmes over a two-day period. It was an example of using technical innovation to maximise the impact of reporting. In 1984 a single extended report made a global impression. Thirty years later, it takes two days of multiplatform coverage to stand out in the media-saturated crowd.

Technology is also allowing those directly caught up in crises to communicate with the world—offering video and eyewitness accounts. The news organisation's role is then to aggregate this "citizen journalism", verify it, and put it in context.

Again in Haiti in 2010, initial reports of the earthquake came through social media. With only two foreign correspondents based on the island, who had to ensure their own safety, the first tweet came just minutes after the quake. Radio, TV, and phone networks were down, but there was some Internet capability and international organisations used the Twitter feeds of those caught up in the disaster to provide coverage for the first twenty-four hours (Bruno, 2011, pp. 6–10).

The use of social media—including graphic phone pictures—in the tsunamis in Indonesia and then Japan provide further evidence of how user content now drives TV's response to humanitarian crises. Again the most graphic images and accounts came not from news organisations—who as Reuters CEO Tom Glocer pointed out, did not have journalists and camera crews on the beaches—but from ordinary people caught up in the crisis (Glocer, 2006). This provides a raw authenticity and sense of the moment which professional coverage struggles to match.

Haiti also provides a strong example of another major change—that of developing countries to report themselves rather than rely on Western organisations to dictate coverage. One early response was from the agency Internews, which set up an FM radio station to report essential information to the survivors as "News you can use" (Hoffman, 2013, pp. 150–160).

The provision of media within developing countries—providing a platform for a greater range of voices at times of crisis—is another essential change. As countries facing crises tell their own stories and accounts they are able to influence global coverage as well.

Crowdsourcing technology can also help to steer TV coverage. The mapping technology Ushahidi brought together updates from blog posts, emails, SMS messages, tweets, and other citizen journalist sources to provide a dynamic and accurate picture of what was happening on the ground in Haiti. This in turn was used by major media on their own websites and informed their decisions on where to go and what to report. It also informed aid agencies on where and how to respond.

In all of these ways, those caught up in crises are able to influence how they are reported to a greater extent than ever before. Either by direct reporting via social media, the provision of first-hand material to news organisations, or the generation of data and information which other parties are able to analyse and use to direct both aid and reporting.

Michael Buerk's report in 1984 was a key moment in the coverage of humanitarian crises. It represented the high-water mark at the time for impact and response, a hugely powerful individual piece of reporting which modern media would struggle to match in a more competitive and fragmented environment. It produced a brief fashion for crisis reporting during which, with hindsight, some of those involved now reflect that their reporting focused too much on empathy and insufficiently on the harder political and conflict roots of crisis.

Since then, the media has grown exponentially, creating greater competition for coverage and the need for greater influence. Media has become more politicised in the interim, with reporting moving from objectivity to empathy, to national voice towards a more authentic tone or attitude influenced by the reach of social media and citizen journalism. Live reporting has become a powerful tool in reporting crises and ensuring continuing impact—although it compounds the bias of TV news towards event coverage over process and background.

At the same time the aid agencies face greater competition for funds and also the need to increase the impact of their campaigns. These two constituencies have developed and refined their relationship and means of engagement over thirty years—but are still entwined in a mutual dependency over the reporting of crises.

At the same time, technology and changes to the media ecology have allowed a greater diversity of voices, better representation on air, and the development of more local media—just as individuals and citizens have had access to the public space as well.

These changes seem certain to continue to drive the changing character and tone of reporting humanitarian crises in the years ahead.

NOTE

1. For detailed analysis of the report and its consequences, see Franks, 2013.

BIBLIOGRAPHY

Ariens, C. (2014, 11 March). NBC takes viewers inside humanitarian crisis of the Syrian War. Retrieved from https://www.mediabistro.com/tvnewser/nbc-news-takes-viewers-inside-humanitarian-crisis-of-syrian-war_b216829

Bruno, N. (2011). Tweet first, verify later? *RISJ*. Retrieved from http://reutersinstitute.politics.ox.ac.uk/publication/tweet-first-verify-later.

Buerk, M. (2004). *The road taken*. London: Hutchinson.

Cooper, G. (2011). From their own correspondent? *RISJ*. Retrieved from http://reutersinstitute.politics.ox.ac.uk/publication/their-own-correspondent

Ellis, J. (2014, 7 January). Vice News wants to take documentary-style storytelling to hotspots around the globe. Retrieved from http://www.niemanlab.org/2014/01/vice-news-wants-to-take-documentary-style-storytelling-to-hot-spots-around-the-globe/

Franks, S. (2013). *Reporting disasters*. London: Hurst.

Fritz Institute & Reuters Foundation. (2004). *Towards news understandings: Journalists and humanitarian relief coverage*. Fritz Institute.

Glocer, T. (2006, 11 October). We media speech. Retrieved from http://tomglocer.com/blogs/sample_weblog/archive/2006/10/11/98.aspx

Hoffman, D. (2013). *Citizens rising*. New York: CUNY Press.

Sambrook, R. (2010). *Are foreign correspondents redundant?* Oxford: Oxford University Press, Reuters Institute for the Study of Journalism.

CHAPTER FOUR

Digital Humanitarianism

PAUL CONNEALLY

I remember standing on the roof of the Ministry of Justice in downtown Port-au-Prince. It was about two meters high, completely squashed by the violence of the earthquake.

For those of us on the ground in those early days, it was clear for even the most disaster-hardened veterans that Haiti was something different. Haiti was something we hadn't seen before. But Haiti also provided us with something else unprecedented. Haiti allowed us to glimpse into a future of what disaster response might look like in a hyper-connected world where people have access to mobile smart devices.

The humanitarian model has barely changed since the early twentieth century. Its origins are firmly rooted in the analogue age. But there is a major shift coming on the horizon. And the catalyst for this change was the major earthquake that struck Haiti on 12 January 2010.

The earthquake destroyed the capital of Port-au-Prince, claiming the lives of some 320,000 people, and rendering homeless about 1.2 million people. Government institutions were completely decapitated, including the presidential palace.

But Haiti was a game changer. Because, out of the urban devastation in Port-au-Prince came a torrent of SMS texts—people crying for help, beseeching us for assistance, sharing data, offering support, looking for their loved ones. This was a situation that traditional aid agencies had never before encountered. We were in one of the poorest countries on the planet, but 80 percent of the people had mobile devices in their hands. We were unprepared for this—and they were shaping the aid effort.

Outside Haiti, also, things were looking different. Tens of thousands of so-called digital volunteers were scouring the Internet, converting tweets that had already been converted from texts and putting these into open-source maps, layering them with all sorts of important information. People like Crisis Mappers and Open Street Map were putting these on the web for everybody—the media, the aid organisations, and the communities themselves—to participate in, and to use.

Back in Haiti, people were increasingly turning to the medium of SMS to say that they were hungry and hurting and to report their need for help. On street sides all over Port-au-Prince, entrepreneurs sprung up offering mobile phone charging stations. They understood more than we did people's innate need to be connected.

Never having been confronted with this type of situation before, we wanted to try and understand how we could tap into this incredible resource, how we could really leverage this incredible use of mobile technology and SMS technology. We started talking with a local telecom provider called Voilà, which is a subsidiary of Trilogy International. We had basically three requirements. First, we wanted to communicate in a two-way form of communication. We didn't want to shout; we needed to listen as well. Second, we wanted to be able to target specific geographic communities. We didn't need to talk to the whole country at the same time. And third, we wanted it to be easy to use.

Out of this rubble of Haiti and from this devastation came something that we call TERA—the Trilogy Emergency Response Application—a SMS text system which has been used to support the aid effort ever since. It has been used to help communities prepare for disasters. It has been used to signal early warning in advance of weather-related disasters. It is used for public health awareness campaigns such as the prevention of cholera. And it is even used for sensitive issues such as building awareness around gender-based violence.

But does it work? We published an evaluation of this programme (Chazaly, 2011), and the evidence that is there for all to see is quite remarkable. Some 74 percent of people received the data; 0.96 percent of them found it useful. Eighty-three percent of them took action—evidence that it is indeed empowering. And 73 percent of them shared it.

The TERA system was developed from Haiti with support of engineers in the region. It is a user-appropriate technology that has been used for humanitarian good to great effect. Technology is transformational. Right across the developing world, citizens and communities are using technology to enable them to bring about change, positive change, in their own communities. The grassroots has been strengthened through the social power of sharing and they are challenging the old models, the old analogue models of control and command.

One illustration of the transformational power of technology is in Kibera. Kibera is one of Africa's largest slums. It's on the outskirts of Nairobi, the capital city of Kenya. It's home to an unknown number of people—some say between

250,000 and 1.2 million. If you were to arrive in Nairobi today and pick up a tourist map, Kibera is represented as a lush, green national park devoid of human settlement.

Young people living in Kibera in their community, with simple handheld devices, GPS handheld devices, and SMS-enabled mobile phones, have literally put themselves on the map. They have collated crowd-sourced data and rendered the invisible visible. People are continuing to layer information upon information, real-time information, tweet it and text it onto these maps for all to use. You can find out about the latest impromptu music session. You can find out about the latest security incident. You can find out about places of worship. You can find out about the health centers. You can feel the dynamism of this living, breathing community. They also have their own news network on YouTube (https://www.youtube.com/user/KiberaNewsNetwork) with 36,000 viewers at the moment.

They're showing us what can be done with mobile, digital technologies. They're showing that the magic of technology can bring the invisible visible. And they are giving a voice to themselves. They are telling their own story, bypassing the official narrative.

And we're seeing from all points on the globe similar stories. In Mongolia, for instance, where 30 percent of the people are nomadic, SMS information systems are being used to track migration and weather patterns. SMS is even used to hold herder summits with remote participation. And if people are migrating into urban, unfamiliar, concrete environments, they can also be helped in anticipation with social supporters ready and waiting for them based on SMS knowledge. In Nigeria, open-source SMS tools are being used by the Red Cross community workers to gather information from the local community in an attempt to better understand and mitigate the prevalence of malaria. My colleague, Jason Peat, who runs this programme, says that it is ten times faster and ten times cheaper than the traditional way of doing things.

And not only is it empowering to the communities, but really important, this information stays in the community where it is needed to formulate long-term health policies. We are on a planet of 7 billion people, 5 billion mobile subscriptions. By 2015, there will be 3 billion smartphones in the world. The U.N. broadband commission has set targets to help broadband access in 50 percent of the developing world. We are hurtling towards a hyper-connected world where citizens from all cultures and all social strata will have access to smart, fast mobile devices.

People are understanding, from Cairo to Oakland, that there are new ways to come together, there are new ways to mobilize, there are new ways to influence. A transformation is coming which needs to be understood by the humanitarian structures and humanitarian models. The collective voices of people need to be more integrated through new technologies into the organisational strategies and plans of actions, and not just recycled for fundraising or marketing. We need to, for example, embrace the big data, the knowledge that is there from market leaders who understand what it means to use and leverage big data.

One idea that I'd like you to consider, for instance, is to take a look at our IT departments. They're normally backroom or basement hardware service providers, but they need to be elevated to software strategists. We need people in our organizations who know what it's like to work with big data. We need technology as a core organizational principle. We need technological strategists in the boardroom who can ask and answer the question, "What would Amazon or Google do with all of this data?" and convert it to humanitarian good.

The possibilities that new digital technologies are bringing can help humanitarian organisations not only ensure that people's right to information is met, or that they have their right to communicate, but I think in the future, humanitarian organisations will also have to anticipate the right for people to access critical communication technologies in order to ensure that their voices are heard, that they're truly participating, that they're truly empowered in the humanitarian world. It has always been the elusive ideal to ensure full participation of people affected by disasters in the humanitarian effort. We now have the tools. We now have the possibilities. There are no more reasons not to do it. I believe we need to bring the humanitarian world from analogue to digital.

This chapter is based on a TEDxRC2 talk, November 2011 https://www.ted.com/talks/ paul_conneally_digital_humanitarianism

REFERENCE

Chazaly, C. (2011). *Beneficiaries communication evaluation: Haiti Earthquake Evaluation*. International Federation of the Red Cross. Retrieved from http://www.ifrc.org/Global/Publications/disasters/ reports/IFRC-Haiti-Beneficiary-Communications-Evaluation-EN.pdf.

PART TWO

Cash, Charity, and Communication

CHAPTER FIVE

'Give us your ****ing money'

A Critical Appraisal of TV and the Cash Nexus

GLENDA COOPER

At 3 pm on 13 July 1985, Bob Geldof, the organiser of Live Aid, burst out on live television: "People are dying NOW. Give us the money NOW.... F*** the address, give us the phone, here's the number."

It was, in fact, the first time such an expletive had been used on such a 'family friendly' occasion (Franks, 2013) Geldof's swearing may have broken boundaries in taste terms—yet after this outburst, giving increased to £300 per second (Geldof, 2014). And Live Aid would, more important, come to symbolise the increasing importance of the cash nexus to the aid industry.

Thirty years on, the relationship between rock-'n'-roll, charity, and money claimed the headlines in a very different way, when at the end of 2013 it emerged that the international NGO World Vision UK had paid Elizabeth McGovern (better known as the Countess of Grantham in TV series *Downton Abbey*) £28,000 to subsidise her band Sadie and the Hotheads, as part of a deal in which she would become an ambassador for the charity. In three decades we have moved from rock stars raising money for aid agencies to aid agencies paying money to rock stars to raise their profile.

This chapter will deal with the increasing importance of the cash nexus in the modern humanitarian agency and how consumerism has become embedded in aid. In this, I use Carlyle's view of the cash nexus of social relationships being reduced to economic gain, then taken on by Marx and Engels, but also the idea as expressed by Dant (2000) of the idea of the cash nexus in the area of personal choice—defining oneself by the NGO you choose to donate to or the NGO product you consume.

It will trace the development from the success of Live Aid as a televisual event to the other forms of media that have been able to marry consumerism with caring. The changes take place with the background of an increasingly competitive environment for international NGOs, coupled with the global financial crisis putting the squeeze on donations.

Today, deals with big corporates to market children's action figures, sponsorship on *American Idol*, paying for a celebrity's vanity rock band—all are now playing a role in how the most successful international NGOs operate, even if that means they find themselves in situations they could not have predicted years ago. As Justin Forsyth, CEO of Save the Children UK, puts it of his organisation's tie-up with pharma giant GlaxoSmithKline, years ago he used to picket the company's annual meeting in protest at their lack of action on HIV and Aids drugs, but in contrast now:

> They are in the forefront of finding new solutions to illnesses such as diarrhea and pneumonia, investing in a malaria vaccine. But also, they're partnered with us in investing in new health workers to administer vaccines. (Cooper, 2012)

GELDOF AND THE REBRANDING OF POVERTY

As far back as 1977, Jorgen Lissner argued there was a destructive internal conflict in NGOs between fundraising and development with the activities of fundraising and education being conflictual and competitive (Lissner, 1997, cited in Lidchi, 2005).

But the seductive success of Live Aid's moneymaking—it raised $150 million (Richey & Ponte, 2008)—opened aid agencies' eyes to the possibilities of television and other media being harnessed. And in the aftermath of Live Aid, Geldof was lauded by thinkers such as Martin Jacques and Stuart Hall, who opined that the cause of the developing world had become one of the major popular movements of its time, in contrast to a Thatcherite selfishness (Allen, 1986; Franks, 2013). Jacques and Hall (1986) saw its popularity as an attack on prevailing sensibilities and Geldof's achievement as a reinvention of Sixties' charitable activism using a combination of rock and politics. There was, they felt, a sea change in public mood.

But even in the early days that reading was disputed, most fervently by Robert Allen, who said that what Band Aid, Live Aid, and Sports Aid had created in contrast was "the first truly effective version of Consumer Aid" (Allen, 1986, p. 34). He went on:

> Consumer Aid is about a product, a packaged disaster, and a client, the individual consumer. The problems and answers of the Third World are only marginally about those

things. Central to the whole of Geldof's campaign was the idea of a sudden disaster and immediate action. This was reflected in the style of presentation, particularly of Bob Geldof himself. There was the frequent emphasis on the word 'now' and a very visual sense of urgency and crisis in the interviews and appeals. (1986, pp. 35–36)

For the aid agencies, however, Geldof's legacy was to cement the link between money and media interest. Pre-dating the much-disputed 'CNN effect', linking political action and media coverage, the connection between donations and disaster coverage seemed clear—for the 'lucky' disasters which caught a journalist or rock star's attention, the effect could be astonishing.

As the former UN Under Secretary for Humanitarian Affairs and Emergency Relief Co-ordinator, Jan Egeland, summed up not long after the 2004 tsunami, disaster victims are caught up in a 'kind of humanitarian sweepstake in which… every night 99 per cent of them lose, and one per cent win' (2005). The Red Cross's *World Disasters Report 2006* estimated that in the case of the tsunami, those affected received on average $1,241 per survivor—50 times as much as the worst-funded crises in that year (Walter, 2006).

In 2007, Eisensee and Stromberg published a study that looked at the US government's response to 5,000 disasters that occurred between 1968 and 2002, claiming 63,000 lives and affecting nearly 125 million people. They deduced that decisions on who gets aid are driven by the intensity of media coverage of disasters. They found that if the first three stories in a news bulletin have 2.4 minutes spent on them—so if it is a busy news day like the Olympics or the Columbine shootings—then that decreases the likelihood a humanitarian disaster will get covered by four percentage points, and then the probability the disaster gets relief by three points (Eisensee & Stromberg, 2007, p. 708).

Like earlier studies, Eisensee and Stromberg found that the number killed or affected does not necessarily affect newsworthiness of stories but that the type of disaster has a direct effect on its 'newsworthiness'. As they put it:

For every person killed in a volcano disaster, 40,000 people must die in a drought to reach the same probability of media coverage. Similarly, it requires forty times as many killed in an African disaster to achieve the same expected media coverage age as for a disaster in Eastern Europe of similar type and magnitude. (2007, pp. 694–695)

But when the media does concentrate on such a disaster the results can be life changing. One example is that of the Niger food crisis of 2005. A combination of drought and locust swarms during 2004 had led to harvest failure in Niger, and by mid-2005, the World Food Programme was warning that 2.5 million people were on the brink of starvation. On 16 May 2005, the UN launched a $16 million appeal. In contrast to the outpouring of money several months earlier for the South Asian tsunami, it was greeted with what Egeland called "near-deafening silence" (Egeland, 2005). By 14 July only $3.6 million had been raised. But then on 18 July, Hilary Andersson of the BBC started a series of reports on Niger for the *Ten O'Clock News* after her editor Kevin Bakhurst had spotted pictures of Niger when looking through Reuters footage to illustrate a Live 8 news package (Cooper, 2007). Within ten days, $17 million had been committed.

Mamadou Tanja, Niger's president, accused journalists of exaggerating the crisis (Aister, 2006). He was widely condemned—but the problem was many journalists who covered the problem had simplified the story so that it did not accurately reflect the situation. Niger did have food—but exporting it had caused prices to rocket. As the *Guardian's* Jeevan Vasagar (2005) pointed out, there were markets full of food. The tone of many of the Niger pieces also caused disquiet within both agencies and the BBC—it was "the worst kind of 'oh my god' dying babies journalism" according to one senior correspondent (Cooper, 2007, p. 16).

THE RISE OF SOCIAL MEDIA—SMS TO SAVE A LIFE

But even as Andersson was reporting from Niger however, a change had already taken place. Television, while still the most influential, was no longer the sole player in the cash nexus. The use of social media, particularly after the 2004 tsunami, and the increasing professionalisation of aid agency press and marketing departments meant that aid agencies were increasingly looking to new ways to raise awareness—with new opportunities for consumerist approaches.

The change over the past four decades was neatly summed up in 2013 by Mitchell Hintz, an experienced NGO fundraiser for more than 20 years.

> In the 70's, fundraisers started "personalizing" NGO fundraising (Mr X, please be a sponsor and save a child). Then, in the 80's, we tried to "commoditize" [sic] it (donate and get your free tote bag), in the 90's we "experiential-ized" it (trek northern Cambodia and save a child), by the millennium 2000 we had "life-styled it" (buy now and 5% of your payment goes to charity) and now, finally, we are "digitizing" it (reply to this SMS and buy a meal for this child). (Hintz, 2013)

The first decade of the twenty-first century saw two key developments. First, as Hintz refers, the growth of multimedia platforms, in particular SMS and Twitter, meant that news coverage and fundraising could be much more easily intertwined. Second, there was a major push towards a consumerist outlook—far beyond the 1980s 'tote bag'—in how aid agencies could sell a solution as an actual physical product—whether a PRODUCT (RED) phone, a stay in a Red Cross Hotel, or a Save the Children television programme.

In the late 1990s up to the millennium, Jubilee 2000, a campaign to write off the external debt of the world's poorest countries, demonstrated how the potential combination of the internet, celebrities, and diffuse structures could reach the public—and policy makers. The campaign—with its link to the new millennium and religious traditions—was, according to Jamie Drummond, its global strategist, a "rebranding" (Drummond, cited by Busby, 2009) of global poverty issues, in much the same way that Geldof had reconfigured the landscape in the 1980s. It paved the way for such movements as the ONE campaign, 2005's Make Poverty History (and the 2013 Enough Food IF campaign, sometimes referred to as 'Make Poverty History 2').

These campaigns were not asking for donations—ONE's slogan was explicit, "We're not asking for your money; we are asking for your voice"—they wanted people to sign up, usually electronically.

It is worth noting, however, that NGOs commonly have a policy called 'conversion'—that is changing those who are willing to sign up for a cause with their email address to giving money regularly. It becomes a grey area. As one NGO fundraiser puts it:

> There wasn't a donation request for those events/campaigns but charities did get people's data. This meant they could contact them at a later stage and ask for a direct money pledge. The fundraising value lies in getting the data and 'upgrading' the ask to a cash donation or setting up a direct debit. (personal communication, 2014)

The game changer of the 2000s, however, was the growth of text messaging to make donations. In the aftermath of the Haitian earthquake the American Red Cross alone received $21 million in text donations in just over a week—compared with $4 million raised by SMS by all US charities in 2009 (Gross, 2010).

The advantage of text fundraising was that it was immediate—and so those moved by the sight of an emotive advert or news story could donate before the feeling receded. It was also simple—it relied on punching in a short code, and then usually a word—HAITI in the 2010 earthquake, or in UNICEF's more recent Syria appeal BLANKET, and a specific amount is suggested. (In UNICEF's case the charity said that for £3, donors could help buy a blanket for a Syrian child.) And there was no need to plug in credit card information; the amount was simply added to your next phone bill.

Research carried out by the Pew Center (Smith, 2012) into those who donated via text to the Haitian earthquake appeal found that donors tended to be spur-of-the-moment givers, many of whom had not given via phone before and were twice as likely to be Twitter users as the general population. It is interesting that more than half went on to donate to other disasters—such as the Great East Japan Earthquake or the BP oil spill—as a result.

This was reflected in the UK by a report by the regulator of premium phone services, which said it saw text donations double in 2012, with one in four 18–34-year-olds having donated by text; the regulator concluded it was a "real growth opportunity for charities" (Warman, 2012).

Added to that, it is far quicker to react to moving stories than traditional media space buying. As another iNGO fundraiser puts it:

> For one food crisis we knew that [our chief exec] was going to be on BBC radio and news, and we knew what time s/he was going to be on, and we said, right, we have an SMS broadcast that we've agreed, time it for this time, because we know s/he will be on—how powerful would that be if you see the CEO of a charity on, and then you get the text, asking you to donate? (personal communication, London, 2013)

THE CORPORATISATION OF CARING

If phones were an integral part of the consumer lifestyle, they were not the only objects deployed. So, for example, Make Poverty History was not just about the sign-up and attending the rally—it was about the white rubber/fabric wristband, sold for £1 each, of which 70 per cent went to organisations such as Oxfam and Christian Aid. (The perils of such a visible consumer object came to light when it was revealed that some of the bands had been made in Chinese factories, which violated the Ethical Trading Initiative [McCormack, 2005].)

These wristbands—also used in the IF campaign—were fairly low-key however compared to the 2006 launch of PRODUCT (RED), a project dreamed up by Bono and Bobby Shriver of ONE. The pair sought to engage the private sector to raise money for HIV/AIDS in Africa by licensing a brand to partner companies such as Nike, American Express, and Apple—the idea as Richey and Ponte put it of "doing good by dressing well" (2008, p. 712). In return for the opportunity to increase revenue through the PRODUCT (RED) license, a percentage of the profit gained by each partner was donated to the Global Fund to Fight Aids, TB and Malaria—ranging from 1 per cent to 50 per cent of profits. But again there was controversy over connections with brands like Gap who had previously faced criticism for their labour standards. As Richey and Ponte elaborate further:

> Product RED, in its positive spin, masks the social and environmental relations of trade and production that underpin poverty, inequality and disease. This process, also known as 'commodity fetishism' (the term was first used by Marx), is not new per se in capitalist relations. What is new in the context of Product RED is its employment by celebrities in connecting consumption and aid. (2008, p. 722)

The profits from RED were only a tiny amount compared to the amount governments gave the Fund or foundations like the Bill & Melinda Gates Foundation. Despite some disquiet, the success of RED was noted by mainstream aid organisations. As Neal Keny-Guyer of Mercy Corps based in the US commented, NGOs were constantly looking for new and innovative approaches to raising funds.

There's a real use of new business models on the fundraising side—we try to strike interesting partnerships with different companies that would have longer-term revenue stream associated with it, whether it's through Affinity credit card or Affinity advertising or sponsorship on American Idol. We just did one with Warner Brothers and Save the Children International and International Rescue Committee around the We Can Be Heroes action figures to raise awareness around the Horn of Africa. (interview via phone, 6 February 2012)

In the UK, one of the most innovative agencies but one which has also faced criticism because of its corporate links, was Save the Children which saw its turnover grow from £140m to £300m in the space of five years according to its chief executive Justin Forsyth (personal communication, 2012). Its No Child Born to Die campaign was named slogan of the year at the 2011 AdSlogans Awards (Campaign, 2011a) and Grand Prix winner at the ThinkBox Planning Awards (Marketing, 2012). A key part of that campaign was the link up with ITV and the 2011 *Born to Shine* TV show, which raised more than £2.1 million for the charity. The six-week series involved children with exceptional talents attempting to teach celebrities a new skill. It culminated with the comedian Jason Manford being crowned the winner. The reviews for the programme were not particularly flattering, and some questioned the ethics of the approach. As Kevin O'Sullivan of the *Mirror* wrote:

> We're all for raising money for worthy causes. But unless every single last penny of the profits—including the channel's vast advertising—revenue—goes to charity it smacks of a cynical ruse. Watch this show or African kids will die. (O'Sullivan, 2011)

Meanwhile the blogger Charity Celebrity questioned whether ITV was pushing the boundaries of Section 9 of the broadcasting code, which rules that charity appeals should benefit a range of charities by featuring Save the Children so heavily (Charity Celebrity, 2011).

More serious was the controversy around Save's close relationship with several corporates. A linkup between Save and GlaxoSmithKline was announced in 2013 worth £15 million, of which £1 million was to be raised by GSK employees themselves (Boseley, 2013a). During a five-year project it was said that the drugs behemoth will train new healthcare workers to vaccinate babies and give essential medicines to children as well as reformulate some of its existing products. But as Boseley puts it: "It raises questions about Big Pharma and about the future direction of NGOs and development as a whole. And it has left a number of people working in aid feeling very uncomfortable" (2013b).

The concerns Boseley raises are whether GSK would lower its prices of HIV drugs or whether this was a Corporate Social Responsibility stunt. These questions were exacerbated by a BBC *Panorama* programme in December 2013 which raised questions about Save's earlier sponsorship deal with British Gas. A former head of news at Save the Children alleged he had been asked to spike a press release condemning price rises (Nutt, 2013) and *Panorama* also alleged that Save the Children had avoided criticism of EDF when it was in consideration for a partnership with the energy company (Milmo, 2013).

Save the Children issued a detailed rebuttal of the claims and categorically denied pulling a campaign on fuel poverty in order to win the EDF staff charity funding ("Our Rebuttal," 2013). But as Matthew Sherrington for Third Sector alleges, many charity workers attacking *Panorama* for raising the issue, missed the point.

> Corporate partnerships are often where values, money and the question of independence come crashing together. Can you take the shilling without compromising your integrity, independence and campaigning voice? You might think so and be confident of that, as Save the Children was, but is that how it will be seen? (2013)

CONCLUSION

It is the perception of the NGOs' relationships with money that has proved key, the confusion of philanthropy and commercialisation. Criticism has grown over the past decade after the problems exposed spending the South Asian tsunami money, when many journalists uncovered waste and underspending for the traditional 'anniversary' articles ("Post-tsunami Chaos Wastes Aid," 2005; Jones, 2006; Callick, 2010), and recent coverage concerning six-figure chief executive salaries (Hope, 2013; Jennings, 2013; Seamark, 2014).

The aid agencies have found themselves caught in an uncomfortable dilemma as a result: by emphasising their new professionalism (the need to recruit the best staff—and pay them well; their new global status to help people as effectively as possible), they inevitably clash with the traditional fundraising and media images they have clung on to which emphasise the individual donation can make a difference (a blanket for £3 or a wristband to show support for a cause) or that a personal connection between a donor and beneficiary (e.g., via sponsorship). A better solution might be to acknowledge this disconnect.

Even the use of celebrity (with inevitable tears as s/he experiences the developing world for the first time) often uses consciously or otherwise a Geldofian framing: rock stars taking action because of being sufficiently moved by a news story, when in reality major aid agencies all now have 'celebrity fixers'—jobs within their PR or media offices specifically tasked to sign up celebrities to their cause.

Which brings us back to the case of Elizabeth McGovern and the World Vision UK donation to her rock band. This was revealed in an excruciating *Daily Telegraph* interview in which a badly-briefed (or ignorant) McGovern confused Darfur and Dakar, appeared to be unclear that WVUK is a faith-based organisation and suggested that "in Africa people have sex more freely than we do back home" (Wallis Simons, 2013).

Not that the McGovern deal was unique: World Vision later revealed that it was paying £106,900 in total to 'artist ambassadors' in the year finishing September 2014, describing it as a "good investment" and "cost-effective" marketing (Rawstrone, 2014).

When *Third Sector* magazine asked celebrities' agents and charities whether celebrities would be paid to be ambassadors for charities, the vast majority of charities said they would not—although curiously the Agents Association and the Big Talent Group said that they would expect celebrities to be paid if they are used as 'marketing tools' (Rawstrone, 2014). What is particularly interesting is the explanation McGovern gives for accepting World Vision money in the *Telegraph* article.

> World Vision has paid her band £28,000 to fund the recording of their latest album and a UK tour, in return for which they have agreed to promote the charity. Without this money, McGovern says, her band would "never survive". (Wallis Simons, 2013)

As Geldof once said, "Give us the money NOW.... F*** the address, give us the phone, here's the number".... But who is the money for now?

NOTE

1. Communications with iNGO fundraisers took place in 2013-4 as part of wider research for the author's PhD thesis. Interview with Neal Keny-Guyer was in earlier draft of Cooper (2012) in bibliography.

BIBLIOGRAPHY

Advertising news—'No child' ad is best slogan. (2011, 2 September). *The Week.*

Advertising news—ITV talent show raises pounds 2.1m. (2011, 25 November). *The Week.*

Aister, H. (2006, 1 February). Can aid do more harm than good? BBC News. Retrieved 29 March 2012, from http://news.bbc.co.uk/1/hi/world/africa/4185550.stm.

Alexander, R. (2013, 17 June). Does a child die of hunger every ten seconds? BBC News. Retrieved 26 February 2014, from http://www.bbc.co.uk/news/magazine-22935692.

Allen, R. (1986). Bob's not your uncle. *Capital and Class, 10*(3), 31–37.

Benthall, J. (1993). *Disasters, relief and the media.* London: I. B. Tauris.

Boseley, S. (2013, 9 May). Save the Children teams up with GlaxoSmithKline. *The Guardian.* Retrieved 18 July 2013, from http://www.guardian.co.uk/business/2013/may/09/save-the-children-teams-up-glaxosmithkline.

Boseley, S. (2013, 10 May). Charity and big pharma make uneasy bedfellows. *The Guardian.* Retrieved 26 February 2014, from http://www.theguardian.com/commentisfree/2013/may/10/gsk-save-the-children-aids-drugs-africa.

Brainard, L., & LaFleur, V. (2009). Making poverty history? How activists, philanthropists and the public are changing global development. In L. Brainard & D. Chollet (Eds.), *Global development 2.0: Can philanthropists, the public and the poor make poverty history?* (p. 9). Washington, DC: Brookings Institution.

Busby, J. (2009). Is there a constituency for global poverty? Jubilee 2000 and the future of development advocacy. In L. Brainard & D. Chollet (Eds.), *Global development 2.0: Can philanthropists, the public and the poor make poverty history?* (pp. 85–101).Washington, DC: Brookings Institution.

Campaign (2011, 2 September). *'No child' ad is best slogan.* London: Author.

Callick, R. (2010, 12 July). Tsunami aid funds wasted by organisational rivalry. *The Australian.* Retrieved 12 March 2014, from http://www.theaustralian.com.au/news/nation/tsunami-aid-funds-wasted-by-organisational-rivalry/story-e6frg6nf-1225890483104.

Charity Celebrity. (2011, 9 August). Does ITV's Born to Shine give an unfair advantage to Save the Children? Retrieved 12 March 2014, from http://www.theguardian.com/voluntary-sector-network/2011/aug/09/born-to-shine-broadcasting-code.

Cooper, G. (2007) *Anyone here survived a wave, speak English and got a mobile? Aid agencies, the media and reporting disasters since the tsunami.* The 14th Guardian Lecture, Nuffield College Oxford, 5 November 2007.

Cooper, G. (2011). *From their own correspondent? New media and the changes in disaster coverage: Lessons to be learned.* Oxford: Reuters Institute for the Study of Journalism.

Cooper, G. (2012, 8 October). Reinventing the International NGO. Devex. Retrieved 18 July 2013, from https://www.devex.com/en/news/reinventing-the-international-ngo/79392.

Dant, T. (2000). Consumption caught in the cash nexus. *Sociology, 34*(4), 655–670.

Egeland, J. (2005, 11 January). The sympathy gap. *ABC News Nightline* [Television broadcast]. New York.

Egeland, J. (2005, 7 August). Niger is dying and the world is merely watching. *USA Today.* Retrieved 29 March 2012, from http://www.usatoday.com/news/opinion/editorials/2005-08-07-niger-edit_x.htm.

Eisensee, T., & Stromberg, D. (2007). News droughts, news floods and US disaster relief. *Quarterly Journal of Economics, 122*(2), 693–728.

Franks, S. (2013). *Reporting disasters: Famine, aid, politics and the media.* London: Hurst.

Geldof, B. (2014). Memorable moments at Wembley Stadium: Raising money. Retrieved 12 February 2014, from http://www.bobgeldof.com/content.asp?id=257.

Gross, D. (2010, 18 January). Red Cross text donations cross $21 million. CNN International. Retrieved 26 February 2014, http://edition.cnn.com/2010/TECH/01/18/redcross.texts/.

Hintz, M. (2013, 25 February). Dear fundraiser, What, exactly, is your 'product'? 101 Fundraising. Retrieved 11 March 2014, from http://101fundraising.org/2013/02/dear-fundraiser-what-exactly-is-your-product/.

Hope, C. (2013, 6 August). 30 charity chiefs paid more than £100,000. *Daily Telegraph.* Retrieved 12 March 2014, from http://www.telegraph.co.uk/news/politics/10224104/30-charity-chiefs-paid-more-than-100000.html.

Jacques, M., & Hall, S. (1986, July). People aid: A new politics sweeps the land. *Marxism Today, 31*, 7.

Jennings, M. (2013, 6 August) Charity CEOs' pay: Let's talk about transparency *The Guardian.* Retrieved 27 January 2015 from http://www.theguardian.com/global-development/poverty-matters/2013/aug/06/charities-ceo-pay-transparency-ngos.

Jones, M. (2006, 19 December). Tsunami funds languish in banks. BBC Newsnight. Retrieved 12 March 2014, from http://news.bbc.co.uk/1/hi/programmes/newsnight/6193737.stm.

Lidchi, H. (2005). Finding the right image. In T. Allen & T. Skelton (Eds.), *Culture and global change* (pp. 88–105). London: Routledge.

Mair, V. (2013, 29 November). DEC sees huge upsurge in text donations for the Philippines appeal. Civil Society. Retrieved 27 February 2014, from http://www.civilsociety.co.uk/fundraising/news/content/16523/dec_sees_huge_upsurge_in_text_donations_for_philippines_appeal.

Marketing. (2012, 13 June). *The best of TV planning 2012*. London: Author.

McCormack, H. (2005, 30 May). Anti-poverty bands made with forced labour, Oxfam says. *The Independent*. Retrieved 25 February 2014, from http://www.independent.co.uk/news/uk/politics/antipoverty-bands-made-with-forced-labour-oxfam-says-6145147.html.

Milmo, C. (2013, 10 December). The price of charity: Save the Children exposed after seeking approval of energy firms. *The Independent*. Retrieved 26 February 2014, from http://www.independent.co.uk/news/uk/home-news/the-price-of-charity-save-the-children-exposed-after-seeking-approval-of-energy-firms-8994225.html.

Nutt, D. (2013, 10 December). Charities need money but they also need principles. *The Independent*. Retrieved 26 February 2014, from http://www.independent.co.uk/voices/comment/charities-need-money-but-they-also-need-principles-8994059.html.

O'Sullivan, K. (2011, 24 July). Which is worse: Born to shine or show me the funny? *The Mirror*. Retrieved 27 February 2014, from http://www.mirror.co.uk/tv/tv-previews/which-is-worse-born-to-shine-or-show-me-the-funny-143521.

Our rebuttal of the allegations made by Panorama and in the Independent. (2013). Save the Children. Retrieved 26 February 2014, from http://www.savethechildren.org.uk/node/3501.

Post-tsunami chaos wastes aid. (2005, 5 October). Thomson Reuters Foundation. Retrieved 12 March 2014, from http://www.trust.org/item/?map=post-tsunami-chaos-wastes-aid/.

Rawstrone, A. (2014, 18 February). Analysis: Paying celebrities—where do charities draw the line? *Third Sector*. Retrieved 19 February 2014, from http://www.thirdsector.co.uk/Fundraising/article/1281101/Analysis-Paying-celebrities-charities-draw-line/.

Richey, L. & Ponte, S. (2008). Better RED than Dead? Celebrities, Consumption and International Aid. *Third World Quarterly, 29* (4) 711–729.

Seamark, M. (2014, 2 February). Fury over £234,000 salary of top boss of Save the Children. *The Daily Mail*. Retrieved 12 March 2014, from http://www.dailymail.co.uk/news/article-2550648/Fury-234-000-salary-boss-Save-Children-Charity-chiefs-huge-wages-reined-say-MPs.html.

Sherrington, M. (2013, 16 December). Panorama, scrutiny and charity ethics. *Third Sector*. Retrieved 26 February 2014, from http://www.thirdsector.co.uk/Communications/article/1224879/Matthew-Sherrington-Panorama-scrutiny-charity-ethics/?HAYILC=RELATED.

Smith, A. (2012, 12 January). Real time charitable giving. Pew Research Internet Project. Retrieved 11 March 2014, from http://www.pewinternet.org/2012/01/12/real-time-charitable-giving/.

Vasagar, J. (2005, 1 August). Plenty of food, yet the poor are starving. *The Guardian*. Retrieved 25 January 2015 from http://www.theguardian.com/world/2005/aug/01/famine.jeevanvasagar.

Wallace, N. (2010, 1 March). Fundraising efforts for Chile off to a slow start. *Chronicle of Philanthropy*. Retrieved 17 July 2013, from http://philanthropy.com/article/Fund-Raising-Efforts-for-Chile/64430/?sid=&utm_source=&utm_medium=en&doc=interstitialskip.

Wallis Simons, J. (2013, 22 December). Downton Abbey: Elizabeth McGovern's African adventure. *The Telegraph*. Retrieved 19 February 2014, from http://www.telegraph.co.uk/culture/tvandradio/downton-abbey/10526655/Downton-Abbey-Elizabeth-McGoverns-African-adventure.html.

Walter, J. (Ed.). (2006). *World Disasters Report 2006*. London: IFRC.

Warman, M. (2012, 20 December). Text message donations double to £66m. *The Telegraph*. Retrieved 11 March, 2014, from http://www.telegraph.co.uk/technology/news/9756485/Text-message-donations-double-to-66million.html.

Westcott, R. (2005, July). What Is Making Poverty History? BBC. Retrieved 27 February 2014, from http://www.bbc.co.uk/music/thelive8event/whylive8/povertyhistory.shtml.

CHAPTER SIX

NGOs, Media, and Public Understanding 25 Years On

An Interview with Paddy Coulter, Former Head of Media, Oxfam

PADDY COULTER WITH GLENDA COOPER

In 1989, Paddy Coulter, former head of media for Oxfam, trustee of Comic Relief, and the man who facilitated Michael Buerk's first trip to Ethiopia, wrote a piece for the New Internationalist *magazine, making a powerful attack on aid agencies of the time for their reliance on backward-looking 'starving children' imagery. This pushed the idea of a passive developing world, and agencies whose intervention was cheap, easy, and risk-free and which failed to mention the indispensable work that local partners did.*

The article, titled 'Pretty as a Picture', was a controversial one, particularly as it was written by an insider. Coulter ended with a plea for agencies to stop seeing fundraising as the dominant, if not primary objective, and to fulfil their responsibilities to educate the public.

To mark twenty-five years on from that piece, we invited Coulter to reflect on the situation then and now, and what developments and differences he sees now in 2014.

EARLY YEARS: FROM DISCRETE ADVERTISING TO ADVERTISING GURUS

Q: Can you start by just filling us in on your experience in seeing how charities deal with publicising disasters?

A: My first involvement with Oxfam came in the early 1970s. I was working in Ethiopia and then in Yemen—I was Oxfam's first country director in Yemen in 1972. The key influences of that time in terms of charity communications were still very much the approaches of early Oxfam figure Cecil Jackson-Cole and his acolyte, Harold Sumption.

These two had pioneered a different approach to advertising. Previously the charities like Save the Children Fund (as it was then) and the Red Cross were very much sedate, establishment outfits, and rarely advertised at all. And when they did, it was very discreet. In comparison, the combination of Jackson-Cole (a businessman-cum-philanthropist), and Sumption, an advertising guru, applied commercial business techniques for the first time.

They used a combination of striking image and punchy copy. Some of this stuff was very much 'child in distress', 'human skeleton' etcetera and Jackson-Cole and Sumption certainly have to take responsibility for that. But they also ran more thought-provoking advertising, saying things like "Oxfam HATES hungry children" or "Help Oxfam STOP feeding hungry children" with "hates" and "stop" in huge bold capital letters. They were aware of the ongoing tension between maximising income and public education, both of which are strong impulses within aid agencies.

TRADITIONAL MEDIA, OVERSIMPLIFIED IMAGERY, AND CHARISMATIC FIGURES

Q: Sumption's influence was marked in the 1950s; what changes did you see in the next decade?

A: Sumption and Jackson-Cole led the innovation in the use of advertising in mass-circulation newspapers. But by the time of the Biafran Emergency of the late sixties we find, for the first time, strong competition from popular television news bulletins for public attention. To see how it had changed, you need to compare Biafran media coverage with that of the Congo in the early 1960s. Congo had been a classic African famine disaster but I can identify only one television interview from that time with an Oxfam official for BBC News and this was extremely stilted. It went on the lines: "Tell me, Mr Oxfam director, is there tremendous need in the Congo?" To which Oxfam's then director, Leslie Kirkley replied, "Yes, there is tremendous need in the Congo," and that was the end of the take. It was a new technology and aid agencies weren't at home with it.

But Biafra was different. If you look at it in the context of Suzanne Franks' book (2013), you can see how a very clever African politician, Odumegwu Ojukwu, duped and outwitted most of the British media, international NGOs, and a lot of the wider world. When you read the Oxfam papers of the time, there were warnings from the very knowledgeable Tim Brierly, Oxfam's country director for Nigeria, who kept saying, 'Hang on, this is getting unbalanced"—as did the chair of Oxfam's Africa Committee—but against this there was a one-sided, seemingly unstoppable media campaign to 'save Biafra'.

Looking back it seems hardly credible now to have the pre-Murdoch *Sun* and the *Daily Express* competing over Biafra stories with journalists of the calibre of Michael Leapman, later of the *Observer* but then of the *Sun*, splashing stories on the emergency. And there was now a new media player, ITN, whose entrance was that of a brash intruder, transforming the staid ways of BBC News. So you had a scenario in the 1960s where the printed press is still top dog, but by the time I first worked in Ethiopia in the early 1970s it was television that had taken over the lead, for example, exposing with the Wollo famine in Jonathan Dimbleby's 'The Unknown Famine' report on ITV in 1973. This takeover by television of course was to culminate in Michael Buerk's BBC Television News coverage of an even more extensive Ethiopian famine a decade later.

But with Biafra you had a situation where the NGOs on the whole got the analysis wrong, as had most of the media. It was presented to the British public as a desperate one-sided race to save children, which was playing into the hands of those wanting a prolongation of the war.

This was exacerbated by oversimplified imagery, a colonial mind set, competition between the media plus the involvement of some very charismatic figures like the writer Frederick Forsyth and the photographer Don McCullin on the Biafran side. Cooler heads got side-lined in the frenzy. A frame was established for how a relief emergency got covered—but it was the wrong frame.

RECOGNISING THE PROBLEM, CHALLENGING THE FRAME

Q: What do you mean by the wrong frame?

A: I think perhaps the most pernicious thing was the frame of whites to the rescue of blacks, and that is one of the most persistent problems in this area, a hangover from an imperial era. Relief agencies know you've got to simplify the situation to catch public attention and engage them but the challenge is to simplify in a way that does not distort.

The principal distortion is as follows: all these relief agencies operate through partnerships with national and local governments, local civil society organisations, church networks and the like—but these tend almost always to get written out of the script in charity advertising. The agency always has to appear top dog. It is the outside relief agency which is made out to have potency, and this is fundamentally misleading.

Q: Do you have personal experience of this?

A: I remember very vividly in 1984 when the Oxfam relief operation was set up, it was an emergency operation which had to be added to an overwhelmingly development-focused programme. There were 108 employees in all, of whom 100 were Ethiopian and only a handful of specialists flown in from outside. The reality was for Oxfam, as for all the other international relief organisations, the main burden of the relief effort was being carried by nationals of that country. But that was very far from the picture that the British public got. Locals get written out of the script very quickly when it comes to fundraising.

The Ethiopian famine was the first time I recall that the internal debate within Oxfam on advertising post-Sumption becoming more sophisticated. I remember the fundraisers sitting down with the campaigners and communications people in an effort to work out a different kind of charity advertising, one which would combine public education with raising the cash which the charity required. We came up with advertising that there were two things you could do for Ethiopia: one was to give money, the second was to sign up to Oxfam's Hungry for Change campaign, which was tackling the deeper issues of trade, arms, and debt. There was a determination to get across some of the complexity.

There was also a kind of frustration that Oxfam had been party to an established frame and by the 1980s we were in danger of being trapped in it. It all too often ended up with Oxfam's veteran emergencies expert, the late Jim Howard, or myself being in front of a camera because we were the people who were most conversant with television interviews. At that time British television journalists would not normally look for Africans to comment and their news organisations didn't care to run interviews on mainstream bulletins with captions and translation—that was not regarded as acceptable for many viewers—with the net effect that we were inadvertently adding to the distortion of 'Brits to the rescue of Africans'.

We did try to challenge this; I recollect that we went back to ITN for a corrective, in a bid to try to get them to interview locals. But to get on *News at Ten* for that, we had to have Glenda Jackson to go out to interview Ethiopians and get their perspectives—we needed a celebrity to do that.

Q: How responsible was Oxfam for this situation though?

A: The fault was in our heads—not being sufficiently conscious of it at the time to insist, for example, on media training for our Ethiopian colleagues in order to give them a much greater familiarity with the most powerful medium. But there was also fault with the conventions of television news that we had to have a British celebrity to introduce Ethiopians to the peak-time British viewing public.

IMAGES OF AFRICA AND THE RED CROSS CODE OF CONDUCT

Q: What changes came about post-Ethiopia?

A: The contradictions on the Ethiopian famine coverage were so overwhelming that it led to a huge debate, which crystallised in *Images of Africa* [the 1987 Oxfam report by Nikki van der Gaag and Cathy Nash] and that ultimately led to the Red Cross Code of Conduct in Disaster Relief of 1992[1]. Today, when you look at the code it may not strike you as being a momentous achievement—it is saying the obvious that people should have dignity in media portrayal, and agencies should be responsible. Before that, the better agencies had had internal principles, but they weren't Holy Writ—they could be overridden in certain situations.

The problem with this is the interagency competition, particularly in the situation of financial recession, when donations drop. It comes down to the argument about how principled you are. You may say, "Well, I'm very principled"—but if you're director of an organisation that has just effectively lost out on millions of pounds of potential charitable income and your trustees are beginning to wonder why they've employed you, you may come to feel that you are too principled. There can be a race to the bottom in charitable advertising.

Q: Did the Code make a discernible difference then?

A: With the 1992 code, all the key humanitarian relief agencies signed up for it and so for the first time ever there was an inter-agency deal on behaviour with media and advertising. I saw the code as a real breakthrough, thinking, 'That's it! That's been fixed!' as it had been something I'd been very irritated about in the '80s. But when I wrote that article in *New Internationalist*[2] in 1989 that there was a sense from some that these problems were going to be resolved. I find myself looking back and feeling that was a very naïve view! It's a bit like looking back at old-fashioned sexist advertising, for example, the use of attractive women in ads to sell cars. It became such a joke—what has a woman's body got to do with the selling of a car?—you thought that nobody would ever again stoop to that. Well, it turns out an awful lot of people would and it has all resurfaced. Similarly with charitable advertising, this battle is never finally won, it's not susceptible to being finally won because simplification is the name of the game—and your simplification is my oversimplification.

Then added to that, we have many completely new aid players coming in, including foundations like Gates, China and the other BRICS countries, sovereign wealth funds and diaspora groups—for instance, committed Muslim humanitarians driving to Syria. None of these new players had been involved in formulating this code. I think in too many charity quarters the argument still remains, "What we have to do is attract the maximum number of eyeballs to this now; the deeper public education can come later but, to paraphrase Bob Geldof, we first absolutely have to have the f***ing money." That's the root problem.

COMIC RELIEF: A CRITICAL TURNING POINT?

Q: Tell me about your experience with Comic Relief. You were involved at the beginning there.

A: I was involved from the very early days of Comic Relief, becoming a trustee of the charity for some ten years. I misjudged the very beginning—when I first met Comic Relief co-founders Richard Curtis, who then had a name as a radio comedy scriptwriter, and Jane Tewson, who was involved with Mencap, made their first visit to Oxfam House and wanted to send comedians to Africa, my first instinct was that sounded like the limit! But I quickly re-thought and saw that was really quite ingenious; someone like Lenny Henry could get over messages in a way that conventional aid agencies couldn't.

And by this stage Oxfam, which had started life as an anti-establishment body, was now a very large organisation, Britain's biggest charitable aid institution. So if comedians could take up this cause, they could have a 'Heineken effect' and reach a public that Oxfam simply couldn't. So I rapidly changed my position 180 degrees.

There is a brilliant early Comic Relief film when there are seven or eight Ethiopians wrapped in *shammas* (a loose wrap) standing in a row outside a typical Ethiopian *tukul* (a traditional circular hut) and the camera pans from left to right and then jerks back and the middle face creases up and the viewer sees that it is Lenny Henry. That makes the point eloquently that Ethiopians are real people (like the Lenny Henry the viewers already know) and as such this piece was probably more effective than our Oxfam initiative with Glenda Jackson. Certainly in the early days of Comic Relief there was innovation after innovation.

Q: But you became uneasy about Comic Relief and resigned as a trustee?

A: I began to worry how unbalanced the fundraising imagery was becoming. The emotiveness, which reaches to the widest possible audience and which gets the money coming in, and the public education aspect had been held in tension at the beginning, particularly for a very creative period in the nineties, but it later got seriously out of kilter. The use of celebrities, which is justifiable in terms of appealing to a very wide audience, was to become ever more strongly focused on the emotions of the visiting celebrity, and less and less on seizing the opportunity to explain the nature of the African partnership. The audience also got the impression of weakness and powerlessness on the part of Africans which I found disturbing. This is a trend that had started to bother me when I was a trustee—I want to give you the example of the film treatment of Ethiopian street children.

THE TROUBLE WITH 'GRAB THE EYEBALLS NOW, EDUCATE LATER'

Q: Tell me about your experience in Ethiopia.

A: As I found when I first turned up in Ethiopia in 1971, street children in Addis Ababa have acute problems of deprivation as well as posing a considerable social problem themselves. I recall that street children back then would demand a couple of dollars to look after your parked vehicle and if you dared not to give them this, when you returned to your vehicle, the exhaust would have been dismantled and you would pay a lot more than a few dollars to get it fixed.

From, I think, the late 1980s Comic Relief started supporting imaginative work with the Addis street children and gave substantial funding over a period of years. This was successful—not just in terms of giving street children a conventional education but also of stimulating their creativity and of training them for employment. Some became successful performers and dancers, doing shows in public, including in the city's main square for public gatherings, Meskel Square, in front of enormous audiences. And there was a film and video training component to the project with help from a couple of committed BBC film producers so the street children could film their own activities.

For a Red Nose Day of the late 1990s, the plan was for the street children project to be visited by a celebrity, in this case the actress and comedienne Julie Walters. When the film team came back from the shoot, I was able as a trustee to review the rough footage and it was clear they had got masses of material of all the different dimensions of the project. However, when I was sitting in on the BBC viewing of the fine cut later on, the focus of the film was limited to the education of the younger street children, with appealing shots of Julie Walters with her arm around a little boy doing his homework by the light of a hurricane lamp.

It was a powerful piece, very emotive and skilfully produced, but where, I asked, were the adolescent children and scenes of their vocational training in performance arts and indeed of their own filmmaking capacities and evidence of their progress? Without some of these elements a sense of the empowerment of street children and what they could go on to achieve was missing. I was told that the insertion of those sequences showing Ethiopian street children as successful dancers or filmmakers would not bring anything like the same amount of money as the more narrowly focused film. And I was reminded that it is very important to Comic Relief that each Red Nose

Day sets a new record total of funds raised. As indeed it is because the achievement gets used by sympathetic politicians and the aid industry more generally every time they are challenged on the popularity of aid to say, "Well, actually Comic Relief has attracted a record amount of money from the British public this year" to back up their claim that there is not a seriously declining public appetite for giving aid.

Now I accept that if the sequences which I favoured were inserted, then Red Nose Day probably wouldn't raise quite as much money as the sequences which had been chosen. On the other hand, it seemed to me the Red Cross code rules out a policy of maximisation of money at all costs. Certainly it was a policy I didn't hold with and so I stepped down as a trustee with these misgivings. I found this personally a very difficult issue because I believed Comic Relief and the setting up of Red Nose Day was a hugely creative and wonderful thing, one which has had such an enormous impact on the school system in the UK that it is almost embedded in the curriculum. I also worried that critical noises might play into the hands of that vocal anti-aid lobby orchestrated by the likes of the *Daily Mail* and serve to undermine public support for development and make the situation worse. But if you ask me directly about my views on Comic Relief's recent fundraising imagery, I have to say that I feel that it's going in quite the wrong direction.

The trouble, in my view, with the 'grab the eyeballs now, educate later' approach is that the education part never really happens, or if it does, it's very subsidiary and short lived and doesn't attract anything like the same resource and effort. So that became a parting of the ways, in sorrow and not anger.

Q: What is your verdict now?

A: The original impulse [of Comic Relief] was so brilliant and creative, but if the only way the level of popularity can be maintained is by ignoring or suppressing inconvenient information because of the need to maximise the cash return, I, for one, would rather accept a smaller return and have a more 'educated pound'. Because aid is not just the crude insertion of cash, it's what is done with it and the relationship you have with your beneficiaries that is crucial. And if the role of beneficiaries is subtly reduced or not so subtly edited out, then I think the public is being given a very partial and distorted view, particularly in the case of Ethiopian street children who turn out to be like teenagers here—or even better than us because some of them have been able to make the leap from being street children to being performers and filmmakers.

Q: Is this a problem confined to Comic Relief?

A: No. I feel this erosion of the Red Cross Code goes on across the charitable sector. Officially when agencies join BOND, the membership body of UK-based development NGOs, they are obliged to subscribe to the code. Yet I was watching television the other day and caught a Save the Children Fund advert that seemed to violate those principles. SCF is a sophisticated agency which knows better than most about the complexity of development, and yet they are wilfully putting out this misleading and reductive messaging.

The SCF ad managed to insinuate most of those messages I objected to in the original *New Internationalist* article—that intervening is risk-free, it's cheap and easy, little or no references to the causes of suffering or its complexities at all, and any partners involved are edited out of the equation. But I know from my own field experience that where Save the Children are at their most effective is where they are working with a national or local government partners or a community group. And then there's the question of the beneficiaries. Are the people involved really aware of how they are being used? I am concerned that agencies pay lip service to the beneficiaries, but the assumption is that if the advertising 'works' in terms of raising money at more or less any price, then that can be justified.

NEW HORIZONS? CHANGING MEDIA, COMPLEX PARTNERSHIPS, POWER DISCONNECTS

Q: What do you see as a solution?

A: There are many questions involved here: Does there need to be a renewal and, indeed, a toughening of these codes, and what is the engine of implementation? What is the regulation of this? Is it self-regulation? Are the trustees regulating? And how much do agencies discuss this with the beneficiaries? The evidence is that people, when they are consulted about how they are portrayed, often do have strong views.

I feel two things really matter here. One is that this issue of enforcement of codes and who regulates needs to be brought right up charity agendas. We've seen with the regulation of the press that it's pretty hopeless relying on people to police their own. I would imagine that if I was back on the Oxfam board I would be wondering 'what price our principles?' when we see Save the Children and others going down this road.

Two, I think we need to see another burst of new creativity over communicating aid and development. When I wrote that *New Internationalist* article I was criticising allies like the UN Association and the *New Statesman* for carrying a UNA ad with a stereotypical image of an African skeletal child. Stephen Platt, the then editor of the *Statesman*, responded to the NI with a letter challenging, "Well, what would Mr Coulter show? What would he do?" That is a good question.

It seems to me looking back on all this that there is a pattern which starts off with a brilliant surge of creative energy, but then you reflect later on the flaws—for example, take Oxfam which, having invented mass charity advertising, by the sixties was re-thinking this as too crude and at odds with basic principles. Then come the

African famines of the 1970s and '80s that reinforce the stereotypes which seem to 'work', at least on a fundraising level. But then, by the time of the Ethiopian famine of the 1980s it becomes so difficult for the agencies that they are forced to reflect much more deeply and then that fresh thinking eventually generates a new inter-agency code. And that seemed to be that, issue done and dusted. But of course it wasn't and it isn't. I have a theory that it goes in cycles over the decades with the pulse waxing and waning. The big question is whether the situation needs to get so much worse at the bottom of a cycle that out of it will come the best new creative thinking.

I can see the internet and social media are allowing people to be their own media, therefore enforcement of codes will become far more difficult in future. But you have nevertheless to develop some very clear principles and have the best creative minds doing something with different approaches, ones that fit the situation. And this is a different situation from before, one where global poverty is overall in decline and if the world were to sustain this trend, extreme poverty could be very radically reduced if not eliminated within the next 15–20 years. The research I've been associated with at OPHI (the Oxford Poverty and Human Development Initiative) shows that the countries that are making the fastest inroads into poverty are some of the poorest countries but it's the middle-income countries like India that have the largest repositories of poor people that are the most sluggish. The challenge is to make innovative partnerships to end poverty a proposition that everyone would want to support.

Q: Why do you think agencies hide their work with partners?

A: If the choice is between an emotive piece with Julie Walters with her arm around a little kid studying with the aid of a hurricane lamp versus a non-engaging mini-documentary, then it's a no-brainer. But why is it not possible to highlight more of the success, to show that people's lives have been transformed by their own efforts and the efforts of supportive partner organisations? Surely that is a genuine 'good news' story?

I wonder if in part it's because the current more professional generation of fundraisers and marketeers have less of a background in relief and development, less direct personal involvement with people and programmes on the ground. Is this separation fostered by career trajectories which mean you are likely to have come up by being a fundraiser or marketeer with some other charity in a different field, and it's this professional expertise that comes across, rather than any necessary identification with poor people and an understanding of how development occurs?

The beneficiaries of aid are a long way away and so on the whole are not going to see the adverts to complain. You couldn't do some of this stuff with a domestic audience who have much more direct access to media and powerful representatives, including MPs. The agencies have a freer hand than would a domestic charity, especially if you are not consulting beneficiaries and not dealing with them directly. There is a power disconnect at the bottom of all this where professional aid careers here are judged not by the adherence to the Red Cross Code, not by their consultation with beneficiaries nor by how far they have been able to take this challenge of simplification and do it in an ingenious way, but—crudely—are they bringing in the loot?

NOTES

1. In particular, article 10 of the Code read, "In our information, publicity and advertising activities, we shall recognize disaster victims as dignified human beings, not hopeless objects". See more at http://www.ifrc.org/en/publications-and-reports/code-of-conduct/#sthash.Zc43Lkvq.dpuf.
2. http://newint.org/features/1989/04/05/pretty/.

REFERENCE

Franks, S. (2013). *Reporting disasters*. London: Hurst.

CHAPTER SEVEN

3,000 Words that Explain How to Build a Powerful Fanbase, Make Your Message Go Viral, and Raise Millions for Your Cause

LIZ SCARFF/FIELDCRAFT STUDIOS

Back in 1971, when the founders of Greenpeace wanted to raise awareness of nuclear testing, they took a boat to Alaska and were able to make a huge international news splash as the media influence was brokered and controlled by a small circle of broadcasters (Greenpeace, 2007).

This wouldn't work in today's media landscape. The monopoly on publishing and participation has been irreversibly broken.

As sites like BuzzFeed re-write the content rules, and YouTube, its multi-channel networks, and media organisations like VICE are re-wiring broadcast media, our rapidly changing media landscape has simultaneously empowered and fractured audiences (or fans[1]) into super niches. The ability to publish and command an audience (or fanbase) is now out of the clutches of the few becoming open to anybody with a talent for telling a good story. As a result, the lines between news reporter, bystander, and NGO have become blurred.

In this new communications paradigm, NGOs should be recalibrating their relationship with both donors and beneficiaries by designing stories that simultaneously unfold over multiple platforms and, crucially, encourage participation that connects and builds a community/fanbase they can then mobilise to take action or donate.

When Harry Jenkins, Director of MIT Comparative Media Studies Program, coined the phrase 'participatory culture' in 1992 for his book, *Textual Poachers*, by his own admission he had no idea how participatory it would get.

"I was trying to set up a basic contrast between the ways that mass media had created a spectator culture, and the ways that fandom was asserting a collective and individual right to participate within media culture, often through the production of new kinds of works—fan fiction primarily, but also fan music and fan video—from the raw materials that the culture industry provided," says Jenkins (Rose, 2013).[2]

But as the lines become blurred between reporter (reporting facts to an audience who passively consume them) and citizen journalist (citizens getting involved in the production and dissemination of news) become blurred, so too has the line between a previously passive audience and a participatory community/fanbase. And while Jenkins may not have predicted the degree to which participation has become embedded in our culture, Jenkins's assertions on fandom ring as true today, as we witness a rise in social media stars, with audiences—or fans—in the millions spawning a whole new media industry.

Creation, promotion, and distribution are no longer in the hands of a few. If fans, creators, and hobbyists are the new publishers they are also our new distributors.

YouTube's head of entertainment, Alex Carloss, suggests that YouTube's power is less about audiences and more about fans at the recent MIPTV Conference in Cannes. "An audience tunes in when they're told to, a fanbase chooses when and what to watch. An audience changes the channel when their show is over. A fanbase shares, it comments, it curates, it creates," he said (Dredge, 2014).

It isn't just the readily available and affordable technological tools that are changing rapidly—it's our culture. The rise and influence of the YouTube star has been significant over the last few years. YouTubers (vloggers) now walk the red carpet with film and TV celebrities, and are sought after by big brands to pimp their products to their audiences of millions. In April 2014 Tanya Burr, a British beauty vlogger with an audience of more than 2 million subscribers, was invited to walk the red carpet at the London premier of *Noah* to help promote the film—Burberry subsequently got in touch and asked if they could dress her. Burr has also launched her own makeup line with Superdrug (http://www.tanyaburr.co.uk/?blog=blogs/archive/2014/04/07/superdrug.stores.for.tanya.burr.cosmetics.aspx).

YouTube even has its own fan-produced industry conference. Vid Con, launched in 2010 by the Vlog Brothers, is now the largest gathering of online video viewers, creators, and industry. The Vlog Brothers are John and Hank Green who began broadcasting on YouTube in 2007. The brothers decided to cease all text-based communication for one year and instead converse by video blogs every weekend. As their popularity increased so did their influence, which in 2013 saw

John Green taking part in a Google+ Hangout with President Obama (https://www.youtube.com/watch?v=kp_zigxMS-Y).

By 2009, a new wave of independent YouTube multi-channel networks began to emerge. Multi-channel networks (MCNs) bring numerous YouTube channels and their owners under one network umbrella. They provide assistance in the form of promotion, channel management, and brand monetisation in return for a cut of advertising revenue from the existing YouTube partner programme.

A series of recent MCN buyouts suggest that larger media corporations are recognising the industry disruption and the power and influence of YouTube, its stars, and community. Maker Studios, established 2009 and which today claims 5.5 billion views a month, was sold last to Disney in March 2014 for a reported $500 million. Awesomeness TV, an MCN aimed at teens and tweens was bought by Dreamworks Animation in May 2013 for a reported £17 million, and Warner Brothers paid $18 million in March 2014 for the gaming MCN Machinima.

Consumption of media via digital and social networks is on the increase (Pew Center, 2014) and top-ranking YouTube stars and their channels are commanding audiences higher than many primetime TV shows. The production principles of a good media story (be you a journalist or NGO PR) haven't changed—but the platforms on which we tell them and our viewing habits have. Social and digital channels like YouTube should not be viewed as just a transit lounge for eyeballs on content—they have their own unique communities that should be nurtured to become super fans of your brand.

For NGOs (and any brand publishing content) this means that understanding your audience or fanbase is essential but as audiences have been fractured into super niches, traditional audience profiling is now not enough. It is vital to understand audiences in the social space, how they group around a topic, niche, or geographical location, and how this relates to your own brand and, in turn, your own burgeoning community.

IF IT DOESN'T SPREAD IT'S DEAD

Cheap and readily available technology has been disrupting creative industries for decades—with broadcast being the latest. When Fieldcraft Studios launched the Medical Innovation Bill via the first live Google+ Hangout from the House of Lords for Lord (Maurice) Saatchi on February 24, 2014, (http://youtu.be/9uxwl0e-DcU), we built a sophisticated portable broadcast quality TV studio in two weeks in order to facilitate a live broadcast across the internet. The House of Lords Google+ Hangout was a truly democratic way to gather public opinion in the heart of the Palace of Westminster. We worked with key partners, both traditional media, such as *The Telegraph*, and new media—via our network of social media influencers—in order to amplify the content.

Whether from the Palace of Westminster or a humanitarian emergency telling real stories of real people in real time, thus allowing the audience to walk in the shoes of an NGO beneficiary and indeed allow the beneficiary to tell their own story, is now not only reserved for the media organisations alone.

In 2014 Sightsavers commissioned Fieldcraft Studios[3] to produce an innovative LIVE broadcast from a hospital in rural Malawi. This LIVE storytelling event unfolded across multiple channels, including social media, Google+ Hangouts/YouTube and press adverts, traditional media and email newsletters.

We invited YouTube star Doug Armstrong to present the first LIVE Google hangout broadcast of a cataract surgery from a hospital in rural Malawi. A global audience watched LIVE as Winesi Marche, 69, blind for two years, received a life-changing 7-minute operation.

The following day Doug hosted the incredible moment the bandages were removed and Winesi, with his sight restored, met his grandson for the first time. Using a custom built portable TV studio, the innovative LIVE broadcasts directly connected the surgeon, health worker and patient with the audience.

Participants on the hangout and via the Twitter hashtag #SeeTheMiracle asked questions of the local surgeon and got answers in real time.

We also produced stunning photography and video that unfolded across social media press ads the week before. Introducing the characters: Winesi, his family and issues facing people with blinding cataracts. Health worker, Madalitso Nyangulu, travelled miles by motorbike along treacherous roads to find and refer Winesi to Dr Msukaw, one of Malawi's few trained eye surgeons who performed the LIVE surgery.

A super-charged audience engagement strategy ensured these complex issues reached a wide audience. Twitter chats, blogger engagement and working with a YouTube star delivered a 10 million reach on Twitter and produced 1,500 blogs—most notably 1,200 from blogging students across the UK, and a 33 million audience reach across traditional media.

Most notably the creative and innovative nature of the project secured DFID match funding and enabled us to partner with Google and *The Telegraph* and raised £10 million in three months.

Also disrupting the traditional broadcast model using Google's hangout technology is entertainment show *The Fox Problem*, launched in March 2013. The chat show, an homage to *The Word* and *TFI Friday*, is significant because it bypassed all traditional routes of commissioning and production. It was delivered through Google+ and YouTube and embedded across G+, Facebook, Twitter, and entertainment blogs.

This democratisation of technology has led to the growth of communities and networks who use their collective power for causes or issues they believe in. As each member has an individual presence on several social media channels they can collectively pack as big, if not bigger, punch as traditional media. The Harry Potter Alliance, a coalition of Potter fans who feel passionate about the power of story to inspire and affect social change, and hacktivist network Anonymous are just two examples—each at the polar opposite end of the participatory spectrum.

Google has recently dubbed this audience Gen C, people who care deeply about creation, curation, connection, and community. They say, "It's not an age group; it's an attitude and a mind-set." And this mind-set, coupled with the right technological tools, is dictating a shift from the organisation-led campaign to a charge led by the people. The challenge for NGOs is to find a symbiotic balance between the two.

In April 2014 terminal cancer patient Stephen Sutton gained media notoriety when his bucket list, which included raising £100,000 for Teenage Cancer Trust, went viral. Stephen inspired and built a community with his daily personal Facebook and Twitter updates. The Teenage Cancer Trust were quick to support Stephen and as his campaign snowballed he raised in excess of £3 million for the charity.

CROWDFUNDING £2 MILLION FOR A CANCER CURE

For most, if not all organisations, it is the organisation, not the supporters, who make the decision on fundraising appeals. In comparison crowdfunding allows a community to fund what matters to them most.

On the first anniversary of Steve Jobs' death, Fieldcraft Studios, along with author Alexander Masters and communications specialist Dominic Nutt, launched a crowdfunding campaign, iCancer, to raise £2 million to fund research into a potential treatment for the cancer that killed Steve Jobs.

The potential therapy, a cancer-busting virus, which if successfully developed could significantly extend the lives of patients with the same cancer as Steve Jobs, was sitting in a freezer in Sweden untested for lack of just £2 million. Without the money, the potential treatment was to be thrown away, placing in jeopardy a therapy that could significantly extend the lives of thousands of NET cancer sufferers.

Fieldcraft Studios run experimental test lab projects and we were keen to test crowdfunding. We worked pro-bono, preparing the campaign and the media plan in just over a week. With the *Telegraph* on board as a launch partner and a solid campaign strategy we launched on the first anniversary of Steve Jobs' death.

As we were not a charity or brand we had no existing supporter base, networks, or community to help us amplify our message and contribute to our goal. We were starting from ground zero. We worked hard to build trust. An existing organisation will have a longstanding reputation built on, among other elements, trust. We had to quickly establish a rapport—to do this we made available all the research papers and produced video testimonies of support from eminent, independent experts.

We also worked hard to ensure that our messaging was inclusive—that our audience knew that we, with them, were all one team enabling medical research and breaking down the stranglehold of big, profit-led pharma together. We did this in the creative production which included tight direction of both the video and the story narrative for the social content—both encouraged our burgeoning community to participate.

We created a digital storm. We achieved significant national and international coverage including Radio 4's *Today* programme, *Financial Times*, *Telegraph*, *The Guardian*, and *Mashable Nature Magazine*. We also received huge celebrity support on Twitter, essential for amplification, and sparked a rich and vocal debate in the cancer research community with our ground-breaking approach to funding medical research.

Our newly formed community started to participate. They created posters, animations, helped spread the word at coffee mornings. One man walked to the shops every day, saving his £1 bus fare. He did that for 30 days and sent a cheque for £30.

Within the first two days we raised $15,000 and the money kept rolling in. More than 4,000 people from around the world contributed and in a few months we raised £250,000. Fieldcraft Studios have developed an 'amplification loop' strategy where social media and traditional media are designed to work together, each feeding the other and thereby increasing exposure. As a result of the campaign publicity a high-net-worth donor approached us and donated the remaining money, giving us a total of £2 million.

"It's about people voting with their wallet for what people really want, rather than letting the gatekeeper decide what the people should have," says Danae Ringleman, co-founder of the San Francisco based crowdfunding site Indiegogo, in an interview with *Aeon* (Masters, 2014). "When we saw your iCancer campaign go up,' she continued, 'everyone here at the office took notice because it's new. It's paving the way for people to think differently about which drugs should come to market."

Crowdfunding enables anybody anywhere to test out an idea—or fund somebody else's. In re-calibrating their relationship with funders and supporters, NGOs would benefit from striking a better balance between gatekeeper and enabler. People want to participate, they want to feel like they are making a difference, that their contribution counts—and they want to be rewarded for it.

BUT HOW IS A THUMBS-UP GOING TO HELP IN A FAMINE?

Does sharing content across social channels achieve anything tangible? Will we at best simply cheer up our internet friends with listicles such as, '28 cats having a worse day than you,' or can it be used to exert political pressure, help shape policy, and drive public opinion?

Yes.

But creating an amplification loop—or symbiotic relationship—between social media, media and political lobbying is key.

Let's jump back to 2010 when we were tasked by Save the Children to raise awareness of the upcoming Millennium Development Goals (MDG), United Nations Summit in New York 2010. Recognising the seismic shift in media and influence, I put together a project that tapped into the social media zeitgeist and took three of the UK's most influential blogging mums to Bangladesh.

Dubbed 'Blogladesh' the idea was to tell the compelling stories of the challenges facing mums—everyday challenges, like treating diarrhoea. The difference being that in Bangladesh these everyday challenges contribute to the 8.1 million children dying of preventable diseases every year.

We constructed a tight schedule and storyline to share their stories minute by minute over the course of a week. The blogging mums told of the heart-breaking moment we watched a child die from pneumonia and spoke to the doctor who, with his limited resources, had battled to save her life, through to meeting the inspiring health workers pounding the paddy fields.

These were real stories of real people in real time. And by working with bloggers with their own large audiences, we got immediate cut through with our target audience. The strategy was that we didn't take just the three mums; we took their whole parenting community (each with their publishing platform, blog, Twitter feed, etc.). And we created a digital storm.

It was the first time a UK charity had taken bloggers on a live-reporting trip and as such it created a huge surprise and support within the blogging community. The project immediately trended on Twitter and reached more than 4.5 million people before the bloggers had even left the UK (see http://fieldcraftstudios.com/portfolio_archive/blogladesh-save-the-children-uk/for full details).

As a result, whilst we were in Bangladesh, we were able to secure key media opportunities with Sky, *The Sun*, and regional print and broadcast outlets. Further amplification was achieved by lining up Twitter support from celebrities including actor Stephen Fry, *New York Times* columnist and Pulitzer Prize–winner Nick Kristof, and author Neil Gaiman. We also hosted Twitter chats and web chats whilst in the field and more than 150 bloggers wrote blog posts in support.

On our return to the UK the fresh angle on child and maternal mortality secured significant media exposure including the BBC *Today* programme, ITN lunchtime, Six and Ten O'Clock news, and *The Times* among many others. As a result of the exposure we were able to secure a meet and greet for the bloggers with Andrew Mitchell, then Secretary of State for International Development, and two meetings with Nick Clegg (deputising for David Cameron who was on paternity leave at the time).

I then took one of the bloggers to New York to the United Nations General Assembly (UNGA) Millennium Development Goals conference. However, this was revealing as it became apparent that the UN conference was out of the blogging communities' frame of reference—and as such the support across social media dipped. This didn't matter because as the project was designed to create an amplification loop between social media and traditional media, Save the Children were able to secure another meeting with Nick Clegg at the summit, which enabled us to get some video footage of the blogger demanding to know what Clegg was going to do about 8.1 million children dying every year. This footage then made its way onto ITV's ten o'clock news.

At the UNGA, the UN launched a worldwide campaign to save 16 million mothers and children over the coming five years and Nick Clegg announced that the UK government were to double the number of women and children's lives saved.

With no advertising spent the results are all earned or organic. In total, the Twitter reach for the Blogladesh campaign was 10 million and the traditional media we leveraged reached an audience of 75 million. One of the key components with this campaign was co-ordination across several internal departments with the media and government relations teams working hard, using the amplification loop created to secure meetings and media.

With such valuable lessons learnt, my next project, Pass it On[4], in 2011, again for Save the Children, tripled this success by mixing up the audiences (parenting and political) and including a YouTube star, wrangling the non-linear storytelling into a linear format, and working hard to create a compelling storyline that would work across multiple platforms that included YouTube, Facebook, Twitter, and blogs, creating an amplification loop that would push the story out into print and broadcast media.

The goal was to raise awareness of a global vaccination–pledging conference hosted by David Cameron in London. I put together a social media storytelling campaign that followed in real time the journey of a vaccination from the warehouse in Maputo, Mozambique, to a rural outreach clinic hosted under a tree.

I took two bloggers, one a parenting blogger and one political blogger, along with a YouTube star. An engagement strategy was designed for each audience to ensure maximum participation. For example, parenting bloggers worked with their children to draw a picture of what they wanted to be when they grow up—the message being that 8 million children will not live past their fifth birthday.

Audience fragmentation also dictates that one blanket-engagement strategy is not enough—if you want people to participate you need to understand the identity of each community. One major reason BuzzFeed was able to drive more than 130 million unique visitors to its site in November 2013 (BuzzFeed, 2013) is that it understands how to make content relate to people. As Jeff Greenspan, BuzzFeed

Chief Creative Officer, told the *New York Times*, "Nobody wants to be a shill for your brand. But they are happy to share information and content that helps them promote their own identity" (Rice, 2013).

#Passiton reached 27 million on Twitter, achieved more than 200,000 YouTube views, more than 200 bloggers writing posts in support, significant national and regional media coverage, including ITN lunchtime news, *Daybreak*, and achieved political influence. With no advertising spend on this campaign the results are all earned or organic.

And during the West Africa food crisis in 2012, I produced a transmedia storytelling project for World Vision UK. Raising funds for a slow-onset crisis is notoriously difficult. The project #ShareNiger was crafted to push the under-reported food crisis into the media spotlight using social media channels, social media stars, and a creative partnership with Cybher, one of the UK's most influential blogging conferences.

The engagement and participation strategy was nuanced across the numerous audiences. These included blogging school children, parenting bloggers, and life-style bloggers, broadsheet newspaper readers (press ads), and ultimately the public at large as the project reached national and international media outlets.

The strength of the project secured UK government match funding, a 10 million reach on Twitter, engagement with school children across the UK, and national and international media coverage. #ShareNiger garnered coverage from *The Telegraph*, CNN news, and BBC, among others, and mobilised the audience to spread the word and raise £810,000.

For Greenpeace in 1971, an inspiring idea for direct action and a press release was all it took to command the world's attention. The gatekeeper for them was the news editor—the human being who would read the press release and ultimately put them on our TV screens or in our newspapers. Today's ultimate gate-keeper is the algorithm. Code written by media behemoth's such as Google and Facebook that serve us content based on our recent searches. Mark Zuckerberg, Facebook's chief executive, once told colleagues that "a squirrel dying in your front yard may be more relevant to your interests right now than people dying in Africa" (Pariser, 2011).

That 'content is king' is a hackneyed phrase that still holds true—yet the art and science of delivering that content to an audience (or message to supporters) is ever evolving.

Entry points to content come from numerous sources. It could be via search, an online newspaper article, an email, something shared by a peer—the user journey for each needs to be shaped and analysed with real-time analytics. And your community/fans as the new publishers and distributors are a key weapon in punching through the noise pushing your message directly to their audiences—and therefore yours.

Social media has flattened the world, giving everybody access to the same communication tools. Campaigns that don't work across multiple platforms, encourage participation, sharing, or creating will become campaigns that are just not worth engaging with.

NOTES

1. Fans: supporters who are enthusiastically dedicated and promote the object of their interest and attention.
2. Interview by author Frank Rose, January 17, 2013, for his own blog, http://www.deepmedia-online.com/deepmedia/2013/01/henry-jenkins-on-spreadable-media.html.
3. Fieldcraft Studios – Million Miracles launch event for charity SIghtsavers.
4. http://fieldcraft.co/portfolio/pass-it-on-for-save-the-children/.

REFERENCES

BuzzFeed. (2013, 2 December). BuzzFeed Reaches More than 130 Million Unique Users in November. BuzzFeed.com. Retrieved from http://www.buzzfeed.com/buzzfeedpress/buzzfeed-reaches-more-than-130-million-unique-visitors-in-no.

Dredge, S. (2014, 8 April). YouTube wants its creators to build 'fanbases' rather than audiences. *Guardian Online*. Retrieved from http://www.theguardian.com/technology/2014/apr/08/youtube-fanbases-jimmy-fallon-psy.

Greenpeace. (2007, 15 May). Amchitka: The founding journey. Retrieved from http://www.greenpeace.org/international/en/about/history/amchitka-hunter/.

Masters, A. (2014). An iCure? *Aeon*. Retrieved from http://aeon.co/magazine/living-together/alexander-masters-crowdfunding-cancer-treatments/.

Pariser, E. (2011, 22 May). When the Internet thinks it knows you. *International New York*. Retrieved from http://www.nytimes.com/2011/05/23/opinion/23pariser.html?_r=0.

Pew Research Center. (2014, 26 March). Key indicators in media and news. *State of the Media*. Retrieved from http://www.journalism.org/2014/03/26/state-of-the-news-media-2014-key-indicators-in-media-and-news/.

Rice, A. (2013, 7 April). Does BuzzFeed know the secret? *New Yorker*. Retrieved from http://nymag.com/news/features/buzzfeed-2013-4/#print.

Rose, F. (2013, 17 January). Henry Jenkins on spreadable media, why fans rule and why the 'Walking Dead' takes on a life of its own. *Deep Media Blog*. Retrieved from http://www.deepmediaonline.com/deepmedia/2013/01/henry-jenkins-on-spreadable-media.html.

PART THREE

The Politics of Pity and the Poverty of Representation

CHAPTER EIGHT

International NGOs, Global Poverty and the Representations of Children

NANDITA DOGRA

International charities or non-governmental organisations (NGOs) bring us a range of messages about global poverty through our letter boxes, newspapers, television screens, and other media. How do they help us visualise and understand global poverty? How do we connect them with our own lives? This chapter draws on a larger study on the media role of UK-based international development NGOs (INGOs) such as Oxfam, Save the Children, ActionAid, Christian Aid, Plan, World Vision, and War on Want (Dogra, 2014).

The analysis of a full annual cycle of INGOs' recent public messages demonstrates that they construct, and connect, the 'first world' or developed world and the 'third world' or majority world of developing countries, mainly of Asia, Africa and South America, through a double logic of 'difference' and 'oneness'. This dualism enables them to show the global poor as different and distant from the developed world and yet like us by virtue of their humanity. INGOs' messages project many colonial discourses even as they ironically erase this period of our connected history and its legacies which continue to shape existing global economic structures, power relations, and the current state of poverty and prosperity across various regions. Shared histories are erased and replaced by shared humanity. Theorised in particular ways, the dualism is projected and reconciled across varied axes and a range of representations of people, space and issues. This is my critical argument.

In this chapter, I illustrate this duality of 'difference' and 'oneness' through the portrayals of the most important set of characters in INGOs' public messages—children. Children, mostly from the majority world but also the developed world, simultaneously project universality and particularity through their varied instrumental and symbolic uses. Images of children work inter-textually in complex ways as factual indicators and metaphors and resonate across discourses of childhood, infantilism, humanism, cosmopolitanism and human rights to connect people of the developed world with the majority world in very distinctive ways. In this introductory section, dualism and details of the study are outlined. The subsequent two sections respectively discuss how 'difference' and 'oneness' are portrayed through children and these are followed by some concluding remarks.

My study focuses on 2005–2006 which was an important year for INGOs. It had summits and disasters leading to a flood of public messages by INGOs with visual imagery at its heart. The Asian Tsunami had occurred on Boxing Day in 2004 and its tremors still lingered in the new year. The unprecedented public response to the appeals of the Asian Tsunami boosted the coffers and profile of INGOs in a similar way to the Ethiopian crisis of 1984–1985. The year 2005 was also the year of 'Make Poverty History', a high-profile joint campaign by INGOs under the aegis of an independent coalition.

The research reviews an annual cycle of fundraising and advocacy communications of these NGOs publicised in the UK's national newspapers, direct mails, and websites. The overall visual analysis consists of a total of 88 messages of twelve INGOs in the newspapers containing 276 images/texts and approximately 7,000–8,000 still images in other formats. Data was analysed through mixed methods of analysis—content analysis, discourse analysis, and semiotics.

The content analysis of INGOs' messages demonstrates that they are people-centred, and nearly four-fifths of the messages showed people. Ordinary majority world people are the most commonly used characters and formed the subject of 71% of messages while 14% of messages showed majority world landscape, animals, maps, or 'developmental' products. Ordinary developed world individuals and famous persons (leaders and celebrities) were shown in 7% and 3% of the messages respectively, and 5% of messages did not contain any images but were text-based.

DIFFERENCE

Majority world children's images form an overwhelming proportion of INGOs' messages at 42% of the total messages showing characters. Images of mothers and children form another 17% of all people shown. This means that nearly three fifths of the images of people show children or infants. Seen in terms of their popularity, children truly are the 'development candy' of INGOs' messages. Their overwhelming dominance projects a 'different' majority world even at a quick glance—overpopulated and inhabited mainly by vulnerable children (and women). Their sheer and pervasive numbers allow children to signify the majority world both empirically and symbolically. This is also contended by both colonial and development discourses and a whole history of colonial imagery that infantilises the non-West (Escobar, 1995; Hall, 2002; McClintock, 1995; Mudimbe, 1988; Nandy, 1983; Shohat & Stam, 1994).

The 'infantilisation' or 'infantilism' argument is supported by Ashis Nandy through the metaphor of childhood in colonial discourse as 'a blank slate on which adults must write their moral codes' which then links it with ideas of growth and development to draw parallels between primitivism and childhood (1983, p. 15). This suggests, and justifies, that the majority world symbolised by a child can, and must, be intervened upon as the INGO is already doing. Such portrayals also fit into W. W. Rostow's well-known model of economic growth that puts the majority world at the first stage of 'underdevelopment'/infancy that should evolve into a 'developed', adult-like stage just like 'the West'. Nandy (1987, cited in Escobar, 1995, p. 30) highlights this development discourse that draws on colonial metaphors as 'the representation of the Third World as a child in need of adult guidance... The infantilisation of the Third World'. Following Nandy, Escobar argues that the portrayal of a hungry majority world child to be adopted for a small change per month signifies a whole discourse of inequality between, and power of, the 'First World' over 'the Third' (1995). Another study, discussing the advertisements of private corporations that use smiling children from Asia and Africa, echoes this to show their symbolic helplessness and dependence—while children are 'enchanting, they present those children as helpless creatures dependent on the bounty provided by corporate conglomerates' (Ramamurthy, 2003, p. 186).

A single child's face, seemingly caught unawares, staring passively, and without any clear expression at the camera is the quintessence of many sponsorship appeals (Manzo, 2008). Given the close-up of the face, such expressions may be read by various viewers as sad, appealing, hurt or complaining (as if saying 'Why don't you help me?'), making them look needy. To be sure, the issue of eye contact with the camera (and thus the viewers) is a blurry area and context-specific. On the one hand, it can convey 'need' via an appeal through the eyes which places the photographed in a 'low' position compared to the viewer connoting his/her availability and servitude (Nederveen Pieterse, 1992, p. 131). On the other hand, it can also suggest the ease and trust the photographed subjects show in their photographer as argued by John and Jean Comaroff in the case of anthropologist Issac Schapera's photographs of children in Botswana taken during his fieldwork between 1929 and 1934—'Bana: Children at Play and Work' (2007).

The need quotient of these INGO images is enhanced by two factors—removal or blurring of the background including any other person in it and a relatively large space occupied by the image in the total space of the advert. The image, cropped to hide the background, lends a quality of isolation to the child and de-contextualises it, thus, adding to the overall sense of need and urgency. A child sponsorship brochure of ActionAid illustrates how 'cropping' is used as a strategy to enhance vulnerability. The cover with the title, "You have the chance to change this child's life forever" and some colourful patterns has a window through which one can see the next page where a girl from 'Africa' wearing a frock stands alone on a mud surface looking slightly downcast. Interestingly, when one turns the page to see the whole picture, one can see shadows of three people on the mud ground implying that the girl was not alone but standing in a group or with her family. So the cover photo, which usually works as a 'hook' to attract readers, cleverly heightens the vulnerability and isolation of the child by hiding parts of the image and achieving a cropped effect on the cover.

When repeated on different dates, some of the messages in newspapers reduce the space used by the image vis-à-vis the space used by written text. A comparison of these sets of adverts illustrates the effect of varying percentages of space occupied by the images in the total advert. The up-close and big images lend a magnified effect, thereby, objectifying the subjects. On the other hand, an attempt is made to 'individualise' or 'personalise' them by 'naming' them so that they do not seem to be unnamed and undifferentiated faces of 'the "teeming masses" of the Third World' (Escobar, 1995, p. 70) but appear as specific human beings.

Another inconsistency reflects the single child versus community debate. Child sponsorship schemes favouring a single child instead of overall benefits to a greater number of people have been criticised for being 'possessive and patronising', that has led many INGOs to move towards a more 'community-oriented approach' (Smith, 2004, p. 743). This is attempted by emphasising the benefits of sponsorship to communities as in the following message:

> Sponsorship will give Saima and her community access to safe, clean water, healthcare and education. These basics, which we take for granted, are so vital in making sure they have a chance of making their dreams of becoming self sufficient come true.
>
> You'll soon notice the difference that you'll make to a community like Saima's, with regular updates from local fieldworkers and messages from the child you sponsor. (ActionAid: Image AA-6 showing 'Saima')

The above message is laden with contradictions. The 'needy' look of Saima, in this message, is symbolically linked to her unnamed community that would gain basic services through the sponsor's help which will make it 'self sufficient'. Here, community, empowerment, and autonomy are emphasised but a quick and easy solution to poverty is also offered. The 'gain' to sponsors in terms of regular updates accentuates its 'win-win' suggestion. The messages suggest that the lack of self-sufficiency of this community is because of lack of basic services and not linked to any wider structures or global relations which make this community economically poor in the first place.

Another set of contradictions is revealed, and reconciled, in the ActionAid appeal titled 'Sponsorship gives her a helping hand, not a handout' (Image AA-1 showing 'Amita') which reflects 'competing ideas of assistance' through 'a critique of both welfare dependency and the demeaning character of handouts' (Smith, 2004, p. 744). It also attempts to minimise the charitable aspect of giving by suggesting that it is a 'helping hand' to a deserving recipient.

A variation of such depictions is the use of linearity to show a chain of interventions with the last stage showcasing the success of the donor's 'helping hand' that allows the NGO to achieve it. One of Plan's inserts in 2005, for instance, contained a series of images on three folds that showed a visual depiction of Plan's intervention 'justifying' the use of sadness and happiness in this way: "Learning from the past...." (shows a sad black baby with runny nose and dirty frock), "...to solve the problems of the present..." (an image of a smiling brown child drinking running tap water), "...and build a sustainable future." (This fold shows a laughing brown child holding a notebook who will be named as "Trung" in another Plan insert.)

One of the interesting things about such ads is that, given their long and extensive use, *all* the stages need no longer be shown always. The familiarity with linear narratives means that even seeing one stage can lead to a chain of semiosis and understanding of the whole narrative. The narrative is simple and like a fairy tale with a situation and protagonists that transform and get transformed by the end of the tale. It also establishes a certain positioning of the developed world as saviour by projecting a problem *before* it intervenes that is solved *after* the intervention leading to a happy ending.

The dominance of children in INGOs' messages evokes implicit binaries. A parent/child status is evoked through an infantilised majority world represented through its children who are the most favoured of characters in INGOs' messages. The sheer number of children suggests an inexplicably overpopulated majority world which in turn also connotes its lack of wisdom and rationality. The messages do not explain the links between poverty, high infant mortality rates and family size. Furthermore, this simplistic overpopulation argument does not reflect the extreme disparities in the per capita consumption and disguises that 'one Euro-American child consumes 183 times what one Third World child consumes' (Spivak, 2007, p. 194), thereby implicitly framing the causes of global poverty as 'internal' to the majority world and 'out there' without any global links.

Children symbolically project the majority world as 'toddlers' still needing the help of the 'adult'/developed nations (Shohat & Stam, 1998) and lacking leadership, towards whom the developed world can be paternalistic and helpful. Such portrayals set the scene for what Hobart (1993) calls 'agentiveness' or outside intervention. John Hutnyk argues that such 'charitable' images, in fact, work as 'trinketisation' of poverty and conceal power and inequality behind 'morsels of aid' (2004, p. 87).

ONENESS

Children's images work in complex and divergent ways as metaphors to symbolise the majority world and childhood per se across axes of 'need', vulnerability, and infantilisation as well as 'universal' appeal, neutrality, innocence and 'hope'. As such, and often contrarily, they project and reconcile both ends of the dualism of 'difference' and 'oneness'. Majority world children are shown not just to highlight their 'difference' but also their 'oneness' and hence their implicit 'deservedness'. This is reflected through the representations of children to project childhood and ideas that stem from the root word 'human' and encompass humanism and human rights.

The logic of the 'universal' appeal of children, to evoke visceral emotions, irrespective of who they are ethnically, as in the slogan 'A Hungry Child Has No Politics' (Cohen, 2001, p. 178) is a part of their appeal. The correspondence of children with emotions is not just in terms of the adults' 'universal' emotional reactions to children but children *themselves* being emotional, natural, and playful thereby symbolising these qualities. Images of children are used to project childhood that takes forms such as 'need', that is, lacking something, as seen earlier in the case of ActionAid's 'Saima' and in the images of malnourished or starving children in food crises appeals, such as 'Halima' in a Concern appeal on the Niger food crisis (Image CW-1), and as idealisation, as it ought to be. The smile is an important way to achieve 'idealisation of the other, permitting the projection of the ideal of the happy life' (Lutz & Collins, 1993). Children such as 'Manu' shown by ActionAid and a girl child in many press ads of Plan are shown smiling broadly. 'Photogenic poverty' is projected through the healthy looks and happy and naughty expressions of these children (Hutnyk, 2004, p. 87).

Apart from the feel-good and 'post–NGO intervention' scenario such images evoke, they also make the viewers identify with them as the children shown look like children from anywhere in the world, including the developed world, supporting their 'universal' appeal. However, all images ensure that this identification, if any, remains partial. This is achieved through projections of some obvious, visible differences between 'our' children and 'theirs' that take the form of the facial features of the children, darker colour of hair and eyes, unkempt state of hair, 'ethnic' jewellery such as earrings and safety pins typically worn in the Indian subcontinent as in the image of 'Saima' discussed earlier. These features not only show 'them' as distinct but also prove their authenticity and the INGO's presence and intervention by combining docu-realism with a happy, idealised childhood. So, on the one hand, there is emphasis on the children *looking* 'different' or 'ethnic', to borrow Cohen's (2001) term, in order to show that they are 'other' children; on the other, they are also supposed to *be* like a child anywhere doing things children must do connoting a sense of *childhood*. In the latter sense, images of children are used to show childhood in various ways—either lacking something, that is, needing something or in a normative sense of how it should be—idealised, innocent (thus 'deserving' of help), happy, engaged in play and study, thereby connoting hope and future.

In sum, the overall depictions of children are as needy (as they should *not* be) or as idealised and happy (as they *should* be). With the sole exception of a Save the Children photograph in an insert that shows majority world children addressing adults in a campaign, they rarely speak for themselves to demand their rights.

In addition to projecting 'oneness' through childhood, representations of children help project ideas related to the 'human' which are crucial to INGOs' work and messages. INGOs use an ideology of 'universal humanism' to nest the dominant portrayals of 'difference' of the majority world within it, seek support from the readers for the same 'different' and 'distant' majority world, and connect the developed and majority worlds on the whole in a neutral and apolitical manner. Roland Barthes' distinction between 'classic humanism' and 'progressive humanism' is invaluable here. INGOs' messages, in general, use the former, not the latter, to rely on 'the solid rock of universal nature' and thus neglect historicity (Barthes, 1993, p. 101).

In his famous critique of a photographic exhibition titled The Family of Man, Barthes showed how it projected the 'myth' of a global human community in two stages—first by emphasising difference seen in terms of exotic diversity of daily lives and, second, by taking it away to show that underneath there is but one human nature and a common human essence (Young, 1990, p. 122). Barthes does not deny that birth and death are 'facts of nature, universal facts' but shows that removing History makes any comment about them 'purely tautological' (1993, p. 101). He illustrates the unfairness of 'classic humanism' through the following example:

> It will never be fair to confuse in a purely gestural identity the colonial and the Western worker (let us also ask the North African workers of the Goutte d'Or district in Paris what they think of *The Great Family of Man*). (1993, p. 102)

The notion of universal humanism (Barthes' 'classic humanism') is spread across INGOs' messages in many forms. These include the 'one-to-one' or individual-to-individual connections that are best exemplified in child-sponsorship messages. A child-sponsorship insert used by Plan through the year contained six images, a world map with Plan's project areas marked out, a table about finances and the text "Sponsorship is about real people helping real people…" The use of adjectives and qualifiers is common in INGO appeals. The word "real" here connotes not fictitious or 'out there' but actual people. The term "real people" is also used for both the sponsors and the beneficiaries linking them into a chain or circle of universal humanism.

Universal humanism is also illustrated by stories about visits to sponsored children by their sponsors, both ordinary developed world people and celebrities. These stories work within the frame of individuals connecting with individuals.

Plan's supplement "Look and Learn" in *The Guardian* contained a story about a sponsor's visit with her son Robbie to Kenya to meet the girl she had sponsored. The images show the sponsored girl Kanini wearing a frock and smiling at the camera in front of a thatched hut; Kanini playing football with Robbie; Kanini and Robbie petting a black lamb while another little girl in a nice white frock looks on with lush green trees in the background; and the sponsor, Harriet Griffey, at a health centre holding a black chubby baby who wears a shiny satin blue frilly frock.

There is 'deliberate positivism' (Lidchi, 1999) in the images with smiling children and idyllic background. The story talks about sponsorship, Robbie's impressions of Africa based on TV shows on wildlife, the friendship he strikes with Kanini, Kanini's family details, and Harriet's visit to a health centre, all of which evoke 'human' connections between individuals. The story briefly disrupts the de-historicised version of humanism to move towards 'progressive humanism' (Barthes, 1993, p. 101) by including a slice of history when it mentions the comfortable life, servants and a large house of British ex-patriates the visitors stay with in Nairobi. These 'ex-pats' had arrived prior to Kenya's independence from Britain in 1963. The text states that while life is comfortable for the whites ("mzungus"), 56% of Kenya's population lives below a dollar a day and Kenya has high national debt. While this part of the text commendably fits into a rare and 'deviant' category of INGO messages, the fact that it is in such small print implies that it is likely to be missed by most readers who tend to scan through messages and only notice the images and the captions. Another evocation of universal humanism can be found in the Asian tsunami update story in Plan's supplement where a celebrity actor, Shobna Gulati, is shown visiting a Plan project in Tamil Nadu, India, and holding the child she has sponsored, which projects an individual, and individualised, connection as human beings.

'Oneness' and solidarity are also manifested in some appeals through the use of a notion of a cosmopolitan club of world citizens. Oxfam's 'I'm in' campaign is a case in point. Launched in January 2006, these appeals seemed to address young people perhaps to consolidate the gains of Make Poverty History (MPH) coalition campaign of 2005. The MPH connection is made clear in the formal stated purpose of 'I'm in' as elaborated in Oxfam's "the little book of communications" (Oxfam, 2006, p. 20): "Building on Make Poverty History, I'm in is founded on Oxfam's belief that poverty is a moral injustice that must be overcome." Poverty here is clearly seen as a moral not a historical issue.

The 'I'm in' series showed individual young men and women from the developed world who had presumably joined or wanted to join the campaign. For instance, an ad in January 2006 showed a young white man sitting on a chair holding a small boy. Both are well dressed and the child looks up to the man projecting the man's ability to take care and the child-parent connection. A bottle of milk can be seen on the floor near the chair. This appeal of a young developed world male looking after a child is also suggestive of a 'new man' cosmopolitan modernity. This is in marked contrast to the near total absence of a 'new man', a majority world male in a nurturing role, in INGOs' messages again projecting 'difference' and 'distance'.

The 'I'm in' campaign continued to show similar ads and posters displayed in the tube and trains and the press with images of various young people connoting a multi-ethnic and aware Britain. All images showed the people in a flattering light—well dressed, young, smart, good looking. These messages deployed a humanistic, cosmopolitan framework to appeal to individuals to join a 'club' of 'global' citizens (Calhoun, 2003), once again without addressing any historical connections outside of the 'human' links. The savvy cosmopolitanism discourse in these messages avoids messy geopolitics and history.

Humanism portrayed in INGOs' messages tends to gloss over the chapters of global history that significantly contributed, and continue to contribute, to current global poverty and disparities. As Barthes said of *The Family of Man*:

> Everywhere here, the content and the appeal of pictures, the discourse which justifies them, aims to suppress the determining weight of History: we are held back at the surface of an identity, prevented precisely by sentimentality from penetrating into this ulterior zone of human behaviour where historical alienation introduces some 'differences' which we shall here quite simply call 'injustices'. (1993, p. 101)

Universality is also expressed through use of concepts of human 'rights' and 'needs' which are occasionally used together as a phrase—'rights and needs' of children, for instance, by World Vision, thereby equating the two words. Similarly a Plan insert states: "Plan's work with communities to promote children's needs and rights." The use of the word 'right' is generally used in this sense to suggest that all children have the right to basic needs. The term 'right' is also used independently, for example, by ActionAid in several messages where it implies universal rights of all human beings to have access to, say, health and education. A direct mail brochure from ActionAid, with details of child sponsorship, illustrates the use of 'rights-based' language:

> Why become a sponsor? Because you believe every child has a right to the fundamentals of life. (ActionAid, direct mail)

The connotations of 'justice' in the use of the term 'rights' again employ a 'humanistic' moral logic which argues that *all* human beings have the right to basic needs. In addition to this understanding of the concept of human rights, conviction in its effectiveness, as expressed on the website of ActionAid during October 2005 under the caption "please give a gift to ActionAid", is noteworthy. The text mentions access to vital services as well as gaining knowledge of their basic rights to change their lives themselves. There is a certain naiveté in such text implying not just faith in 'rights' but that if 'they' know their rights 'they' would do something about it themselves, and in this sense it connotes 'their' ignorance. It is useful here to compare the works of authors such as John Rawls and Charles Beitz on the ethics of international aid, global justice, and human rights and their counter-criticisms from scholars such as Thomas Pogge.

Comparing charitable donations with foreign aid, Beitz states that aid has been regarded as a kind of international charity, like charitable contributions, and hence understood as morally discretionary but it should be considered as a part of global redistributive obligations founded on justice (1999). His notion of justice is based on, what he terms, 'cosmopolitan liberalism' that looks beyond nation-state to give primacy to each human no matter where he/she may be. It

> does not take societies as fundamental and aims to identify principles which are acceptable from a point of view in which each person's prospects, rather the prospects of each society or people, are equally represented. Because it accords no privilege to domestic societies or to national (or multinational or nonnational) states, cosmopolitan liberalism extends to the world the criteria of distributive justice that apply within a single society. (Beitz, 1999, p. 215)

Discussing political imperialism and economic dependence, that is, the issue of causality, Beitz adds that 'it make[s] little moral difference whether the regime is imposed by other members of their own community or by foreign agents' (1999, p. 119). Beitz finds it necessary to undervalue both historical and current, and, domestic and foreign factors to place the concept of 'justice' (as in justice for individual human beings) as the core issue. Rawls, similarly, adopts a universal human principle when he insists that 'peoples have a duty to assist other peoples living under unfavourable conditions that prevent their having a just or decent political and social regime' (1999, p. 37). This is commendable but it overlooks something crucial. Pogge challenges Rawls's suggestion of 'duty of assistance' to the global poor by objecting to the notion of 'assistance' because it is based on the assumption that the causes of severe poverty are internal to poor countries and not due to foreign influences such as historical processes of enslavement and colonialism and their legacies (Pogge, 2004).

This debate on charity or assistance versus justice resonates in the human rights discourse in INGOs' messages. A combined term, 'human rights' as 'rights' is a legal category and as 'human' a moral one which together stands for 'moral rights or claims by individuals' that entitle people to certain minimum standards of treatment by various institutions (Douzinas, 2007, p. 9). To be sure, many consider the notion of poverty as a violation of human rights as a step in the right direction. By endorsing the connections of basic social and economic rights with civil and political rights, it makes state and non-state actors legally obliged to uphold the right of poor people not to live in poverty. However, this is one of the approaches to human rights and is based primarily on the notion of duties of humanity. The other approach, based on the notion of justice, looks at poverty that is the violation of human rights as injustice caused by the culpable conduct of others. 'Human rights' is not a magic mantra containing an intrinsic notion of justice but justice should form an integral element of the term. I do not suggest that these two approaches are inherently contradictory. In fact, accommodating both approaches within the notion of 'human rights' is likely to optimise both the theoretical and practical potential of the term as both humanity and justice can (and must) work against poverty (Campbell, 2007). The case of a natural disaster may require a humanitarian reaction based on the notion of 'one' humanity but a similar explanation in the case of global poverty caused by deep historical and structural factors tends to make 'human rights' an abstract notion that merely avoids the issue of justice and causality. As Tom Campbell states:

> It is the failure to alleviate poverty as well as complicity in or actually causing poverty that should be regarded as violating poverty-related human rights. (2007, p. 62)

The use of the phrase 'human rights' in INGOs' messages suggests the former approach of a universal moral basis for individuals who are a part of humanity but not historically located within a specific place (country/region) that is linked to the rest of the world, notably the developed world. In other words, the notion of rights is based on a de-historicised notion of mankind as 'one' which does not accommodate any context, namely past and/or present macro-level connections of a specific set of people. The complete absence of a relational aspect, thus, keeps it located within a broadly charitable discourse and does not raise it to the discourse of justice despite the use of the language of human rights.

CONCLUSIONS

A dualism of 'difference' and 'oneness' is the master code that underlines INGOs' representations of global poverty. This is reflected in many ways, especially portrayals of children who dominate INGOs' messages. Use of majority world children in such large numbers empirically and symbolically infantilises the majority world and attributes to it several contradictory ideas associated with children such as innocence, blamelessness and neutrality as well as paternalism, overpopulation, ignorance, lack of leadership and under-development which undermine INGOs' values and aims. The connotations of overpopulation and irrationality assign the blame solely to the majority world and lower the 'deservedness' by making the same innocent children, who promise hope and a future, less deserving of help. By reproducing these myths, such portrayals not just limit any 'outside the box' thinking of majority world problems and solutions, but also contradict INGOs' own messages, especially their portrayals of majority world children as 'deserving', leading to inconsistencies and incoherence in their messages. Such representations also negate the advocacy aims of NGOs aimed at 'root causes of poverty'.

The primary mode of making connections in INGOs' messages is through the notion of 'one' universal humanity. Oneness is evoked through certain ideas, foremost being universal humanism which claims that all human beings are one. This oneness does not have any place for historicity. The humanism deployed works as a sentimental unifier and an ideology that is devoid of historicity to place human beings in a universal, de-historicised space. It is linked to and conflated with an analogous notion of cosmopolitanism that similarly echoes a humanist idea of 'one family of man' and 'world citizens'.

Other concepts used to evoke oneness are those of rights and justice which are used to support a bottom line argument where facts are stated about the current problems but *not* how and why this situation came about. The situation is then labelled unfair with the declaration that something must be done about it. The end result of these concepts is the loss of continuities and lessons embedded in history and structures. This projects the myth of a majority world 'out there'. It is *another* world, historically unconnected to 'us' except in a universally humanistic way where good developed-world human beings help good majority-world human beings. The humanistic approach in INGOs' messages, that, following the Italian clothing company Benetton's slogan, I call 'united colours of humanity', projects a sanitised, fuzzy and non-conflictual realm where humanity is shared but not history.

REFERENCES

Barthes, R. (1993). *Mythologies.* (A. Lavers, Trans.). London: Vintage.

Beitz, C. R. (1999). *Political theory and international relations.* Princeton, NJ: Princeton University Press.

Calhoun, C. (2003). The class consciousness of frequent travellers: Towards a critique of actually existing cosmopolitanism. In D. Archibugi (Ed.), *Debating cosmopolitics* (pp. 86–116). London: Verso.

Campbell, T. (2007). Poverty as a violation of human rights: Inhumanity or injustice? In T. Pogge (Ed.), *Freedom from poverty as a human right* (pp. 55–74). Oxford: Oxford University Press.

Cohen, S. (2001). *States of denial: Knowing about atrocities and suffering.* Cambridge, MA: Polity.

Comaroff, J. L., & Comaroff, J. (2007). Introduction: The portraits of an ethnographer as a young man. In J. L. Comaroff, J. Comaroff, & D. James (Eds.), *Picturing a colonial past: The African photographs of Isaac Schapera* (pp. 1–18). Chicago: University of Chicago Press.

Dogra, N. (2014). *Representations of global poverty: Aid, development and international NGOs.* London: I. B. Tauris.

Douzinas, C. (2007). *Human rights and empire: The political philosophy of cosmopolitanism.* Abingdon, UK: Routledge-Cavendish.

Escobar, A. (1995). *Encountering development: The making and unmaking of the third world.* Princeton, NJ: Princeton University Press.

Hall, C. (2002). *Civilising subjects: Metropole and colony in the English imagination 1830–1867.* Cambridge, MA: Polity.

Hobart, M. (1993). Introduction: The growth of ignorance? In Mark Hobart (Ed.), *An anthropological critique of development: The growth of ignorance* (pp. 1–30). London: Routledge.

Hutnyk, J. (2004). Photogenic poverty: Souvenirs and infantilism. *Journal of Visual Culture, 3*(1), 77–94.

Lidchi, H. (1999). Finding the right image: British Development NGOs and the regulation of imagery. In T. Skelton & T. Allen (Eds.), *Culture and global change* (pp. 88–104). London: Routledge.

Lutz, C. A., & Collins, J. L. (1993). *Reading* National Geographic. London: University of Chicago Press.

Manzo, K. (2008). Imaging humanitarianism: NGO identity and the iconography of childhood. *Antipode, 40*(4), 633–659.

McClintock, A. (1995). *Imperial leather: Race, gender, and sexuality in the colonial contest.* New York: Routledge.

Mudimbe, V. Y. (1988). *The invention of Africa: Gnosis, philosophy and the order of knowledge.* Bloomington: Indiana University Press.

Nederveen Pieterse, J. (1992). *White on black: Images of Africa and blacks in Western popular culture.* New Haven, CT: Yale University Press.

Nandy, A. (1983). *The intimate enemy: Loss and recovery of self under colonialism.* Oxford: Oxford University Press.

Oxfam. (2006). *The little book of communication.* Oxford: Oxfam.

Pogge, T. (2004). "Assisting" the global poor. In D. K. Chatterjee (Ed.), *The ethics of assistance: Morality and the distant needy* (pp. 260–288). Cambridge: Cambridge University Press.

Ramamurthy, A. (2003). *Imperial persuaders: Images of Africa and Asia in British advertising.* Manchester: Manchester University Press.

Rawls, J. (1999). *The laws of peoples.* Cambridge, MA: Harvard University Press.

Shohat, E., & Stam, R. (1994). *Unthinking Eurocentrism: Multiculturalism and the media.* London: Routledge.

Shohat, E., & Stam, R. (1998). Narrativizing visual culture: Towards a polycentric aesthetics. In N. Mirzoeff (Ed.), *The visual culture reader* (pp. 37–59). London: Routledge.

Smith, M. (2004). Contradiction and change? NGOs, schools and the public faces of development. *Journal of International Development, 16*(5), 741–749.

Spivak, G. C. (2007). Interview with Gayatri Chakravorty Spivak. In N. Shaikh (Int.), *The present as history: Critical perspectives on contemporary global power* (pp. 172–202). New York: Columbia University Press.

Young, R. (1990). *White mythologies: Writing history and the West.* London: Routledge.

CHAPTER NINE

Underline, Celebrate, Mitigate, Erase

Humanitarian NGOs' Strategies of Communicating Difference

SHANI ORGAD

Non-governmental organizations (NGOs) are amongst the central producers of representations of humanitarianism in the contemporary global mediated space. Their messages rely heavily on symbolically representing 'the other'—victims of atrocities, natural disasters and human rights abuses, and children and women in the global South—to elicit care, compassion, and action from audiences primarily in the global North. This paper expands debate on representation of distant suffering and international development by exploring how NGO practitioners' frames of thinking and understanding inform their communications practices and shape particular choices of how to portray difference and otherness. It examines four strategies employed by NGOs in their planning and production of communications of international development, humanitarian aid, and human rights abuses, namely underlining, celebrating, mitigating, and erasing difference. The discussion is based on a thematic analysis of in-depth interviews with 17 NGO professionals in 9 UK-based organizations, responsible for the design and production of international development, humanitarian crisis and human rights abuse communications, and an analysis of 12 communication items selected by representatives of those NGOs.

REPRESENTATION OF 'THE OTHER' IN NGO HUMANITARIAN COMMUNICATION

Existing research focuses on how NGO communication of humanitarian emergencies and international development shapes spectators' understanding and judgement of distant others. It explores how representations cultivate/inhibit relationships, distance/proximity, compassion and solidarity between spectators in the global North and 'beneficiaries' in the global South (e.g., Orgad, 2012; Boltanski, 1999; Chouliaraki, 2012; Fassin, 2012). Using visual and textual analysis, studies examine the patterns, formulas, modes, and conventions employed in NGO representations of distant suffering (e.g., Chouliaraki, 2012; Lidchi, 1993; Smith & Yanacopulos, 2004; Wilson, 2011). They show how depictions of distant others are rooted in colonial, racialized 'regimes of representation' (Hall, 1997, p. 232), while at the same time NGO communications have changed significantly over the years.

One change concerns the shift from 'negative' to 'positive' images of distant others (Benthall, 1993; Cohen, 2001; Dogra, 2006). Negative imagery depicts needy, passive, helpless, and vulnerable victims and often shocking and distressing images. Since the 1970s, this representational paradigm has been criticized as patronizing, orientalising, and dehumanizing. It has been argued that images of starving children with 'flies in their eyes' deprive people of agency and dignity, decontextualize their misery, and perpetuate a distorted view of the developing world as a theatre of tragedy and disaster (Cohen, 2001). Largely in response to this criticism, since the 1980s 'positive imagery' was encouraged: depicting distant others as self-sufficient, dignified, active agents, situated within their communities and social contexts, it is hoped, would contribute to telling a more complex story of social justice and progress, and to evoking solidarity with distant strangers based on justice rather than need and its relief (Orgad, 2013).

Another change consists of increasing adoption in NGO communication of neoliberal logic, market discourses, and corporate techniques and styles (Chouliaraki, 2012; Koffman & Gill, 2013; Richey & Ponte, 2011; Vestergaard, 2008; Wilson, 2011). It is linked to a move towards 'post-humanitarian' communication: from communications demanding solidarity with vulnerable others based on pity, to articulation of this demand for solidarity as irony, based on a focus on 'us' in the global North rather than the other, and marginalizing questions about justice, global inequality, and the root causes of suffering (Chouliaraki, 2012).

Despite this large body of work, whose review is beyond the scope of this chapter (see Orgad & Seu, 2014), most studies do not link analysis of representations to the actual thinking and practices that underpin their production by NGOs.[1] This chapter seeks to make this connection by juxtaposing analysis of NGO representations of otherness and difference, with analysis of accounts of the NGO practitioners who produce them to reveal some of the thinking and 'frameworlds' (Silverstone, 2007, p. 7) that underpin their communication strategies and practice.

THE STUDY

The following discussion combines elements from two larger-scale analyses: (1) thematic analysis of interviews with NGO practitioners; and (2) semiotic analysis of NGO communications.

Interviews

The author conducted open-ended, in-depth (1.5–2 hour) interviews in 9 UK-based humanitarian, human rights, and international development NGOs, with 17 NGO professionals engaged in planning, designing, and producing humanitarian and development communications. The sample included a mix of NGO size and longevity, positions/roles, levels of seniority, and departments (6 from communications and campaigns, 3 from fundraising, 4 from marketing and branding, 2 from media relations, and 2 from advocacy and policy).

Interviews aimed at exploring practitioners' thinking about goals, practices, and experience of communication planning, design, production, and dissemination. They were open-ended to allow practitioners to describe what they saw as most central, important and/or challenging, and difficult in their practice. Interviews began by giving interviewees a broad description of the study's purpose (to investigate how NGO practitioners and the UK public perceive and experience humanitarian communication) and asking them to describe their role in the organization; subsequently, the interviewer's interventions were minimal.

Interviews were audiotaped and transcribed. Thematic analysis of the interview transcripts identified broad topics and the issues practitioners prioritized in their accounts. These themes were not prompted by specific questions; they were discussed in idiosyncratic order and manner by individual participants. Further thematic analysis was guided by interest in how practitioners account for their practices of representing 'the other', specifically the views, ideas, and claims that inform and are used to justify their choices of how to depict their 'beneficiaries'. Substantively, the analysis aimed to expand and complement previous research on humanitarian communication that relies heavily on analysis of mediated images and texts.

NGO Communications

The sample consisted of 12 communication items, including appeals, leaflets, and newsletters. Representatives from the participating NGOs were asked to select the communications items they considered to best represent their ethos and current work. This NGO-led selection of items was used to create a sample that showcased the explicit intentions and goals of NGOs in communicating their cause. Using semiotic analysis of visual communication (Jewitt & Oyama, 2001; Kress & Van Leeuwen, 1996), and drawing on Hall's (1997) discussion of the signification of difference, the selected 12 items were examined for the ways they signify 'others' and the meaning potentials they generate.

For the present discussion, I combine selected elements from these separate analyses, aimed at demonstrating how NGO producers think about and explain representations of otherness and difference they produce, how this thinking informs their practices and, vice versa, how particular ways and modes of signifying otherness and difference in NGO communications are explained and justified —explicitly and/or implicitly—by their producers. I was looking deliberately for connections and similarities in the analyses of the two sets of data, for example, how remarks made by one or more interviewees about their practice of depicting 'the other' was illustrated in the ways difference and/or otherness were communicated in the selected materials. Details that could identify speakers and/or NGOs were removed and the analysis does not explicitly link communications items and speakers from the same organization. Although this constrains specific comments about the differences between types of NGOs and professional roles, it enables reflection on NGO communication practices and patterns of thinking beyond individual organizations, affiliations, and specific remits.

Ultimately, I seek to offer a contextualized understanding of four strategies employed by NGOs in their production of humanitarian communications. Each strategy involves the mobilization of specific signifiers of social and cultural difference, underpinned by particular ethical and instrumental motivations. The distinction among strategies is analytical; they can overlap and can be used simultaneously within single messages or campaigns. I first explore the strategy of 'underlining difference' at some length since (as I will show) it constitutes a point of reference for the formation and articulation of the other three strategies. The conclusion offers some overall observations about the relations among and implications of these four strategies.

ANALYSIS: NGO STRATEGIES OF COMMUNICATING DIFFERENCE

Underlining Difference

Underlining difference centres on marking otherness[2] and exploits cultural and social difference signifiers mostly from the colonial representational regime. A notable signifier of difference is dirt—used (in 5 of 12 items) in representations of children and women in the developing world in conjunction with familiar racial signifiers of cultural difference, connoting disorder and being out-of-place (Douglas, 1966). A UNICEF appeal to help children get off the street is illustrative of this strategy. Though the text refers to 190 countries where UNICEF works to help street children, its front cover shows a dark-skinned, Asian-looking child, possibly a boy (only the text inside the leaflet confirms it is a girl). The child is in the foreground of the picture, leaning on a bar, and framed by another two bars of what looks like a gate. She looks sad, bedraggled, and her face is pockmarked. The upper part of her body is naked, and her lower half is clad only in pants, which appear dirty. The child is standing in *contrapposto*, with one hand behind her back and the other to the fore in the centre of the picture—a posture reminiscent of iconographic connotations of suffering in Christian art. Her stomach is bloated and mud-spattered, and with a protruding navel. Her hair is matted and unkempt. She looks down, away from the camera, and her blank expression casts her as in a separate 'zone'—removed from the viewer.

The image recalls and reproduces racialized representations of the 'unwashed poor' such as in nineteenth-century imperial soap advertisements. Soaps

> apparently had the power to wash black skin white as well as being capable of washing off the soot, grime and dirt of the industrial slums and their inhabitants—the unwashed poor—at home, while at the same time keeping the imperial body clean and pure in the racially polluted contact zones 'out there' in the Empire. (Hall, 1997, p. 241)

The UNICEF appeal for a £2-a-month donation carries a strikingly similar message, promising the spectator in the global North to 'put it right' and rescue the child from her backward society, while keeping the spectator 'pure' and safe in the 'zone of contact' (Chouliaraki, 2006, p. 141)—the mediated encounter with the suffering.

However, Hall (1997, p. 268) observes that 'what is declared to be different, hideous, "primitive", deformed… is at the same time being obsessively enjoyed and lingered over because it is strange, "different", exotic', thus licensing 'an unregulated voyeurism'. This fetishist voyeurism is enacted by presenting the viewer with a second image of the same child inside the leaflet. It is a close-up 'demand' picture (Kress & Van Leeuwen, 1996) of the child, photographed from below, looking from inside the picture frame at the viewer (similar demand images are used in six other items in the sample). The close-up accentuates the child's 'primitiveness', while her unwashed, unkempt hair, dark-coloured, dirty face render her exotic, strange, curious, and to be gazed at.

Similar representational practices of 'othering' are evident in other NGOs' representations (in the sample, and more broadly, see, e.g., Dogra, 2012; Wilson, 2011). But practitioners appeared reluctant to acknowledge this. Most interviewees regarded such 'negative images' of passive helpless victims as exploitative, dehumanizing, and inadequate. Almost all interviewees were denying of their and their organization's employment of such representations,[3] while some accused other organizations of doing so. A communications and campaigns manager commented:

> You see some organizations… putting out quite deliberately shocking images of dying children… It does raise, I think, an important question about, how for the public, those traditional aid modalities are perpetuated, the deserving poor, the sense of 'other' with no agency of change or ability to change. And the sense of an endless pipeline of aid, being pumped full of money at a time when many communities in the west are increasingly marginalised if not suffering. (interview 1)

Furthermore, most practitioners failed to recognize that this approach is not exclusive to 'negative imagery'. Half of the sample included 'positive images' which employ signifying practices that perpetuate otherness. For instance, an ActionAid 'cold mailing' brochure depicts three women, identified in the caption as a 9-year-old Guatemalan girl, her grandmother, and her mother. The figures are framed by wooden poles at their sides and stand behind three wooden bars. The child is in the centre of the picture and is standing on a bar with the other two standing on either side on the ground, making the child appear taller by some 5 or so inches. The women look at the girl with pride; the girl is smiling, and looking confidently towards a horizon beyond the frame. The message is clear: the girl is taller, that is, more advanced and better off than her mother and grandmother; she can look towards a future, out of the bars that symbolically imprison her mother and grandmother, while they can look only at her. The text below the picture quoting the mother reinforces this message: 'I send my daughter to school so she can do much better for herself, so she can have a brighter future than me'.

Although a 'positive' colourful image of three smiling characters connoting hope and optimism, it is replete with racial and stereotypical signifiers: all three figures are reduced visually to a few, simple, essential characteristics: they are dark skinned, with dark eyes, dark hair tied back, barefoot ('primitiveness'), dressed in the same pleated skirts ('traditionalism'), against a backdrop of a horse or cow and rich tropical foliage ('exoticism'). The mother is in a somewhat sexually evocative posture; she wears a revealing chemise and has a hand to one of her breasts—a depiction that exploits deep-seated practices of sexualizing and fetishizing 'the other'.

Some NGO practitioners did (albeit implicitly) admit to their own and their organization's use of practices that accentuate otherness in similar ways. Three explanations and/or justifications were provided for this representational strategy. First, it constitutes part of the habitus within the NGO communications professional field; 'it's kind of what we know to do', a certain way of thinking and set of practices internalized by individuals working in this industry more through experience than active learning. A campaigns manager observed:

[It is] very, very depressing. But that's where we are at the moment. And the NGOs themselves are culpable for that. You know we've had, 50 years of just churning out the same message about gravity of need, need, need, need, need; and the way to respond to that is give, give, give, give money. (interview 12)

This observation (elaborated later in this interview) alludes to a second explanation for the continuing use of such practices by NGOs, namely that they are believed effective for fundraising. Practitioners referred to an unwritten but widely shared 'formula': the more the communication, and especially the imagery, convey 'the gravity of need' (as in the quote above) through practices of othering and victimization, the more it is likely to 'pull at the heartstrings' and generate a response (money donations). While practices associated with the depiction of 'the gravity of need' were derided as unethical and their employment by NGOs as a 'shitload of backsliding' (communications manager, interview 15), they were also considered to 'work', and interviewees referred to pressure from NGO fundraising departments to use them (Orgad, 2013).

A third justification offered by some practitioners for representational practices that emphasize otherness is ethical: presenting the other's extreme vulnerability and underlining radical differences from the spectator, some argued, are crucial for stirring spectators' consciences. A media director defended the ethicality of depicting naked, malnourished children:

I think within the context of many cultures it will be offensive to show them [children in the global South] naked. But I don't believe that you shouldn't show a very, naked or... a very malnourished child. I do believe people need to see those images because it's shocking and that's a reality... I think that part of our job as advocating on behalf of children means that we should also show the awfulness of what children have to endure, and I don't think we help them by... putting a wall between that reality and the general public... if we filter it because we think by doing so that's in the best interests of the child, then we lose some of our actual function, which is the outrage on behalf of children. (interview 7)

Thus, although most NGO practitioners appeared reluctant to acknowledge the legitimacy and use of the strategy of underlining difference in their communications, analysis of their communications and their own accounts reveals its continuing salience.

Celebrating Difference

Celebrating difference is a deliberate reversal of underlining difference. It is rooted in rejection of the wider representational paradigm of (racialized) othering in NGO communications since the 1980s and 'inverts the binary opposition, privileging the subordinate term... It tries to construct a positive identification with what has been abjected' (Hall, 1997, p. 272). Specifically, celebrating difference seeks to eradicate the much-derided (by NGOs and critics) historical depictions of 'emaciated babies' with 'flies in the eyes' and replace them with 'positive images' that depict and revere distant others as self-sufficient, dignified, and active. A campaigns director explained his NGO's approach as a response grounded in acute awareness of the colonial baggage of NGO representations and a deliberate effort to acknowledge and celebrate distant others in their own right and on their own terms:

> They [the NGO's beneficiaries] are not victims, and we, the NGOs, tell about victims, and we should be talking about heroes. That's a nice way of putting it.... It actually lauds them... You've got to be careful of the noble savage sorts of... there's the kind of colonial thing about it. (interview 2)

A Disasters Emergency Committee (DEC) Pakistan floods appeal (2011) illustrates this strategy. Three men (with several blurred figures in the background) are waist high in rushing flood waters. They are in the prime of life. The picture shows only men—a 'corrective' response to criticisms of infantilizing depictions of women and children as a condition for identification as '100% victims' (Cohen, 2001). The men are shown wading through the water—a depiction that endows them with agency and categorizes them as deserving of pity (Chouliaraki, 2006). The man in the middle is bearded, dressed in white traditional robe, and is carrying a very young child, whose back and bare buttocks are shown: we assume he is the child's father. This conjures up one of the universal symbols of humanity in Western imagination: fatherhood.[4] In this composition, bearded and moustached men wearing traditional Muslim robes, signifiers that in mainstream media are associated with largely negative meanings (terrorism, 'primitivism', etc.), are reversed to construct a positive identification. The man in the middle looks at the camera, his demand for compassion and help reinforced by captions in black, white, and red capitals, above and below the picture—'DEC PAKISTAN FLOODS APPEAL/MILLIONS STRICKEN BY FLOODS/PLEASE HELP NOW DEC.ORG.UK', occupying a third of the frame. The sepia brown photograph and the use of light and shade add dramatic effect that endows the image with out-of-the-ordinariness and urgency.

This image belongs to a genre that NGOs use frequently: 'hero image'. The term, borrowed from the creative industries, refers to a set of features such as eye level—the distant other in the image must 'look us straight in the eye' (interview 15), full-length picture (no cropping of the body), and people in a family or social context rather than alone and isolated (Orgad, 2013). A communications director explained:

> If I hire a photographer who hasn't worked in this sector before, the thing I always say is, you have to remember that people are heroes in their own stories. You are not the hero, I'm not the hero, they are the heroes in these stories... we don't paint ourselves, the outsiders, as the heroes of this story. (interview 15)

Heroic depictions of subjects are sometimes reinforced by quotes that 'give voice' to the other describing her devastation and emergence from suffering thanks to personal agency. Out of the 12 items in the sample 7 use such quotes to try—as interviewees explained—to 'personalize' the issue and create identification with the other as a particular human being in need. However, these quotes often reverberate Western neo-liberal values: in their emphasis on the individual and her agency, self-resilience, and empowerment, and their adoption of a 'makeover paradigm'—a narrative of individual transformation through self-discipline—they may fail genuinely to acknowledge and respect difference (Orgad, 2012), a point I return to in the conclusion.

Mitigating Difference

Mitigating difference also seeks deliberately and explicitly to eschew the symbolic marking out of otherness and its association with victimhood, helplessness, backwardness, and disorder that historically characterized NGO communications. Rather than foregrounding distant others' difference, the mitigating strategy tries to soften the other's (perceived) difference by 'balancing' signifiers of social and cultural difference with signifiers of Western culture.

A representational practice frequently used by NGOs to mitigate difference is the inclusion of a 'mediator'. Several practitioners described using images of aid workers and/or celebrities in their communications as 'proxies' that help 'create affinity and closeness' (interview 11), offer 'a bridge' (interview 11), and 'make connections for people [in the UK]' (interview 7). For example, the front image of a Medecins Sans Frontières (MSF) insert aimed at recruiting new donors shows a naked black baby lying on a camp bed in what looks like an improvised field hospital. The baby appears vulnerable; she stares wide-eyed at the viewer. These signifiers of difference and otherness suggest the baby's total helplessness and passivity and demand pity; they belong to the colonial regime of representing others discussed earlier. However, the baby is being examined by a black woman wearing jeans and a white shirt bearing the MSF logo, which identifies her as a doctor. A stethoscope seen on the bed next to the baby in the foreground of the picture—an iconic tool of a doctor in Western medicine—represents help from someone like 'us'. The doctor's hand is on the baby's belly and since their skin colours are similar, it is difficult to distinguish the outlines of the doctor's hand and the baby's body—a visual convergence that symbolically represents the humanitarian ethos of a common humanity. The text to the left of the image anchors (Barthes, 1977) the photo's image and 'fixes' (Hall, 1997) its meaning with the notion of 'common humanity': 'Angolan? Mozambican? Colombian? Rwandan? Haitian? Human.' Thus, elements of the 'underlining difference' strategy are 'balanced' by signifiers relating to the figure of the woman doctor that are familiar to spectators in the global North.

Mitigating difference seems to have emerged as NGOs' reflexive response to criticisms of the limitations and pitfalls of the other two strategies. Underlining difference is seen by most practitioners as damaging and largely unethical (although still used to varying degrees). It represents, in Silverstone's (2007, p. 480) terms the 'too far': 'the representation of the other… as beyond the pale of humanity… an example of the irresponsibility of distance'. Using imagery that highlights otherness in this way is also argued by some to repel audiences and fail in its ambition of connecting audiences in the global North with distant others in the global South. As a communications director put it: 'People… they're turned off by stuff that looks depressing or, god forbid, worthy, you know. Worthiness is something we try and avoid' (interview 11).

The second strategy, celebrating difference, is seen by some practitioners as also too far, in the sense that it fails to convey the relevance to and resonance with 'the other' to the spectator's life; 'it's so far out of people's realms of what is their reality that they can't possibly begin to imagine' (interview 3), explained a communications director. It is 'too up in the clouds' (interview 9), 'stepping too far' (interview 15), and, thus, practitioners argued, ineffective at connecting spectators 'here', in the global North, to distant others 'there', who demand their compassion and action.

Mitigating difference emerges as a 'third way' among these two strategies. It seeks to communicate difference in ways that practitioners believe (on the basis of intuition, experience, and some research they cited) to be relatable to the UK audiences whose lives are so radically different from those 'others'. In the attempt to move away from representations of difference that evoke 'worthiness'—a term used by the above-cited interviewee (interview 11), echoing Victorian discourses of deserving and underserving poor—NGOs modify difference in the 'original' image. Their communication effort is geared towards 'making the other less other', as put by the same communications director (interview 11).

However, this drive to lessen otherness, compounded by other pressures and factors, may have pushed NGOs to blur or sometimes completely omit the other in their communications. This strategy I call 'erasing difference', which is discussed next.

Erasing Difference

Erasing or eliminating difference involves degrees of symbolic exclusion of the other and replacement by a visual and/or textual focus or reframing on 'us', spectators in the global North. Chouliaraki (2012) argues that this tendency has become increasingly salient in recent NGO communications:

> The presence of the vulnerable other tends… to recede in contemporary humanitarian genres. Appeals shift towards a focus on 'us' rather than the other, or represent this other in aesthetic genres associated with new media fiction—computer games or advertising. (p. 179)

The images included in an Action Aid child-sponsorship booklet demonstrate this strategy. Page 3 is a full-page close-up image of a girl. The subtext in small font identifies her as 'Sallimatou Diallo, age[d] three, Kegneto Peulh village, Senegal'. She is round-faced, suggesting she is well nourished, and looks well kempt and neat. She is appealing and her prettiness conforms to Western heteronormative beauty. Her hair is braided and she wears earrings and a clean sky-blue tee shirt which contrasts with her dark complexion. She looks straight at the viewer and her eyes seem to be smiling although her mouth is closed, suggesting she is posing for the photograph mimicking old-fashioned portrait photos of children in the West. The photo and the girl's pose emphasize mainstream Western notions of child-hood in advertising and popular culture rather than cultural specificity and tradi-tion. The background (albeit blurred, since the focus is on the girl's face) shows a line of washing—a recognizable symbol in Western advertising of cleanliness, tidiness, and happy childhood.

The image depends for its meaning on being read intertextually, not in rela-tion only to Western advertising and popular culture but also significantly in rela-tion to other images of the global South. The signifiers of cleanliness and tidiness contrast starkly with dirt, a central historical signifier of otherness (as discussed in relation to the first strategy). Unlike the figure in the UNICEF appeal analysed earlier whose gender is ambiguous, the earring and the braided hair clearly identify Sallimatou as a girl. The Afro coiffure of the 'dancing girl'—the iconographical symbol of black people as 'childlike and happy-go-lucky' (Van Leeuwen, 2001, p. 103)—is 'restrained', 'tamed' and neatly braided.

To the left of the girl, in childish cursive English handwriting are the words 'our world', forming an almost symmetric graphic with a longish tail on each side, alluding to Sallimatou's ability/potential to learn to read and write and become a functional member of *our* world, in the global North. The writing is in English, the language of *our* [Anglo-Saxon] *world*. The visual composition of this image and its relation with the caption construct the clear message to UK viewers: she might be *our* child. She could be a member of *our* world. Unlike the UNICEF image, which constructs a sharp distinction between the viewer 'here' (in the global North) and the suffering child 'there', this Action Aid image erases this distinction, succumb-ing the message to the values and terms of 'our world' in the global North. While the distant other is shown visually, the message centres on us, viewers, rather than her. It exhibits Silverstone's (2007, p. 47) powerful critique of 'the elision of the different to the same': denial and/or reduction of difference and its legitimacy in the contemporary media space.

In some current NGO representations, efforts to remove connotations of oth-erness eliminate the distant other altogether, replacing her with the figure of the viewer (the potential supporter/donor). Action Aid's postcard, part of its 2011 What a Feeling campaign, is illustrative. The front of the postcard is a photograph of a delighted Caucasian woman in her early 40s set against a wallpaper designed like gift-wrapping paper. She is wearing casual, non-gender specific black jeans, and a bottle-green tee shirt. She looks excited, endorsed by a multi-coloured caption on the right side of the picture, bearing the message 'What a feeling'—reminiscent of slogans for cosmetics or foodstuffs, and echoing the emphasis in consumerist-psychological language on emotional satisfaction. The reason for her happiness is not immediately obvious. In the top right corner of the photo we note the cause: Act!on Aid (and the playful inversion of the first 'i' to form an exclamation mark intensifying the focus on 'I' rather than the other). The back of the postcard provides text describing her as: 'Silvia, Supporter of Action Aid and a force of nature', suggesting it is her charitable action, stemming from her (maternal, Victorian) 'goodness', that 'force of nature', that has promoted her blissful state.

The communicative strategy of erasing difference emerged as the result of a series of pressures on NGOs and changes in the cultural politics and workings of humanitarianism (Chouliaraki, 2012). The interviews with practitioners reveal that, paradoxically, the impulse to erase difference is partly a reflexive ethical response by NGOs to criticisms of the inadequacies of the representational paradigms that governed their earlier work and their constructions of difference and otherness. In reducing or eliminating 'the other' in their communication, NGOs are attempting to avoid the pitfalls of orientalizing, dehumanizaing practices of othering by turning UK audiences' eyes inwards:

> [We decided to focus] on the role of the supporters; focusing on the people but on this end rather than the people at that end.... It came from that thinking:... it's not about desperation and the desperate, great poverty; it's about inspiration: inspiring people to act, inspiring people to give. (campaigns director, interview 12)

Erasing difference also came out of NGOs' endeavours to address the problem of UK audiences' lack of interest in and empathy with social and cultural difference, claimed by fundraising practitioners and borne out by some NGO in-house research. A fundraising director explained the rationale of a campaign he helped to design that focuses on UK supporters (rather than beneficiaries):

> The idea is that *it's someone like me*. So I'm sat at home in my house in [a name of a town in the UK] and this TV advert comes on and *I'm not seeing foreignness, I'm seeing someone like* me and I'm engaging in that story because I would probably behave in that way.

> ... it's a much better strategy—we hope—to take one of those people [UK supporters] and go: well, look, we're going to drop you into this situation and see how you react and your reactions will be much better at *communicating to people like you* than ours would. (interview 10, emphasis added)

As a consequence, somewhat oddly, NGOs, whose communication task is to communicate social and cultural and difference, are focusing inwards. 'I would like this [my NGO's communications] to be as much about who *we* are in this country... as [about] *their* suffering' said a campaigns director (interview 2, emphases in original), adding that the goal of his work is 'finding *our* own new voice' (emphasis added).

CONCLUSION

Analysis of humanitarian representations juxtaposed by producers' accounts of the thinking that underpins their communication practices reveals a paradox. On the one hand, NGOs seek to spotlight cultural and social differences to convey need and deprivation and to elicit compassion and action from audiences in the global North. Thus they continue, with some variations, to draw on colonial and racialized 'regimes of representation' of difference (Hall, 1997). On the other hand, they want to obliterate difference, stress similarity and commonality with (global North) spectators, and promote an ethos of 'common humanity'—a desire driven concurrently by ethical and instrumental (to engage their audiences) motivations. This paradox propelled the development of four communication strategies which often are employed simultaneously, in overlapping and contradictory ways, and are intertwined with organizational, cultural and financial tensions, ambivalences, and struggles that characterize NGOs' work (Orgad, 2013). While NGO practitioners often stress the importance of an internal coherence in their organizations' messages (Dogra, 2012), and in the communication within the humanitarian sector more broadly, the analysis suggests a field characterized by tensions, contradictions, and lack of coherence. Indeed, organisations such as Oxfam UK, Bond, WWF, and UK Aid urge, in a series of publications (e.g., 'Common Cause', 'Finding Frames'), a radical collaborative and collective transformation of the frames that NGOs (as well as the media and the UK government) employ in their communications: from a transactional short-term approach underpinned by what they call 'negative values', to a 'positive value'-based framing oriented towards in-depth engagement with global poverty.

However, whilst the strategies discussed present a range of approaches to the symbolic representation of difference in humanitarian communication, and are cast by practitioners as reflexive responses to critiques, there are some notable absences. First, despite NGO rhetoric about 'giving a voice' to their beneficiaries, their voice is largely missing. As the analysis shows, the 'underlining', 'mitigating', and 'erasing' strategies often emphasize Western notions, values, and understandings, failing to recognize the specific concrete meanings of the other's difference and their irreducibility or attend to how 'the other' wants to express her/himself. New media technologies, and especially social media, promise to challenge the absence of others' voices by enabling marginalized groups to express themselves on these platforms. However, as Cooper (2014, n.p.) argues, the gate is yet to be unlocked: 'While NGOs are clear that beneficiary voices have to be heard, there is still reluctance and nervousness about how best to achieve this'. While the focus of the debate on social media is on voice in its textual/oral sense, the concept of visual voice—the capacity of the other to express herself visually, and for her voice to be acknowledged—holds great promise, particularly with the expansion of mobile telephony allowing individuals to photograph themselves and publish these pictures online. Humanitarian NGOs are important 'feeders' of public imagination of 'the other' in the global media space, and thus, consideration of the significance and signification of voice—both visual and textual/oral—and seeking ways to allow it through their 'gate' seem a crucial task.

Second, in all four strategies of communicating difference there is limited problematization of the current global order.[5] Acutely aware of the colonial baggage and other criticisms of their representation practices on the one hand, and under enormous pressures to raise funds on the other, practitioners admitted that the communications they produce seek to create a sense among their UK audiences of 'gaining' something from caring and acting about distant others. Representations of the other's helplessness and vulnerability that *underline difference* are argued to seek giving viewers a sense of their own agency (interviews 4, 7, 9, 10); communications that *celebrate difference* are seen as educational and as helping viewers to realize their identities (interviews 2, 4, 15, 16) and 'have a clearer sense of themselves in the world' as one campaigns manager described it (interview 2); representations that *mitigate difference* are seen also to give viewers a sense of agency and to foster their self-identity through an emphasis on the similarity between 'us' and 'them' and their avoidance of making spectators feel too upset or guilty (interviews 1, 3, 6, 10, 11, 13, 14, 16); and messages that *erase difference* are considered to give viewers a sense of pleasure and good feeling—congratulation for their generosity (interviews 4, 5, 10, 12). The contemporary marketing-driven, competitive, mediated environment, and the immense pressure on and scrutiny of NGOs internally and by the UK government and media, the public and global actors (Orgad, 2013), seem to have pushed NGOs to stress in their communications reassurance, comfort, and sustenance rather than disruption of the existing social order. Representations of oppression and exploitation that potentially might be disturbing to spectators are consequently being obscured.

Humanitarian NGOs' communication seeks to invite audiences in the global North to make an 'imaginative leap' (Cohen, 2001, p. 183) to the lives of distant others that are radically different from their own. At a time when NGOs seem to be engaged in serious self-critique and analysis of their practice as symbolic producers of difference and otherness in a global world, they might benefit from a rethinking of how symbolically to mobilize difference and otherness to better facilitate the symbolic leap between 'here' and 'there', 'us' and 'them'.

NOTES

1. For exceptions see Benthall's (1993) important, but now somewhat dated study; Cottle and Nolan's (2007) examination of how NGO communication strategies designed to raise awareness, funds and support, have been assimilated in the current, pervasive, and competitive mediated environment; and Dogra's (2012) study which seeks to establish a link between the NGO representations and the institutional dimensions that shape them.
2. For a useful distinction between otherness and difference, see Pickering (2001).
3. This discourse functions to perform a reflexive response to post-colonial criticisms of this regime of representation that dominated NGO communications in the 1980s (see Orgad, 2013).
4. See Chouliaraki (2006, p. 124) for a similar argument about motherhood.
5. See also Wilson (2011).

BIBLIOGRAPHY

Barthes, R. (1977). *Image, music, text*. London: Fontana.

Benthall, J. (1993). *Disasters, relief and the media*. London: I. B. Tauris.

Boltanski, L. (1999). *Distant suffering: Morality, media and politics*. Cambridge: Cambridge University Press.

Chouliaraki, L. (2006). *The spectatorship of suffering*. London: Sage.

Chouliaraki, L. (2012). *The ironic spectator: Solidarity in the age of post-humanitarianism*. Cambridge, MA: Polity.

Cohen, S. (2001). *States of denial: Knowing about atrocities and suffering*. Cambridge, MA: Polity.

Cooper, G. (2014, January). *Unlocking the Gate? How NGOs Mediate the Voices of the Marginalized in Social Media Context*. Paper presented at the annual MeCCSA conference, Bournemouth, UK.

Cottle, S., & Nolan, D. (2007). Global humanitarianism and the changing aid field: 'Everyone was dying for footage.' *Journalism Studies, 8*(6), 862–878.

Dogra, N. (2006). 'Reading NGOs visually'—Implications of visual images for NGO management. *Journal of International Development, 19*(2), 161–171.

Dogra, N. (2012). *Representations of global poverty: Aid, development and international NGOs*. New York: I. B. Tauris.

Douglas, M. (1966). *Purity and danger: An analysis of the concepts of pollution and taboo*. London: Routledge.

Fassin, D. (2012). *Humanitarian reason: A moral history of the present*. Berkeley & Los Angeles: University of California Press.

Hall, S. (1997). *Representation: Cultural representation and signifying practices*. London: Sage.

Jewitt, C., & Oyama, R. (2001). Visual meaning: A social semiotic approach. In T. Van Leeuwen & C. Jewitt (Eds.), *Handbook of visual analysis* (pp. 134–156). London: Sage.

Koffman, O., & Gill, R. (2013). 'The revolution will be led by a 12-year-old girl': Girl power and global biopolitics, *Feminist Review, 105*(1), 83–102.

Kress, G. R., & Van Leeuwen, T. (1996). *Reading images: The grammar of visual design*. London: Routledge.

Lidchi, H. (1993). *'All in the Choosing Eye': Charity, Representation and Developing World*. Unpublished PhD Thesis. London, Open University.

Orgad, S. (2012). *Media representation and the global imagination*. Cambridge, MA: Polity.

Orgad, S. (2013). Visualizers of solidarity: Organizational politics in humanitarian and international development NGOs. *Visual Communication, 12*(3), 295–314.

Orgad, S., & Seu, I. B. (2014). The mediation of humanitarianism: Toward a research framework. *Communication, Culture & Critique, 7*(1), 6–36.

Pickering, M. (2001). *Stereotyping: The politics of representation*. London: Palgrave Macmillan.

Richey, L. A., & Ponte, S. (2011). *Brand aid: Shopping well to save the world*. Minneapolis: University of Minnesota Press.

Silverstone, R. (2007). *Media and morality: On the rise of the mediapolis*. Cambridge, MA: Polity.

Smith, M., & Yanacopulos, H. (2004). The public faces of development: An introduction. *Journal of International Development, 16*(5), 657–664.

Van Leeuwen, T. (2001). Semiotics and iconography. In T. Van Leeuwen & C. Jewitt (Eds.), *Handbook of Visual Analysis* (pp. 92–118). London: Sage.

Vestergaard, A. (2008). Branding the humanitarian: The case of Amnesty International. *Journal of Language and Politics, 7*(3), 200–216.

Wilson, K. (2011). 'Race', gender and neoliberalism: Changing visual representations in development. *Third World Quarterly, 32*(2), 315–331.

CHAPTER TEN

Solidarity in the Age of Post-humanitarianism*

LILIE CHOULIARAKI

INTRODUCTION

From the Asian tsunami to the Haiti earthquake, recent debates about how vulnerable others are represented in the media illustrate the significance of spectacles of suffering in communicating solidarity—the moral imperative to act towards suffering others without the anticipation of reciprocation (Linklater, 2007).

It is this focus on corporeal vulnerability as the clearest manifestation of 'common humanity' that has historically informed the rise of human rights, leading to the emergence of secular humanitarianism (Halttunen, 1995) and contributing to the formation of solidarity bonds within and beyond the West. Indeed, if solidarity, following Arendt's definition, articulates the moral commitment to act on vulnerable others by reference to a 'common shared world', be this a Christian fraternity or the Marxian proletariat, then *cosmopolitan* solidarity, in particular, thematises the universality of vulnerability in order to broaden its conception of a 'shared common world' beyond specific communities of belonging and towards the human species as a whole (d'Entrèves, 2006).

Yet, even if vulnerability has been regarded as a catalyst for the cosmopolitanization of solidarity, it has simultaneously been held accountable for failing to articulate a legitimate ethics of suffering. Rather than motivating solidarity, the proliferation of images and stories of suffering, critics argue, ultimately lead to generalized suspicion or even apathy amongst media publics (Chouliaraki, 2006, for an overview). Central to this critique is the very *corporeality* of vulnerability that also evokes the 'universal' morality of solidarity. Insofar as solidarity is artic-ulated through heartbreaking images of starving children or wounded civilians, the argument goes, it deprives sufferers of their humanity as political and moral agents and evacuates the context of their misfortune of its historical specificity (Silverstone, 2007). Suspended, thus, between common humanity and de-human-isation, cosmopolitan solidarity seems to occupy an unstable space that constantly struggles to reclaim the former whilst avoiding accusations of the latter.

In this article, I approach humanitarian discourse as a crucial site upon which this struggle takes place, in order to argue that solidarity today replaces 'common humanity' with 'the self' as the privileged morality of solidarity—towards, what I call, 'post-humanitarian' discourse. Whilst this discourse proposes a self-reflexive sensibility of utilitarian altruism as a response to the impasses of 'common human-ity', I show that post-humanitarianism ultimately fails to address the key accusa-tion of cosmopolitan solidarity: its de-humanisation of vulnerable others (*section 1. Cosmopolitan solidarity as pity* and *section 2. Beyond pity: The post-humanitarian dis-course of solidarity*). This is because, rather than regarding human vulnerability as a politics of injustice, post-humanitarianism views vulnerability as a politics of iro-ny—a pragmatic solidarity aware of its own contingent foundations (Rorty, 1989). Far from a purely philosophical affair, this transformation is co-nascent with the neo-liberal commodification of solidarity in the global humanitarian market, which, by turning solidarity into self-centred consumerism, ultimately reproduces rather than challenges the existing relations of power between the West and the global South (*section 3. Cosmopolitan solidarity as irony*). Solidarity, I conclude, should instead be predicated upon the recognition that it is this very asymmetry of power that must become the principle of solidarity upon which we act on vul-nerable others. This is an Arendtian solidarity of 'agonism', where the problem of de-humanisation is resolved neither through sharing our 'common' humanity nor through sharing each other's emotions, but through communicating vulnerability as a political question of injustice and engaging with vulnerable others as others with their own voice (*section 4. Conclusion: Beyond pity and irony?*).

COSMOPOLITAN SOLIDARITY AS PITY

What the instability of humanitarian discourse between common humanity and de-humanisation reveals is a fundamental problem in the very relationship be-tween humanitarianism and politics. Boltanski sees this problem as a consequence of the tactical use of humanitarian argument in the service of political interest that often discredits the appeal to suffering as a universal moral cause (2000). For my purposes, Boltanski's argument is helpful not so much as a critique of contempo-rary global politics but as an analytical insight into the very nature of the political.

Contemporary Western politics, founded as it is on the Enlightenment imperative to protect the vulnerable, draws its legitimacy not simply from its adherence to principles of democratic governance but also from its adherence to a universal conception of corporeal welfare; from the articulation of justice with pity. Whereas this moral emphasis on pity has enabled a significant alleviation of suffering among large populations in modern times, it has simultaneously established a dominant discourse about public action that relies on the visuality of suffering and its emotional language of emergency (Halttunen, 1995). It is this reliance that, in Arendt's famous critique, displaces politics into the 'social question'—it displaces the long-term concern with establishing structures of justice with the urgent concern for doing something for those who suffer (1963/1990, pp. 59–114).

Whilst the inadequacy of this conception of the political tends, again, to be understood as an inadequacy of political practice, a failure of global institutions to address injustice, or alleviate suffering, this is not, in fact, the case; on the contrary, despite criticisms, humanitarian NGOs continue to be an important part of global governance structures and to nourish the moral imagination of the West (Calhoun, 2008, pp. 73–97). Instead, the inadequacy of this conception of the political needs to be understood, at least partly, as the historical subordination of justice to pity, which ultimately fails to associate the vulnerability of the sufferer with the question of injustice, whilst it manages to conceal the inevitable partiality of its own morality as 'universal'. This is a morality that appeals to our 'common' humanity as a justification for action, yet, by unequally distributing the quality of humanity across the globe, perpetuates the historical relationships of power between the West and the developing world, under the guise of cosmopolitanism (Douzinas, 2007). From this perspective, the contemporary 'crisis of pity' (Boltanski, 1999) could be defined as a crisis of a particular conception of politics, where the justification of solidary action ignores the historical power relations of human vulnerability and takes place in the name of 'common humanity'—mobilising a language of indignation or guilt that blames the immediate perpetrators or of sentimental gratitude that evokes appreciation for the benefactors, as in disaster relief or development aid initiatives.

The trajectory of humanitarian appeals, for instance, reflects a long history of colonial and interventionist policies of the West, which attempt to communicate the humanity of suffering under the unifying tropes of 'bare life' (in the imagery of emaciated bodies) or 'assimilated' humanity (in the imagery of smiling children).

Relying on two key representational features, the aesthetics of photorealism, which conveys the 'truth' of the sufferer, and the language of emergency, which urges us towards indignation for the extremities of bare life or tender-heartedness for the dignity of the sufferer, both styles of appealing confront us with human vulnerability in two of its 'prototypical' forms: shocking destitution and hopeful self-determination. Yet, as critics say, this persistent evocation of 'common humanity' as a cause for action in the West ultimately occurs at the expense of misrepresenting the humanity of non-Western others—a humanity that cannot be contained in imageries of radical otherness or tamed agency (Chouliaraki, 2013).

The genre of appeals is not, as we shall see, the only one that fails to represent the humanity of suffering others in the moral imagination of the West. It clearly illustrates, however, the inadequacy of the politics of pity to challenge the relationships of injustice between the West and the 'rest'. Insofar as its claims to solidarity reproduce a self-assured, yet Orientalist morality of conviction, the cosmopolitan morality of pity belongs to

> '... a vision of technocratic, Enlightenment universalism, largely untroubled by concerns of cultural difference... and populated by orderly, rational, co-operative moral agents who had transcended all cultural particularity.' (Tomlinson, 2011, p. 355)

It is in the context of this failure of pity to sustain a legitimate claim of cosmopolitanism that we should situate the recent changes in the representation of human vulnerability away from 'common humanity' and towards the self as the new morality of humanitarianism.

Beyond Pity: The Post-humanitarian Discourse of Solidarity

The assumption that informs the study of humanitarian discourse is that, by investigating its emerging strategies of representation, we may learn something important about the moral claims of solidarity that these strategies articulate and the implications of these moral claims for our possibilities to engage in acts of solidarity.

Rather than strictly contained in the genre of appeals, however, solidarity is articulated through a broad communicative structure of popular genres that, in speaking about vulnerable others, simultaneously also raise the political question of action upon those others. Let me then discuss, in turn, the changing representational strategies of humanitarian discourse not only in the genre of appeals but also in celebrity advocacy and disaster journalism.

Humanitarian Appeals

If earlier NGO appeals relied on the truth of bodily suffering, appeals today focus on playful representations of the Western lifestyles of (relative) privilege and urge us to take a reflexive distance from them, not through moral argumentation but through the affective estrangement that these representations enable. The 'Be Humankind' Oxfam appeal (2008), for instance, introduces the imperative to act on vulnerable others through a graphically animated story of a senior citizen who, indifferent as she initially appears to be towards the mediated spectacles of suffering available in the streets of her hometown, ultimately realizes the consequences of her indifference for her own life and joins fellow citizens in her town square to confront the 'monster of injustice'. As they all 'speak out' against the monster, a phantasmagoria of fireworks wrapping up the planet concludes the appeal. The only linguistic text of the campaign is the 'Be Humankind' slogan, accompanied by the Oxfam brand and web address.

Two textual choices are dominant in this appeal: the aesthetics of graphic animation and the absence of suffering others. *Graphic animation*, part of a range of playful textualities that break with the traditional aesthetics of photorealism, fictionalizes the context of 'our' everyday living and, through a strategy of estrangement from our mundane habits, enables us to contemplate on the consequences of our denial. *The absence of suffering others* (except in the doubly mediated form of 'news on suffering' within the appeal) addresses compassion fatigue, the de-sensitizing impact of earlier iconographies of suffering, by avoiding the representation of the other and focusing instead on the Western actor. Whilst the fictionalization of this actor invites a reflexive identification with the self as a catalyst for dispositions of 'human kindness', the absence of suffering others maximizes the distance between 'us' and 'them', rendering their existence irrelevant to the justification of 'becoming humankind'.

Even though the replacement of photorealism by artful textualities can be explained as a response to the failure of pity to represent the humanity of suffering others, this change in the representational strategies of appeals should also be associated with the market logic that today informs organizational responses to compassion fatigue (Calhoun, 2010). Reflected in minimalist and elliptical texts, which avoid explaining the cause of solidarity and foreground the NGO brand, humanitarian 'branding' has today become the privileged communication tool of the humanitarian sector (Chouliaraki, 2013). The idea that the market can remedy the moral tensions of solidarity might have been met with fierce skepticism in the past, yet today, it enjoys universal acceptance—as demonstrated in the words of former UN secretary-general Kofi Annan: 'Let us choose to unite the power of the market with the authority of universal ideals'[1].

Celebrity Advocacy

The commodification of humanitarianism, however, is nowhere clearer than in the re-invigoration of UN celebrity advocacy—a humanitarian genre with a history of success associated with major Hollywood icons, such as Audrey Hepburn (1988–1993) and, more recently, Angelina Jolie (2001–present)[2]. The advocacy of such star figures has always relied upon an ambivalent performativity of humanitarian discourse, which combines 'impersonation', the celebrity's testimony of the suffering of others, with 'personification', the infusion of such testimony with the celebrity's star aura (King, 1985/2006, pp. 230–235, 244–246).

What differentiates contemporary from past articulations of advocacy, however, is the tendency of the former to privilege a 'confessional' communicative structure of celebrity. Unlike the professional formality of earlier forms of celebrity advocacy, confessional performativity rests upon '*intimacy at a distance*'—a feature of today's popular culture that refers to our mediated access to the intimate sphere of celebrity lives, rendering this sphere an inherent aspect of their public personae (Thompson, 1995).

Hepburn's personification, for instance, builds upon a dispassionate public persona that places her Hollywood aura at the service of her professional role as a UNICEF Ambassador. Hepburn, as her emotionally disciplined style demonstrates, hardly ever mixed her private life, Hollywood history, or intimate feelings with her testimonial performance—though she did draw upon her experience as a UNICEF aid recipient, in post–WWII Europe. Even though her advocacy has been accused of focusing on stories of pity rather than explanations of poverty, Hepburn's discursive strategy of '*de-celebritisation*', that is, of the conscious self-effacement of her celebrity status, means that her discourse prioritised the voice of suffering others over her own feelings about it, rendering them, rather than herself, the focus of her testimonial narratives (Chouliaraki, 2013).

Compared to this strictly professional performance of UN ambassadorial humanitarianism, Jolie's discourse is radically personalised. This is because, I argue, her performance draws upon a more complex public persona, which deliberately fuses her UNHCR-related work with her private life as the mother of children adopted from developing countries *and* with her professional life as a human rights films' actress and as an entrepreneurial activist of development projects around the world (Littler, 2008). This strategy of '*hyper-celebritisation*', further framed within a highly emotional body language ultimately re-centres the voice of those people around the celebrity's own voice of self-development. An important consequence of this confessional performativity is that it is the emotional interiority of the 'hyper-celebrity', or her humanity, that we are now asked to identify with as moral actors, rather than the suffering others as others with their own humanity (Littler, 2008).

Rather than simply a rhetorical practice, 'hyper-celebrity' should be understood as yet another manifestation of the commodification of humanitarianism (Cooper, 2007). Whilst the earlier style of celebrity advocacy subordinated the Hollywood brand to that of the UN, today's style strives to build a powerful brand alliance between the two, with important mutual benefits of association and affect—a 'win-win' situation, where the UNHCR maximizes its visibility whilst Jolie legitimizes her public image as a humanitarian (Dickinson & Barker, 2006). A magnet of public attention as it may be, this market strategy, nonetheless, has a significant cost insofar as, in the process, it denies refugees the legitimacy of their own voice. Solidarity becomes, instead, a practice of voyeuristic altruism, which intensifies our engagement with the pleasures of show business whilst it reproduces the moral distance between 'us' and 'them': 'when most people think of the UN now', as a UN employee puts it,

> 'they think of Angelina Jolie on a crusade, not the work that goes on in the field… celebrity is at the heart of every UNICEF campaign and the association is being sold incredibly cheap.' (McDougall, 2006)

Disaster news. Institutional claims to solidarity, however, are further articulated through the genre of the news. Whereas broadcast news relies largely on professional on-location reporting, particularly in the satellite era of 24/7 news, offering NGOs controlled access to their global audiences, post-television news has changed the terms of reporting in favour of more inclusive, multi-authored production of news—the first case of disaster reporting being the 2010 live blogging of the Haiti earthquake[3].

Rather than relying upon the live immediacy of television footage, organised around the professional testimony of the reporter, live blogs draw instead on non-professional witnesses, as their 'real-time' messages (tweets, emails, mobile recordings) are collated online by major news networks in a timeline of cable-like updates. These stories are characterized by their *interrupted textualities*, consisting of a timeline of unrelated and heterogeneous short texts and hyperlinks; and by their *decentralization of voice*, introducing the testimony of NGOs and ordinary people as the key truth claim of newsmaking. Instead of an 'objective' portrayal of the scene of disaster, the claim of live blogging is to a multi-perspectival 'truth', where distant suffering is represented as a fragmented, situated, and open-ended narrative, constituted by snippets of people's own stories (Matheson, 2004, p. 461).

By drawing its authority from the voices of disaster rather than from the voices of the institution, post-television news promises, thus, to challenge the selective indifference to human vulnerability that, hidden as it was behind claims to journalistic 'objectivity' in television broadcasting, reproduces hierarchies of place and human life (Moeller, 1999; Chouliaraki, 2006). In so doing, post-television news further promises to renew the democratic deficit and declining public trust of traditional broadcasting—or, as the ex-director of the BBC World Service put it, 'When major events occur, the public can offer us as much new information as we are able to broadcast to them. From now on, news coverage is a partnership' (Sambrook, 2005).

On closer analytical inspection, however, this decentralisation of voice reflects a re-configuration of Western voices as authors of the news, insofar as the majority of ordinary postings in the Haiti live blog consists of citizens in Europe and the USA communicating their emotions about the suffering of others (Chouliaraki,

2013). The continuing proliferation of such emotional postings ultimately places the suffering in Haiti within a discourse of therapy that speaks about the West's trauma of hearing the news. The compassionate West, consequently, takes the suffering of Haitians to be its object of communication yet places its own emotions about their suffering at the centre of its rituals of communication. This is, as Castells puts it, a case of 'mediated mass self-communication… self-generated in content, self-directed in emission, self-selected in reception by many that communicate with many' (2007, p. 248).

Post-television news is, then, similar to campaigns and celebrity advocacy, insofar as it replaces the 'objectivity' of live footage with the 'truths' of the self, thereby instituting a new distance between those who speak and those who are spoken for. What this dominance of Western citizen voice suggests is, indeed, that the systemic distance between the zones of safety and suffering re-emerges online, as material inequalities in the distribution of communication technologies is now coupled by symbolic inequalities in the distribution of voice across global information flows. *Pace* celebratory accounts that welcome the participatory nature of post-television news as a '*collaborative project*', we should, therefore, re-evaluate its cosmopolitanising potential in the light of the new political economy of Western journalism. This is a fiercely competitive global economy that celebrates global voices, yet ultimately relies on the technological capacities, literacies, testimonies, and, not least, unpaid labour, of the West (Scott, 2005).

The graphic animation of campaigns, the hybrid performativity of celebrity and the 'interrupted' narratives of live blogging are but three of the many strategies of representation in post-humanitarian discourse. They all seek to represent human vulnerability in innovative ways that break with the 'universal' morality of pity and adopt a morality of contingency. This shift may appear to be a creative response to the generalised disaffection of Western publics towards institutional calls to solidarity.

Yet, insofar as post-humanitarianism places self-imagery, confession, and testimony at the heart of its discourse, it risks substituting the public justification of solidarity with narcissistic self-expression. Let me elaborate on this point by theorising post-humanitarianism as a neo-liberal version of solidarity that articulates a particular cultural sensibility—the culture of irony.

COSMOPOLITAN SOLIDARITY AS IRONY

The new genres of post-humanitarianism are a response to the realism of earlier appeals, the dispassionate celebrity, or in the objectivity of broadcast news. Even though, as I argued earlier, these influential genres of pity have traditionally educated the West in the name of 'common humanity', they have, simultaneously, been criticized for de-humanizing vulnerable others and for naturalizing the power relations of humanitarianism.

It is this distrust towards pity that informs the rise of post-humanitarianism. What post-humanitarianism intends to do is challenge pity's 'truth' of suffering and focus on our many 'truths' of suffering as part of the very appeal to act upon it. In this way, post-humanitarianism transform the confident morality of pity into a fragile and modest morality that, according to Rorty, 'combines commitment with a sense of contingency about (our) own commitment' (1989, p. 61). Turning, thus, distrust from problem into promise for a renewed solidarity, this morality of contingency further situates post-humanitarianism within a specific cultural sensibility, the culture of 'irony' (Rorty, 1989).

Grounded as it may be on contingency, the culture of irony nonetheless differs from the radical relativism of post-modernism in that it recognizes in human suffering that minimal, yet crucial, moral claim to other people that remains irreducible to any language game and defines the nature of sociality in our culture. The post-humanitarian discourse of solidarity, in this sense, flourishes within a world of situated meanings, not in the form of a 'universal' truth, but in the form of stories of suffering that, by way of *sentimental education*, mundanely cultivate the virtue of 'being kind to others as the only social bond that is needed' (Rorty, 1989, p. 93).

However, this profound shift in the epistemological basis of solidarity away from the moral justification of distant action as action on suffering humanity and towards a reliance to our own 'truths' as a justification for such action is more than a shift in discourse. It is also, as I argued earlier, an ambivalent political project, grounded on the politics of neo-liberalism and its aggressive commodification of spheres of action that had hitherto remained outside the remit of global capitalism (Lemke, 2001). The corporate appropriation of solidarity refers, here, to the increasingly managerial practices that regulate the communicative structure of humanitarianism with a view to increasing its economic efficiency in a competitive media market (Cottle & Nolan, 2007)—a process that, for Calhoun, signals 'the end of the humanitarian field… as it came to be conceived over a longish history and as it flourished especially in the four decades after 1968' (2010, p. 18).

Whereas the commodification of the communicative structure of solidarity is evident in the new textual strategies, discussed in the previous section, the commodification of the proposals to solidary action can be identified in the individuated ways by which Western publics are today asked to engage with vulnerable others: the online activism of campaigns, evident in the invitation to join Oxfam's website, the hyper-celebritisation of UN advocacy that turns commitment into fandom, and the invitation for people's e-testimonies that turn news co-production into an emotive call. Far from claiming that these proposals fully control public response to humanitarian emergencies, a question open to empirical research, they do indicate that ironic solidarity responds to the challenges of compassion fatigue, by replacing an ethos of conviction to a cause with a modest altruism of the everyday.

Two properties of solidarity define the discourse of irony: solidarity as *private choice*, which treats our action on suffering as public but keeps the justification of such action private; and solidarity as *self-fulfilment*, which construes our action on suffering as the realisation of our humanity whilst keeping the humanity of the sufferer out of view. Both these properties of ironic solidarity are informed by an instrumental logic of market consumerism that subordinates the politics of suffering as injustice to a de-politicised practice of sentimental self-expression.

Solidarity as Private Choice

The contingent morality of everyday habits, celebrity emotions, and ordinary testimonies originates in the subjectivist epistemology of neo-pragmatism (Rorty, 1989). As there is no knowledge outside the self, neo-pragmatism claims, there can be no moral appeal to solidarity beyond the stories *we* produce so as to imagine ourselves as altruistic actors within our own communities of belonging.

It is Rorty's figure of the 'liberal ironist' that best exemplifies the subjectivism of this moral discourse (1989, p. 15). Much like the post-humanitarian activist who expresses solidarity with distant others from the comfort of her living room, the liberal ironist treats, what Rorty calls, the *'vocabulary of justice'* as a private matter, enabling her/himself to both remain skeptical of any claims as to the justification of solidarity and, simultaneously, to engage in solidary action on vulnerable others as part of her/his own project of moral self-fulfillment. Whilst, therefore, the imperative to reduce suffering marks the liberal's commitment to the public realm of solidarity, the question of justification that informs this moral imperative is treated as un-resolvable in public and, hence, as belonging to the private realm of the ironist (1989, pp. 73–95).

Insofar as it turns the morality of solidarity into a private affair that concerns only ourselves, irony further privileges the cultural dimension of solidarity, self-expressive stories that speak to our commitment to suffering others, over the political dimension of solidarity, argumentative stories that help us understand and judge the conditions of vulnerability. This is because, if it is through our own stories of suffering that we become accustomed to a 'vocabulary of justice' rather than through the argumentative justification of justice (the latter being a cause of skepticism rather than commitment), then solidarity cannot but be a matter of 'training the soul' rather than a matter of critically engaging with questions of vulnerability as injustice.

It is, as mentioned, this view of solidarity as sentimental education that dominates the post-humanitarian genres. What the introspection of campaigns, the intimate life of celebrity, and the therapeutic discourse of disaster reporting demonstrate is that, by ceasing to rely on these others, ironic solidarity becomes a matter of crafting artful stories that situate the self at the heart of their communicative structure.

This does not mean that the vocabulary of justice is absent from post-humanitarianism. It could be argued, in fact, that it is the very proliferation of this vocabulary that enables these genres to emerge in the first place. The elliptical character of humanitarian branding, for instance, presupposes our familiarity with a vocabulary of justice and taps upon our already existing awareness of global poverty as a cause for action; the entrepreneurial activism of Jolie rests on criticisms of Hepburn's de-politicized Good Samaritanism, which prioritized the alleviation of suffering at the expense of local development, whilst citizen journalism often links the co-creation of news with the de-Westernization of journalism.

Even though these systematic references to justice could be seen as a series of 'democratic iterations', that is a chain of moral claims that catalyze debate and action in the mediated public realm (Benhabib, 2007, p. 31), they do not, I believe, constitute a resource for the exercise of judgment. What renders judgment marginal to the communication of ironic solidarity is the *textually implicitness* of such iterations. These references to justice, in other words, remain fully embedded in the storytelling conventions of the post-humanitarian genres and are, thus, always subordinate to the dominant references to the self as the only legitimate source of claims to knowledge.

Rather than providing us with the resources to judge the predicament of vulnerable others as a cause for our action, therefore, these genres present us with shortcuts to judgment, hinting to a vocabulary of justice whilst engaging with corporate persuasion: Amnesty International promotes its global brand to maximize consumer loyalty; Jolie, herself a mega-brand of the film industry, increases the authority of the Hollywood star system; and BBC reporting on Haiti's earthquake markets citizen journalism as the 'new democracy' of global broadcasting networks. This marginalization of judgment, in turn, allows no space for solidarity as a project of social change; by being prevented, as McCarthy puts it, 'from even thinking... the thought that the basic structures of society might be inherently unjust in some way, that they might work to the systematic disadvantage of certain social groups' (1990, p. 367), solidarity as self-distance favours a complacent view of culture populated by self-expressive ironists and devoid of visions of social change.

Solidarity as Self-fulfillment

Online petitions, celebrity fandom, and citizen reporting are some of the proposals to solidarity available in the post-humanitarian genres. In their refusal to engage our capacity for judgment, these proposals speak to the liberal ironist—a figure suspicious of the moral 'truth' of suffering, yet harbouring a visceral sense of care towards vulnerable others. At the absence of argumentative justification, however, how do these genres appeal to solidarity as a meaningful practice for the Western actor? They do so, I argue, by construing solidarity as a matter of self-fulfillment.

This is evident in campaign slogans, which focus on the promise to enhance our social consciousness and improve our moral conduct ('be humankind'); in post-television news, where the therapeutic sharing of voice is celebrated as the power of ordinary people to author the news; and in the entrepreneurial individualism of celebrity, whose philanthropy is hailed as the most effective model of solidarity activism today. If, then, personal choice is responsible for keeping the justification of solidarity private, self-fulfillment is further responsible for construing this private choice as a matter of a personally rewarding moral life.

However, insofar as solidarity is presented as a matter of self-gratification, rather than (also) as an act oriented towards those who suffer, then the communication of solidarity ceases to be about educating Western publics into the cosmopolitan sensibility of acting towards distant others without anticipating reciprocation. Under conditions of global market competition, the communication of solidarity becomes, instead, an effort to seduce publics into selecting the better brand—be this Oxfam or the UN. The tearful celebrity, Oxfam's 'Be Humankind' and the Twitter hype on Haiti function, in this context, as sentimental discourses of the humanitarian market, which value lies not in showing us how to relate to the world beyond 'us' but 'in the attempt of one will to align the attitudes, feelings, preferences and choices of another with its own' (McIntyre, 1981/2006, p. 24).

To the extent that we are addressed as primarily sentimental publics, whose personal preference for a cause depends on the branding strategy of a campaign or the star appeal of a celebrity, ironic solidarity treats us more as a means to the accomplishment of certain ends—sign, donate, or buy online—and less as ends in ourselves—as citizens who may engage with the cause of distant suffering because we feel committed to do so. In the ironic solidarity of self-fulfillment, as McIntyre would put it, 'others are always means, never ends' (1981/2006, p. 24).

Yet, solidarity as self-fulfillment does not only instrumentalise Western publics, it also construes vulnerable others as 'annihilated' figures who have no voice of their own (Silverstone, 2007). Campaigns avoid or aestheticise the presence of vulnerable others, live blogging refracts the voices of victims through the voices of people like 'us' and celebrity appropriates distant suffering in her own confessional personification of this suffering. Even though they may employ a rhetoric of dignity, these representational choices fail to construe vulnerable others as historical beings who struggle to come to terms with a legacy of colonial disenfranchisement and, hence, as figures who are endowed with voice and political will.

Consequently, post-humanitarianism may aim at combating the fatigue towards the traditional genres of pity, yet, ultimately, they distribute the quality of humanity unequally among its communicative figures. Whilst their promises to self-fulfilment over-humanise the Western actor, be this a celebrity or an ordinary blogger, their silencing of vulnerable others de-humanizes those who already lie outside Western centres of power and visibility. Far from cosmopolitan, then, ironic solidarity is an ethnocentric solidarity that encourages identification with others like 'us' but employs strategies of annihilation in the sphere of trans-national politics. Instead of enabling us to hear their voice, it treats distant others as voiceless props that evoke responses of self-expression, but cannot in themselves become anything more than shadow figures in someone else's story.

In summary, the discourse of irony reflects the commodification of solidarity, in the context of the neo-liberal expansion of humanitarianism. As market practices are increasingly infusing non-economic spheres of activity with corporate rationality, solidarity becomes a practice of self-expression, which treats the imperative to act on vulnerable others as a matter of free choice at the service of our moral self-fulfillment.

Seeking to address the failure of pity to sustain the cosmopolitan imperative, the imperative to act towards distant others without the anticipation of reciprocation, irony ends up proposing a 'new' ethnocentric cosmopolitanism that addresses us as sentimental publics with little capacity for judgment, whilst it reduces vulnerable others to voiceless figures without humanity.

CONCLUSION: BEYOND PITY AND IRONY?

Pity and irony, the two paradigmatic discourses of humanitarianism, fail to sustain a legitimate appeal to action on vulnerable others. Pity is associated with a solidarity of 'universalism', which articulates a morality of 'common humanity' that, ultimately, de-humanises vulnerable others, whilst irony is associated with a solidarity of contingency, which, by turning self-expression into the source of morality, reproduces an equally de-humanising discourse on these others. Both discourses, I have argued, have proved to be unproductive proposals for cosmopolitan solidarity.

Would it not be possible, however, to imagine a different communicative structure of humanitarianism that navigates beyond pity and irony and escapes both the arrogant universalism of the former and the narcissistic self-expression of the latter? Is it not possible to produce an alternative vision of solidarity? The answer is yes, provided that we reconsider the imperative to act on vulnerable others on the basis of neither universalism nor contingency.

Silverstone uses the term 'proper distance' to speak about cosmopolitan solidarity as 'a space of imagination', that goes 'beyond the individual and the solitary self' so that it 'opens the doors to understanding and in turn to the capacity to make judgments in and through the public world' (2007, p. 46).

Instead of maintaining the strategic distinction between imagination and judgment, characteristic of the ironic preference for self-expression as playfully imaginative and its marginalization of judgment as irrelevant to solidarity, Silverstone's proper distance favours, instead, the co-articulation between judgment and imagination as the only way in which solidarity can go '*beyond the solitary self*' and become a practice of the '*public world*'. Proper distance, for him, requires therefore a dual engagement with human vulnerability, which both enables us to reflect upon this vulnerability as a political question of justice and invites us to relate to the vulnerable other as an other with her or his own humanity (Silverstone, 2007). It is precisely this recovery of the public world as a site where we both think about and imagine the other that promises to renew cosmopolitan solidarity today.

Deeply aware of the asymmetrical distribution of humanity between the West and the global South, however, Silverstone's claim is not that we all equally participate in the public world but, rather, that the task of actively construing the world as 'common and shared' to all is a moral stake in its own right and itself an act of solidarity. This active and continuous reassertion of the world as-if it were 'common and shared' to all, what Arendt refers to as the 'agonism' of the public world, should, I propose, become the starting point for a new vision of solidarity—'agonistic' solidarity (Arendt, 1958/1998; Silverstone, 2007). Against the contingent morality of irony that reduces the world-beyond-us to our own 'truths' about ourselves, agonistic solidarity re-asserts this world as distinct from us and re-appreciates the role that *judgment* and *imagination* can play as key requirements for cosmopolitan solidarity.

The first requirement, *judgment*, treats the imperative to act on vulnerable others as a matter of public justification rather than private preference. This is because, far from private, such justification as, for instance, the promise to self-empowerment, is itself constitutive of solidary action and cannot be arbitrarily separated from it. The moral imperative to 'be humankind', let us recall, construes action as the private choice of a Western consumer, yet remains itself fully public, insofar as it bears effects not only upon the enactment of solidarity, by reducing Western activism into a consumerist practice of brand recognition, but also upon vulnerable others, by silencing their voice and annihilating their humanity.

The neo-liberal attempt to separate private from public dimensions of solidarity should, therefore, be seen as itself serving a specific project of power that, by construing solidarity as self-empowerment, ultimately legitimises the instrumental rationality of the market that informs such action in the first place (Connolly, 1991). Instead of approaching the question of solidarity from a (neo-)pragmatist perspective, as a claim to action that denies its own interest, agonism approaches solidarity as a claim that is always driven by interests and, therefore, as always open to struggle over which of these claims are to be heard and seen, praised or criticized, accepted or rejected: 'being seen and heard by others', as Arendt puts it, 'derive their significance from the fact that everyone sees and hears *from a different position*' (emphasis added). The voicing of standpoints, as claims to public interest rather than self-expressions, as claims to private morality, is, therefore, crucial to a solidarity of agonism.

Far from arguing that the communication of solidarity should become a heavy-handed lesson in the complexities of aid and development politics, the requirement of judgment suggests, rather, that, contra *irony*, agonistic solidarity becomes explicit about the social values that inform its calls to action and problematizes human vulnerability as a question of global injustice, collective responsibility, and social change. It also suggests that, *contra pity*, agonism does not subordinate solidarity to the 'universal' morality of corporeal suffering but, instead, opens up the symbolic space wherein the questions of what to do, where, and why are openly articulated. It is by carving out the communicative space wherein the radical plurality of these standpoints becomes the object of politics, that is to say the object of public deliberation and collective judgment, that agonistic solidarity may be able to galvanize the sensibilities of Western publics towards other-oriented, rather than self-oriented, expressions of solidarity.

The second requirement of agonistic solidarity, imagination, relies in challenging the Western bias inherent in the playful genres of irony. Rather than nurturing a cosmopolitan orientation to distant others, I have shown how these ironic textualities invite identification with those who speak our own voice but ignore the voices of others. Whilst the imagination of the self as a more fulfilled human being may well serve the consumerist logic of neo-liberalism, it can hardly educate Western publics to engage with the plight of those who live in zones of danger and deprivation. Instead of the imagination of the self, it is the imagination of the other that becomes crucial to solidarity—now, not by means of 'the rigorous logical unfolding of an argument but rather', as Villa puts it, '(through) imaginative mobility and the capacity to represent the perspective of others' (1999, p. 96).

This 'imaginative mobility' necessarily starts from the voice that matters most in the communication of solidarity, the voice of vulnerable others. The inclusion of this voice is instrumental in the humanisation of the sufferer, since, as I have argued earlier, the quality of humanity cannot be taken for granted as a 'universal' property of our species but is constructed through choices of representation that selectively privilege certain figures rather than others as worthy of our imagination and action. This suggests that, *contra* irony, the vulnerable other should be portrayed as a historical agent—someone who actively strives to manage her life, yet under conditions severely constraint by historical structures of injustice. It also means that, *contra* pity, this other escapes the 'universalist' imageries of powerless destitution or hopeful self-determination, characteristic of the traditional discourse of pity. Agonistic solidarity, in this sense, may rely on more complex but also, perhaps, more discomforting representations of distant others, made possible today through the mediated textualities available in the communicative structure of humanitarianism. Rather than using these new media genres primarily as a means for self-expression, an important ethico-political task ahead is, therefore, to re-think the ways in which the current economies of global communication may be used to facilitate empathetic connectivities, by encouraging more plural and dialogic encounters with these others.

The solidarity of agonism, in this sense, will be neither about sharing the same humanity for all nor about sharing our own feelings for distant sufferers with each other, but about the communication of human vulnerability as a political question of injustice that can become the object of our collective judgment and empathetic imagination.

ACKNOWLEDGEMENT

* This chapter has also appeared as 'Cosmopolitanism as Irony: A critique of post-humanitarianism.' In: Rosi, Braidotti and Patrick, Hanafin and Bolette, Blaagaard, (eds.) *After Cosmopolitanism*. Routledge, London, UK, 77-96. ISBN 9780415627214.

NOTES

1. Available at htttp://www.unglobalcompact.org.
2. Celebrity advocacy took a new impetus as a UN communication strategy under Koffi Annan's leadership towards the attainment of the Millennium Goals (UN Press Release SG/SM/7595; October 23, 2000).
3. The Haiti earthquake website (BBC, January 13, 2010), http://news.bbc.co.uk/1/hi/8456322.stm.

REFERENCES

Arendt, H. (1958/1998). *The human condition.* Chicago: University of Chicago Press.
Arendt, H. (1963/1990). *On revolution.* London: Penguin Books.
Benhabib, S. (2007). 'Democratic exclusions and democratic iterations. Dilemmas of 'just membership' and prospects of cosmopolitan federalism.' *European Journal of Political Theory,* 6 (4), 445–462.
Boltanski, L. (1999). *Distant suffering: Politics, morality and the media.* Cambridge: Cambridge University Press.
Boltanski, L. (2000). The legitimacy of humanitarian actions and their media representation: The case of France. *Ethical Perspectives,* 7 (1), 3–16.
Calhoun, C. (2008). 'The imperative to reduce suffering.' In M. N. Barnett & T. G. Weiss (Eds.), *Humanitarianism in question: Politics, power, ethics* (pp. 73–97). Ithaca, NY: Cornell University Press.
Calhoun, C. (2010). 'The idea of emergency: Humanitarian action and global (dis)order.' In D. Fassin & M. Pandolfi (Eds.), *Contemporary states of emergency: The politics of military and humanitarian intervention* (pp. 29–58). Cambridge, MA: Zone.

Castells, M. (2007). 'Communication, power and counter-power in the network society.' *International Journal of Communication*, 1 (1), 238–266.

Chouliaraki, L. (2006). *The spectatorship of suffering*. London: Sage.

Chouliaraki, L. (2013). *The ironic spectator. Solidarity in the age of post-humanitarianism*. Cambridge, MA: Polity.

Connolly, W. (1991). 'From irony to prophecy to politics: A Response to Richard Rorty.' *Michigan Quarterly Review*, 10 (10), 259–266.

Cooper, D. (2007). Celebrity Diplomacy and the G8: Bono and Geldof as Legitimate International Actors. Working Paper No. 29, CIGI, University of Waterloo.

Cottle, S., & Nolan, D. (2007). Global humanitarianism and the changing aid-media field: 'Everyone was dying for footage'. *Journalism Studies*, 8(6), pp. 862–878.

D'Entrèves, M.P. (2006). "To think representatively': Arendt on judgment and the imagination.' *Philosophical Papers*, 35 (3), 367–385.

Dickinson, S., & Barker, A. (2006). 'Evaluations of branding alliances between non-profit and commercial brand partners: The transfer of affect.' *International Journal of Non-Profit and Voluntary Sector Marketing*, 12(1), 75–89.

Douzinas, C. (2007). *Human rights and empire: The political philosophy of cosmopolitanism*. Oxford and New York: Routledge-Cavendish.

Halttunen, K. (1995). 'Humanitarianism and the pornography of pain in Anglo-American culture.' *The American Historical Review 100* (2), 303–334.

King, B. (1985/2006). 'Articulating stardom.' In P. D. Marshall (Ed), *The celebrity culture reader* (pp. 229–251). London: Sage.

Lemke, T. (2001). 'The birth of bio-politics: Michel Foucault's lectures at the College de France on neo-liberal governmentality.' *Economy and Society, 30* (2), 190–207.

Linklater, A. (2007). 'Distant suffering and cosmopolitan obligations.' *International Politics*, 44: 19–36.

Littler, J. (2008). 'I feel your pain': Cosmopolitan charity and the public fashioning of celebrity soul. *Social Semiotics*, 18 (2), pp. 237–251.

Matheson, D. (2004). 'Weblogs and the epistemology of the news: Some trends in online journalism.' *New Media & Society, 6* (2), 443–468.

McCarthy, T. (1990). 'Private irony and public decency: Richard Rorty's new pragmatism.' *Critical Inquiry,16*, 355–370.

McDougall, G. (2006, November 26). 'Now charity staff hit at cult of celebrity.' *The Observer*.

McIntyre, A. (1981/2006). *After virtue*. London: Duckworth.

Moeller, S. (1999). *Compassion fatigue: How the media sell disease, famine, war and death*. London: Routledge.

Rorty, R. (1989). *Contingency, irony, solidarity*. Cambridge: CUP.

Sambrook, R. (2005). Citizen journalism and the BBC. Nieman Reports. Retrieved from http://niemanreports.org/articles/citizen-journalism-and-the-bbc/.

Scott, B. (2005). 'A contemporary history of digital journalism.' *Television and New Media, 6* (1), 89–126.

Silverstone, R. (2003). 'Proper distance: Towards an ethics for cyberspace.' In G. Liestol, A. Morrison & T. Rasmussen (Eds.), *Digital media revisited: Theoretical and conceptual innovation in digital domains* (pp. 469–490). Cambridge, MA: MIT.

Silverstone, R. (2007). *Media and morality*. Cambridge, MA: Polity.

Thompson, J. (1995). *Media and modernity*. London: Polity.

Tomlinson, J. (2011). 'Beyond connection: Cultural cosmopolitan and ubiquitous media.' *International Journal of Cultural Studies* 14(4), 347–361.

Villa, D. (1999). *Politics, philosophy, terror: Essays on the thought of Hannah Arendt*. Princeton, NJ: Princeton University Press.

PART FOUR

NGO Communications: Impacts, Audiences, and Media Ecology

CHAPTER ELEVEN

From Pictures to Policy

How Does Humanitarian Reporting Have an Influence?

SUZANNE FRANKS

News coverage does not in itself determine policy despite what proponents of the CNN effect might contend. But it does wield influence in the democratic interaction between public and government. (Seib, 2002)

The degree of influence of media coverage upon policy is part of a longstanding debate. There are many and varied strands to these relationships and the way that media coverage may or may not influence political decision making in relation to foreign policy. Trying to separate out the precise impact of media effects is invariably complex and often opaque. This chapter analyses the state of the contemporary debates. But it also uses historical analysis to assess the arguments about how media influence affected decision making in the period after the television coverage of the Ethiopian famine in the 1980s, which was a key moment in the way that television reported humanitarian crises.

CNN EFFECT DEFINED

The term 'CNN effect' was first formally used during the first Gulf War in 1991 to describe the way that real-time news coverage of foreign stories appeared to affect the decision making of political elites, either directly or through the influence upon domestic audiences. It was defined as a 'generic term for the ability of real-time communications technology via the news media to provoke a major response from domestic audiences and political elites to both global and national events'

(Robinson, 2002). But versions of this argument that media coverage influences foreign policy had been around already for years.

The distinction which arose in the early 1990s was not just the wider question of media influence upon policy, but specifically the way that real-time live pictures, often transmitted via newly emerging 24-hour-news TV channels, might potentially have a role in shaping decision making (Robinson, 2011). And in recent years this has widened into a consideration of how an ever-changing range of online and social media might influence considerations of foreign policy. Yet in the period since 1991, as the debates surrounding the CNN effect developed, there have been many further discussions about cases, where retrospectively media coverage may have appeared to have had an effect upon foreign policy or at least prompted action in relation to foreign events. There have been considerable debates between those who highlighted the effects of media reporting upon political decision making and those who downplayed the role of the media (Robinson, 2000).

So the overall term 'CNN effect' subsequently became used retrospectively to analyse the more widespread effects of media coverage upon previous foreign crises, in a period long before the advent of 24-hour real-time news coverage. It is particularly linked to so-called humanitarian reporting and the presentation of extreme suffering as a driver for politicians to react. But the question of how this mechanism might operate, let alone whether there is in fact a causation between pictures of humanitarian distress and policy response is complex and often unresolved.

In fact according to this interpretation versions of a CNN effect (when defined as the wider impact of media upon policy) were already discernible even centuries earlier, where there are examples of press coverage of a crisis stimulating a response to 'do something' among readers and politicians. The Bulgarian atrocities in the nineteenth century are an early example. In the mid-1870s there was dramatic newspaper coverage of the Turkish slaughter of Bulgarian Christians, in the reporting of the American journalist A. J. MacGahan for the *London Daily News* and by W. T. Stead in the *Northern Echo* (Goldsworthy, 2006). These articles prompted former prime minister William Gladstone to produce a famous pamphlet *The Bulgarian Horrors and the Question of the East*. And the reporting ultimately inspired Gladstone to return to active politics and to campaign energetically on behalf of the Christian population in order to persuade the British government, in spite of Disraeli's initial indifference, to become involved (Little, 2012). The media coverage of the Turkish atrocities was a critical catalyst in Gladstone's campaign for Western intervention and the establishment of the Christian state of Bulgaria. So although the term was only invented during the first Gulf War in 1991, the phenomenon has been around in different versions for a very long time.

DIFFERING VIEWS OF INFLUENCE

In general politicians have tended to be critical of what they regard as the over-weening and inappropriate power of the media—and in particular television pictures—as a catalyst for public pressure, especially on foreign policy. The former UK Conservative foreign secretary Douglas Hurd felt strongly about the inappropriate pressure of media coverage as an influence in policy making in particular during the Balkan crises of the 1990s. He gave a speech in 1993 titled *The Power of Comment* which the *Times* reported as 'Foreign Secretary warns of Media role' ("Douglas Hurd Speech", 1993) and the *Daily Telegraph* as 'Hurd Hits out Again at Media' (1993). And the American journalist George Kennan made similar disapproving observations about US policy and intervention in Somalia. Writing in the *New York Times* he argued that the media was effectively dictating foreign policy making and had triggered the ill-thought-out US intervention (Kennan, 1993). Two years later, in 1995, the former Secretary-General of the United Nations Boutrous Boutrous Ghali went as far as saying that CNN operated like the sixteenth member of the UN Security Council.

> We have 16 members in the Security Council: the 15 country members plus CNN. Long-term work doesn't interest you because the span of attention of the public is limited. Out of 20 peacekeeping operations you are interested in one or two… And because of the limelight on one or two, I am not able to obtain the soldiers or the money or the attention for the other 17 operations. (Smillie & Minear, 2004)

In 1999 Tony Blair, the British Prime Minister, made a similar observation in his Chicago speech on foreign policy when he remarked that politicians were 'still fending off the danger of letting wherever CNN roves be the cattle prod to take a global conflict seriously' (Blair, 1999).

Summarising the various complaints by politicians, Piers Robinson points out 'the CNN effect has been asserted rather than demonstrated… and became an untested and unsubstantiated "fact" for many in foreign policy and humanitarian circles' (Robinson, 2002). These continual assertions about the inappropriate influence of media coverage on foreign policy decision making were important in encouraging a substantial academic examination of the matter.

Over recent decades there has been a vigorous debate about how instrumental media coverage really has been in affecting foreign policy. An early example of this had been a retrospective reassessment of the role of the media in the Vietnam War. Perceived wisdom had always asserted that the media had a major effect upon the conduct of the war. The images of civilian suffering combined with the 'body bag' pictures of the US military were supposed to have affected the decisions in Washington on the conduct of the war. And in later years, during the Iraq War for example, access to this kind of material of returning bodies was, as a result of these sensitivities, much more limited. However Daniel Hallin, in the *The Uncensored War* (1986), argues that the effect of the media during Vietnam was, in fact, far more subtle than originally assumed and that the media were actually reflecting a consensus against the war that had already been reached within important parts of American society and politics at the time. In other words it was not the direct effect of the media upon domestic American opinion that caused popular opposition to the war, which then influenced politicians.

This more-measured view of the CNN effect and a modification to the way that the causation really works has continued in more recent times. Nik Gowing (1994) and Steven Livingston (1997) have argued that it is only in the case of weak governments and indecisive policy that the impact of media coverage will change directions of foreign intervention. Media reporting will have an effect if there is a policy vacuum or moments of 'policy panic'. According to Philip Seib, quoting the US TV correspondent Peter Jennings, 'Political leadership trumps good television every time. As influential as television can be it is most influential in the absence of decisive political leadership' (2002). So the CNN effect will only take place in a policy vacuum. Seib concludes unambiguously that the argument that 'televised images especially heart-wrenching pictures of suffering civilians will so stir public opinion that government officials will be forced to adjust policy to conform to that opinion' may sound appealing, but although 'there is a certain logic to the theory and it cheers (some) journalists who like to think that they are powerful... there is a fundamental problem: it just ain't so at least not as a straightforward cause and effect process' (2002).

The Western intervention in support of the Kurds in Northern Iraq during the period following the first Gulf War in 1991 is sometimes cited as an example of a CNN effect, because policy appeared to shift in reaction to media coverage (Shaw, 1996). There were grim pictures of Kurds huddled on cold mountains, which supposedly were significant in the formation of the policy of creating safe havens pursued by John Major's government. Shaw distinguishes this crisis and the way the media were influential as an example of policymaking on the hoof in response to dramatic media pictures. A gradual consensus emerged from these various analyses that television pictures do inspire public opinion, but if they result in a (successful) call for action they are much more likely to trigger calls for aid and humanitarian assistance. It is less likely that they are the source of pressure for sustained political intervention or military force.

Nevertheless, Susan Carruthers is not so certain that media is so limited in its impact on policy—she also casts doubt upon a methodology that is all about interviewing politicians and asking them how much they were swayed by dramatic media coverage (2011). Her argument is that any politician worth his or her salt will say that they remained steadfast despite being unreasonably pressured by the media. This puts the comments by politicians like Douglas Hurd in a different context. When they complain about a CNN effect they are really talking about feeling under pressure, not that they necessarily give in to the pressure. Carruthers frames the issue as the diffuse effect that media coverage has upon public opinion, which then in turn may influence democratic leaders. Yet here again the kind of intervention is far more likely to be a call for humanitarian assistance rather than direct military involvement, especially ground troops. Andrew Natsios also observes,

> The CNN factor may have consequences for fundraising for NGOs and for sustained congressional funding but is not essential to early (military) intervention except where troops for security are critically important. Even then media coverage may not be sufficient to force a robust international response. (1996)

This is consistent with Michael Ignatieff's observations. He characterises the CNN effect not as a real trigger for action to change. He argues that television pictures are more likely to give us a moral drama with sentimental tales of suffering using a poor country as a backdrop, which serves to stimulate exercises in generosity and even reinforces the donor's sensation of moral superiority, so that the 'CNN effect will have little effect to drive policy but will have a big effect to promote humanitarian intervention' (Ignatieff, 1998; Harvey, 2012). If the media does have a role in prompting military action it is at most able to influence the timing of an intervention. So, for example, the Kosovo crisis in 1999 is deemed to be an example where media coverage prompted intervention (Bahador, 2007). But Rupert Smith argues that in the case of Kosovo the use of force would have happened anyway and the effect of the media pressure was that it potentially speeded up the process (Smith, 2006). In the Syrian crisis during the period 2011–2013 once again there was plenty of impetus for humanitarian assistance, but the media images did not result in the use of outside military force despite what some politicians in Western nations may have wanted.

So the consensus is that large-scale international relief efforts and also a 'something must be done' urgency to intervene may be affected by media coverage, and especially pictures, but it is not clear that this extends beyond the impulse to donate aid, either to persuade governments to commit aid or for the public to make their own contributions. Furthermore there are some instances where governments might even encourage media coverage as a way of gaining public support for a policy which they were already keen to promote.[1] This use of the CNN effect by politicians as an enabling effect is another dimension discussed by both Robinson and Shaw. Nicholas Wheeler points out how the media can be used by policymakers to build support for an intervention that they want to pursue for non-media reasons (Wheeler, 2003). This was discernable in the question of whether the West should intervene in the Syrian crisis in August 2013, following the use by the Syrian regime of chemical weapons. Media coverage was prompting humanitarian assistance both in private donations and encouraging governments to act. However there was less enthusiasm for any kind of official military intervention, as had been the case in Libya eighteen months earlier. The UK government under David Cameron tried to create a consensus towards military support for the Syrian rebels and media coverage (much of it obtained from locally based citizen journalists) formed a key part of this, since it was the only way that the Western public could engage with the crisis. Nevertheless, despite the powerful media images of suffering and atrocities, this was not sufficient and the consensus amongst the public (demonstrated in opinion polls) and the formal rejection of a motion in the UK Parliament showed that there was not national support for military intervention, despite the Government's view.

MEDIA AND HUMANITARIAN APPEALS

What is now apparent is that there are in fact a number of variants of a CNN effect and the way it might impact upon policy. The narrow view is only concerned with direct foreign policy responses as a reaction to media coverage. Here the consensus is now that there is limited connection, with the exception of humanitarian intervention. However there is also a wider interpretation of a CNN effect which concerns the influence of media coverage of foreign events on mainstream domestic opinion and responses—in particular the role of philanthropy. In this case there does however appear to be a correlation between the nature and level of media coverage and the overall scale of humanitarian assistance. In the article 'Humanitarian Crises: Testing the CNN effect', Olsten, Carstensen, and Hoyen contrast the coverage of the Orissa flooding following the cyclone that hit India in late 1999 with the Mozambique floods in early 2000 (Olsen & Nils Carstensen, 2003). The Indian authorities severely restricted media access to the flooded areas in Orissa and there was very little television coverage. Meanwhile the Mozambique flooding attracted dramatic coverage, with helicopters rescuing people from the tops of trees. Its climax was the remarkable rescue by a passing South African helicopter of a woman giving birth. The international aid response to the Mozambique floods was substantial whereas the response to the floods in Orissa was far more limited by comparison. There was a Disasters Emergency Committee (DEC) appeal for funds to Mozambique, launched in March 2000, which raised more than £30 million—at that point the third highest total for any of their broadcast appeals. Beyond this there was substantial official aid offered to Mozambique—including of course the helicopters from South Africa that made possible the remarkable rescues. Mozambique welcomed international relief assistance but this was largely dependent upon sufficient media coverage of the disaster, which it was prepared to facilitate.

There had also been a DEC appeal in November 1999 for the flooding in the Eastern Indian state of Orissa. Although it will accept official charitable donations to disasters, the Indian government does not usually request international assistance for disaster aid, which may be part of the reason that it was not concerned to give media access to the affected area. In contrast to Mozambique this appeal raised a mere £7 million. Moreover the Orissa appeal happened first which would suggest that there might have been a sense of déjà vu by the time the Mozambique appeal took place. And the Orissa appeal was in the comparatively 'fruitful' Christmas period, when charitable donations are traditionally more forthcoming. Yet clearly other reasons led to the Mozambique appeal yielding a higher level of donations. The images are critical in inspiring assistance. The DEC were aware in their assessment that the limited media coverage of the Indian crisis would result in a lower level of donations than for other emergencies but still felt the appeal was worth making. In the official request to the BBC chairman to authorise the broadcast appeals it was pointed out that over the previous year there had been appeals for the Kosovo crisis and a hurricane in Central America, 'however... the scale of human distress is actually greater (in Orissa) than in either of these other two emergencies'.[2] This view was supported by the Department for International Development (DfID) and the estimates were that 10 to 15 million people were affected and 2 million were homeless with millions at risk of cholera and other epidemics. The Kosovo appeal was launched in response to overwhelming media coverage of the refugee crisis. It is interesting that this appeal with its repeated images of (light-skinned) refugees on cold mountains yielded £53 million, which was at that time the highest-ever level of donations to a broadcast appeal.[3]

However an interesting contrast with the Orissa appeal occurred a year later when a devastating earthquake affected the state of Gujarat in northwest India. Once again the Indian government said that it would accept charitable donations and appeal was launched by the DEC in February 2001. Tony Vaux, who once worked for Oxfam and later wrote about the role of NGOs, produced an assessment of the Gujarat appeal contrasting the response to the two Indian disasters of the Gujarat earthquake with the Orissa floods (Vaux, 2001). There was far greater television and media coverage of the earthquake and the public response in the UK was correspondingly three times greater than for the flooding. The DEC appeal for Gujarat raised £24 million, more than three times as much as the total for Orissa. Although the UK has closer links with Gujarat than Orissa it is still hard to explain this discrepancy, except through the images. The response to different disasters is so variable because 'there is no objective reason but simply a subjective response to selected images'.[4] Vaux argues that the reason that donations to emergency appeals constantly break new records is that the global media are better and better at producing shock and horror images. The coverage of the Asian tsunami at the end of 2004 was a prime example, exceeding all previous totals. Hilary

Benn as international development secretary observed in 2006 that fundraising appeals yielded $10 per head for the humanitarian crisis in the Congo compared with $1,000 a head for the Asian tsunami, a difference he attributes to the media coverage.[5]

In the wake of extensive media coverage of a crisis, Smillie and Minear comment on the intense pressure that governments may face in being seen to do *something* to alleviate suffering, even if it is, practically speaking, of little use. In the case of the Mozambique floods, the UK Government responded by sending some helicopters. This entailed a huge cost because of the long distances, and anyway the helicopters arrived too late to be of much use, 'giving the media a second stick with which to beat the government' (Smillie & Minear, 2004). It would have made more sense to contribute towards the helicopters easily accessible from South Africa.

In recent years the CNN effect has not even been perceived as a necessary stimulant to humanitarian action. Political interests and proximity are cited as more powerful stimulants to the decision to send official aid (Smillie & Minear, 2004). Examples cited are those such as the case of North Korea where there is almost no media coverage and yet because of strategic interests there is still significant humanitarian assistance. Similarly according to Smillie and Minear, the conflicts in both Angola and Sudan were for many years the subject of minimal media attention and yet they received a reasonable amount of aid. The current consensus is that just as the CNN effect is most likely to affect foreign policy where there is no strong political direction, it is most likely to influence humanitarian intervention where there are no particular strategic interests involved. In those cases the media may have a substantial effect on prompting calls for wide-scale assistance and aid. As the strategic certainties of the Cold War eroded during the 1990s, media coverage was more effective at prompting humanitarian relief. It appears therefore that the media might be a sufficient but not always a necessary trigger to sending official aid, even if they are much more crucial in the galvanising of individual and private donations.

So the history of the CNN effect is that the original view (held by politicians and some self-important journalists) was that the media coverage could play a critical role in pushing governments in foreign-policy decision making. Then there was an academic consideration of the problem which broadly concluded that it is only in cases of policy uncertainty and lack of direction that the media could have a more significant effect. This was far less likely to have been the case during the Cold War period when foreign policy was more likely to be driven by overriding global strategic concerns. An exception was made for humanitarian suffering and relief where the literature concluded that the CNN effect was powerful, but it is important to understand that this is largely because of the way in which it was refracted through public opinion. However in more recent years, it seems that this conclusion too may be tempered so that even in matters of sending official foreign aid there is not necessarily a strong relationship to media pressure, provided governments have a strong strategic goal.

CNN EFFECT AND ETHIOPIA—A CASE STUDY?

The media coverage of the Ethiopian famine in 1984–1985 is one of the best-known examples of humanitarian coverage which is generally assumed to have had an influence and impact upon decisions about aid policy. Although many scholars agree that there is now very often a doubt about the extent of media effects on the overall policy process, in particular the degree to which coverage can result in a military intervention, there has nevertheless been considerable consensus between Robinson and others that in the case of *humanitarian assistance* the media is more likely to have a substantial effect. Despite uncertainty about the way that media coverage might influence wider foreign policy there was some agreement that in the case of stimulating humanitarian action there is a discernable link to the influence of the media reporting of a crisis. Indeed Robinson even calls the Ethiopian famine in 1984 'a seminal case of the CNN effect where media coverage led to an apparent dramatic humanitarian intervention' (2002).

The benefit of hindsight provides some interesting insights. Through examining archival records and conducting interviews with those who were involved at the time it is possible to illuminate the precise ways that media coverage influenced policy, because this kind of analysis uncovers motivations and causations which were taking place inside government at the time, despite other claims that might have been made, for public consumption. A series of documents available through Freedom of Information requests as well as those released to the National Archive and available in the written BBC archives at Caversham are useful in shedding light upon this question: to what extent did the powerful media coverage, in particular images of suffering, have an effect upon decision making within government?

What becomes apparent is the persistent issue that so often foreign policy is influenced by and cannot be uncoupled from domestic concerns, that is, responding to the voters. In more recent times the memoirs of Bill Gates, the former US Defense Secretary, made the same observations that so often it is domestic political pressures which are pivotal concerns in the framing of foreign policy (Gates, 2014)—in his case the US involvement in Iraq and Afghanistan. As is often the case from examining FOI material it is also evident from studying the contemporary documents that there was a distinct contrast in the ways that the crisis in 1984 was being discussed in public by the UK government from the concerns and pressures that were being raised within private documents and conversations.

Both the US and the UK Government, by late 1984, had already known about the famine in Ethiopia for months, if not years, before the global media coverage arising from the BBC TV report by Michael Buerk and Mo Amin on 23 October. The documents make clear that diplomats on the ground had, on many occasions, warned their superiors of the problem.[6] An urgent cable had been sent from the US embassy in Addis to the State Department on 4 April 1984, about the prevailing food situation. It stated that 'a very serious situation could develop in Ethiopia this year and we will be remiss if we are not adequately informed and prepared.'[7] Meanwhile British diplomats had urged that senior figures from the UK should visit and observe the impending crisis, but to little avail. NGOs had tried to lobby government based upon the evidence they had received from their staff working in the north of Ethiopia, but once again this yielded no response. Indeed even a junior minister, Malcolm Rifkind, responding to these reports, had written to colleagues warning of extreme food shortages.[8] Yet senior officials and ministers did not react to these warnings and there was a distinct unwillingness to engage with the issue.

However on 24 October, the day after the BBC TV news report of the famine, the foreign secretary, in a specific response, announced in an emergency statement to the House of Commons that in the light of the news about this crisis, the government would donate £5 million to famine relief in Ethiopia. The documents make clear that not only had the government long known about the famine, they were specifically sponsoring some research in Ethiopia into food security issues.[9] But it was only when the media images appeared on TV that the government chose to respond. This is a compelling and clear example of a CNN effect. But the question is really, how much substance was there in the response?

An Ethiopian Drought Group was convened by the Overseas Development Administration within the foreign office after the media coverage, which met twice a day and had links to Downing Street and the Ministry of Defence. Yet the overwhelming emphasis was to respond to public concerns. A contemporary note indicates that within a week of the BBC news reports, letters to the prime minister were running at 200 a day (quite substantial in a pre-email and social media era).[10] And this was taken as an indication of the need to acknowledge public concern.

The principal form of assistance that the UK Government and notably the prime minister wanted to provide was airlifts of food by the Royal Air Force. It is evident from the contemporary notes and documents[11] that there was an insistence that the aid should take this form, even if it was not necessarily what was being requested or suggested from those on the ground by the Ethiopian Relief and Rehabilitation Commission or the NGOs who were most closely involved. Furthermore contrary to perceptions, even after the media coverage, it is now evident that government provided virtually no additional money and certainly no long-term assistance. There was even an instance of that familiar government trick of re-announcing the same funding to make it appear as if it was a fresh initiative—so that the minister had then to apologise for misleading MPs.[12] And the Foreign Affairs Select Committee (under a Conservative chairman) delivered a stinging report criticizing the government for its meanness in dealing with the famine and refusing to authorize any new funding.[13]

Meanwhile a letter from the prime minister's office made clear that the airlifts were specifically to be funded by the MOD and the ODA and 'they must settle the costs between them.'[14] This edict led to considerable inter-departmental bickering.[15]

It is not surprising that the famine and requests for emergency aid recurred in Ethiopia a couple of years later. Moreover the policy which the UK government did pursue was not a reaction to the facts of the famine itself or even media coverage of the famine, but a reaction to public opinion's dramatic response to the media coverage. The Government had strong ideological (i.e., anti-Soviet) grounds not to help and so explicitly did what made them look good domestically and reaped the best possible public relations benefit.[16] Ethiopia was firmly within the Soviet Union's sphere of influence, receiving immense military support from it. The regime of Colonel Mengistu operated on extreme authoritarian Communist principles and identified with the East European regimes. The guest of honour at the regime's 10th anniversary celebrations in 1984, when the media reports first emerged, was the East German leader Erich Honecker. This background was reinforcing the resistance of the UK Government towards providing aid on the basis that if Ethiopia was so firmly within the Communist camp, then any assistance needed to be carefully weighed with that in mind.[17] These calculations are evident in the way that the Downing Street and the Foreign Office sought to formulate a policy, once the media images had made this an imperative.

CONCLUSIONS

In contrast to the contemporary media perception the government aid provided to Ethiopia was pretty much existing money that was reconfigured and, despite appearances, there was no 'new money' (Franks, 2013). The UK Government rejected any longer-term, ongoing engagement and was just concerned with short-term emergency relief, appearing to be generous in reaction to disturbing media images. Furthermore, ministers were concerned that the relief that was provided (airdrops of food by RAF planes) should garner the maximum possible domestic political benefit and reap the best political dividend vis-à-vis Cold War adversaries.[18]

It is apparent from this analysis that the ability of the media coverage to produce change in official policy and official assistance was less apparent than might first have appeared. Ultimately the impact of the coverage was far more significant upon driving public opinion and (with the advent of Band Aid) in the way it changed the nature of charitable giving and private philanthropy. So that in terms of policy effects the media on this occasion appears to have a greater effect upon the policies and institutions of the voluntary sector and NGOs. If the 1980s is considered the 'decade of the NGO' (Hellinger, 1987), then the response to the media coverage of Ethiopia played a key part in this expansion.

Thus, we can see that in response to the media coverage of the Ethiopian famine the ability of news coverage to push official policy was far less substantial than may have appeared at the time. When in successive academic debates the Ethiopian famine is considered historically as a case of a 'strong CNN effect' that is not strictly speaking true. Public policy did not shift as a result of powerful media coverage of suffering. Official humanitarian assistance was severely limited and there was no change of heart about development aid.

Despite superficial appearances not really that much changed as a result of the government reaction to the media coverage of Ethiopia. There was a substantial reaction in the short term but what the government did was in response to domestic public opinion, which was, in turn, reacting to the media coverage. It is evident from FOI documents cited earlier that the facts about the famine were well known within the government long before autumn 1984. However once there was a public reaction to the sudden media coverage this made officials and politicians want to be seen to care. So in this case it appears that although there was a CNN effect which might have prompted humanitarian action by government, it was primarily for short-term domestic political effect which was reacting to public opinion within the UK. At this point in the Cold War and under a Conservative Government there was a strong strategic direction to politics which meant that policy decisions were far less likely to change or be influenced by media coverage. This is consistent with the literature over the past ten years which points to the rather more nuanced influence of the media on wider foreign policy decisions. So that even though the CNN effect is perceived to be more likely to happen in the case of providing humanitarian aid, in response to media portrayal of suffering, this has not necessarily been the case to the extent that has been hitherto anticipated.

NOTES

1. In a keynote speech by Gordon Brown at a Vatican seminar on development 9 July 2004, Brown recognised the importance of popular pressure on aid policy, and also after the July 2005 Gleneagles G8 summit he acknowledged the role of international media pressure on those governments initially reluctant to agree to the debt relief proposals. Professor Paul Collier, author of *The Bottom Billion* (2007) has also spoken about the growing role of 'the street' in influencing politicians on development issues. Hay Festival 29 May 2007. www.hayfestival.com/archive.

2. BBC Written Archive Centre RX27 B114-4-5 Appeals Disasters Emergency Committee-India Note from Wendy Jones, Deputy Secretary, to the BBC Chairman, 4 November 1999.

3. BBC Management Registry B114-4 undated memo on 'DEC key aspects' Kosovo appeal was in April 1999.

4. Interview with Tony Vaux, June 2005.

5. Hilary Benn, Secretary of State for International Development, speaking at Media and Politics seminar, Nuffield College, Oxford University, 13 October 2006.

6. For example, see the paper headed 'The Drought in Africa', prepared for Tim Raison, Minister for Overseas Development, 26 July 1984. Obtained under FOI.

7. Peter Cutler presented his research as *The Development of the 1983–85 Famine in Northern Ethiopia*, unpublished PhD thesis, University of London, 1988.

8. The National Archives Public Record Office ODA 53/5 memo from Malcolm Rifkind to Sir Geoffrey Howe 8 October 1984, and memo from Malcolm Rifkind headed 'Famine in Africa', 17 October 84. Obtained under FOI.

9. Cited in Cutler (1988).

10. TNA PRO OD 53/8, 3 November 1984.

11. Letter from Charles Powell (foreign affairs advisor to PM) to C. R. Budd at Foreign Office, 29 October 1984. Obtained under FOI.

12. TNA/PRO OD 53/11. Letter from Timothy Raison, ODA minister to Sir Anthony Kershaw, Chairman of the Foreign Affairs Select Committee, 10 December 1984 (about an announcement made by Foreign Secretary Sir Geoffrey Howe on 23 November 1984).

13. *Famine in Africa 1984-85*, House of Commons Foreign Affairs Select Committee HMSO Session 1984/5.

14. Letter from Charles Powell (foreign affairs advisor to PM) to C. R. Budd at Foreign Office.

15. TNA PRO OD 53/7 letter from Timothy Raison's private secretary to the private secretary of Lord Trefgarne at the MOD, 2 November 1984.

16. See, for example, confidential briefing note for a House of Commons appearance by Tim Raison. Undated but appears to be late October 1984. Obtained under FOI. 'Pity that Soviet assistance to Ethiopia is mainly military: their contribution to famine relief so far sadly inadequate. They must play their part, not least because Ethiopia professes to be a Marxist government.'

17. FCO confidential paper, 'The Ethiopian Famine: Policy Problems', 29 October 1984. Obtained under FOI.

18. TNA PRO OD 53/10, 'Ethiopia and Longer Term Aid', Background briefing note to Minister, 21 November 1984.

REFERENCES

Bahador, B. (2007). *The CNN effect in action: How the news media pushed the West toward war in Kosovo*. New York: Palgrave Macmillan.

Blair, T. (1999, 22 February). *Doctrine of the International Community—Chicago Speech*. Retrieved 22 January 2015, from http://www.britishpoliticalspeech.org/speech-archive.htm?speech=279.

Carruthers, S. (2011). *The media at war*. New York: Palgrave.

Franks, S. (2013). *Reporting disasters: Famine, aid, politics and the media*. London: Hurst.

Gates, W. (2014). *Duty. Memoirs of a secretary at war*. New York: Knopf.

Goldsworthy, S. (2006). English nonconformity and the pioneering of the modern newspaper campaign including the strange case of W. T. Stead and the Bulgarian horrors. *Journalism Studies, 7*(3), 387–402.

Gowing, N. (1994). *Real time television coverage of armed conflicts and diplomatic crises: Does it pressure or distort foreign policy decisions?* Joan Shorenstein Barone Center on the Press, Politics and Public Policy Working Paper Series, John F. Kennedy School of Government, Harvard University.

Hallin, D. (1986). *The uncensored war: The media and Vietnam.* Berkeley: University of California Press.

Harvey, D. C. (2012). *The Invisible Genocide: An Analysis of ABC, CBS, and NBC Television News Coverage of the 1994 Genocide in Rwanda.* Master's thesis, The School of Graduate and Postdoctoral Studies, University of Western Ontario, London, Ontario, Canada.

Hellinger, D. (1987, October). NGOs and the large aid donors: Changing the terms of engagement. (Special Supplement) *World Development, 15.*

Hurd hits out again at media. (1993, 10 September). *Daily Telegraph* (London).

Douglas Hurd speech to the Travellers Club. (1993, 10 September). *The Times* (London).

Ignatieff, M. (1998). The stories we tell: Television and humanitarian aid. In J. Moore (Ed.), *Hard choices: Moral dilemmas in humanitarian intervention* (pp. 287–302). Lanham, MD: Rowman & Littlefield.

Kennan, G. (1993, 30 September). *Somalia through a glass darkly. New York Times.*

Little, T. (2012, 17 April). The Midlothian campaign. Retrieved 26 February 2014, from http://www.liberalhistory.org.uk/?s=The+Midlothian+Campaign&submit=Search.

Livingston, S. (Ed.). (1997). *Clarifying the CNN effect: An examination of media effects according to type of military intervention.* Research Paper R-18, Joan Shorenstein Barone Center on the Press, Politics and Public Policy, John F. Kennedy School of Government, Harvard University.

Natsios, A. (1996). Illusion of Influence: The CNN effect in complex emergencies. In R. Rotberg & T.G. Weiss (Eds.), *From massacres to genocide: The media, public policy, and humanitarian crises* (pp. 149–168) Washington, DC: Brookings Institution.

Olsen, G. R., & Nils Carstensen, K. H. (2003). Humanitarian Crises: Testing the CNN effect. *Forced Migration Review, 16,* 39–40. Retrieved 22 February, 2014, from http://www.fmreview.org/en/FMRpdfs/FMR16/fmr16contents.pdf.

Robinson, P. (2000). World politics and media power: Problems of research design. *Media, Culture & Society, 22*(2), 227–232.

Robinson, P. (2002). *The CNN effect: The myth of news, foreign policy and intervention.* New York: Routledge.

Robinson, P. (2011). The CNN effect reconsidered: Mapping a research agenda for the future. *Media, War & Conflict, 4*(1), 3–11.

Seib, P. M. (2002). *The global journalist: News and conscience in a world of conflict.* Lanham, MD: Rowman & Littlefield.

Shaw, M. (1996). *Civil society and media in global crises: Representing distant violence.* New York: Pinter.

Smillie, I., & Minear, L. (2004). *The charity of nations. Humanitarian action in a calculating world.* Bloomfield, CT: Kumarian.

Smith, R. (2006). *The utility of force: The art of war in the modern world.* London: Penguin.

Vaux, T. (2001). *Independent Evaluation: The DEC Response to the Earthquake in Gujarat.* Humanitarian Initiatives, UK. Retrieved 26 February 2014, from http://www.recoveryplatform.org/assets/publication/evaluation%20of%20DEC%20gujarat%20earthquake.pdf.

Wheeler, N. (2003). *Saving strangers: Humanitarian intervention in international society.* Oxford: Oxford University Press.

CHAPTER TWELVE

Learning from the Public

UK Audiences' Responses to Humanitarian Communications

IRENE BRUNA SEU

This chapter reports on a study[1] investigating empirically how audiences understand and respond—cognitively, emotionally, and through actions—to communications from humanitarian and international development NGOs[2], and how these responses relate to audiences' everyday morality and biography. The 182 participants taking part in 20 nationwide focus group discussions were asked to comment on a selection of communications from the following NGOs: ActionAid, Amnesty International, Disasters and Emergency Committee (DEC), Medicine Sans Frontier (MSF), Oxfam, PLAN UK, Save the Children, and UNICEF.[3]

As it is impossible here to do justice to the complexity of the wide range of participants' emotional and cognitive responses and even more so of their actions and inaction in response to humanitarian communications, I will apply the theoretical frameworks of denial and dynamic equilibrium (Seu, 2013; Cohen & Seu, 2002; Cohen, 2001) to ascertain which communications manage to break through denial and which generate acknowledgment. In doing so I do not intend to offer a linear and mechanistic correlation between communications and actions, nor do I consider monetary donations as the benchmark of 'acknowledgement'. Indeed, here and elsewhere, the assumption that making a donation is intrinsically symptomatic of engagement is questioned (Seu, 2014b; Seu & Orgad, 2014) as, on the contrary, it can be a shortcut to a quick and fleeting engagement followed by disengagement with a clear conscience (Seu, 2014a,b).

Instead I will concentrate on the initial stage of breaking through denial (Seu, 2013; Cohen, 2001) in the limited but important sense of exploring how and through which means particular communications succeed, however temporarily, in turning 'not knowing' into 'knowing'. Similarly, the kind of 'acknowledgement' discussed here refers to communications that foster a psychosocial connectedness; that is, the capacity to hold in mind humanitarian and international development issues and their potential integration into participants' sphere of awareness and preoccupations.

With these caveats in mind, this chapter asks the following questions: In which ways do humanitarian communications impact positively or negatively on audiences? That is, through which mechanisms do they manage to persuade, or not, members of the public to engage with, donate to, or become actively involved in humanitarian causes?

The aim is modest. What is discussed here covers only a small part of very complex and multi-layered psychosocial processes as it focuses exclusively on the initial moment of contact between members of the public and the humanitarian communication. As a key pre-requisite for intervention, particularly in the case of appeals, it is a necessary condition but, alas, not necessarily sufficient to guarantee action. Yet, as a necessary condition it deserves careful attention.

The study found that:

1. Because of a widespread climate of 'appeal fatigue', it is essential for the communication to make a good first impression. A non-formulaic presentation, a technically good and arresting image, and a reader/viewer-friendly format are effective qualities for getting through the fatigue barrier.
2. Members of the UK public wish humanitarian communications to go 'back to basics'—that is, to be Other-centred, rather than self-centred, in their focus to evoke empathy for the suffering Other, and to connect to altruistic and Universalistic moral principles.

Accordingly, the chapter is divided into two parts, discussing participants' comments on communications and appeals, and the perceived and hoped for purposes of the communication, including particular perceptions of agencies by members of the public. All the themes were mentioned frequently, by several participants and across different focus groups.

This chapter does not offer quick fixes or universally applicable formulas. The exploratory study was as an initial step towards engaging empirically with audiences' complex responses to humanitarian communications, a field severely under-researched empirically. Furthermore, these findings need to be contextualised within a crisis in the relationship between the UK public and NGOs, which was identified in the study as one of the key blocks to audience actions (Seu & Orgad, 2014). A particularly relevant aspect of this crisis is the public's widespread distrust in NGOs and a perception that their communications are manipulative and self-serving.

ANALYSIS

1. Content and Style of the Communication

Participants' accounts offered clear evidence of a widespread sense of 'appeal fatigue' due to the perceived ubiquitous presence of humanitarian communications and appeals and that, because of this, the presentation of the appeal mattered. Jonathan's extract summarises and elaborates on issues mentioned by most of the participants throughout the focus groups.

> *Jonathan:* I almost couldn't get into what they (the communications) were actually about, because the way it was approached, I've seen a thousand times, and I think there's something to be said for the fact that when people keep churning over the same ground, we have this, I think, just naturally, we start to build up this immunity.

Jonathan is implicitly referring to the well-known psychological phenomenon of desensitisation due to habituation from over-exposure (Seu, 2013), in short, fatigue. Notwithstanding that this could also be a case of a psychologically informed vocabulary of denial, it seems crucial to find ways of breaking through the 'immunity' barrier. To this end, first impressions, style, and presentation of the communications are terribly important in stimulating the viewer's interest in the topic. As Damien put it "they need to grab the attention."

Making an impact. Many commented on the role of pictures in making an initial impact and 'hooking' the reader. Although this does not guarantee a positive response when the initial interest is counteracted by a formulaic and repetitive content of the communication, making a strong impact on the viewer is nevertheless important, particularly for readers who are not regular donors, are not existing supporters of the agency, and/or don't already know the agency. Lane, for example, said: "Yes. I haven't actually heard of those (agency in question)… but I saw the picture on the back first and it's quite a, like, compelling picture, makes you look."

There were several 'aesthetically savvy' comments which made reference to technical qualities of the picture or other graphic details in the appeal. Yet, because of the pervasive climate of suspicion about the intentions behind the communication and the widespread alertness to the possibility of being manipulated, whilst audiences are attracted by a good quality picture, they resist and resent the use of Photoshop.

> *Nick:* However, going to the shock tactics with the child with the very big white eyes I feel that's enhanced somewhat. I don't think it's the true picture and I don't like that at all. I don't trust it one little bit.… I don't like that one little bit, no. It looks like it's been edited.

> *Bruna:* So you think that that child doesn't actually look like that?

> *Nick:* It's just the eyes and the way the camera flashes. The camera flash is very bright in the face but then the railings behind her have got no light on them whatsoever and it's definitely enhanced I would say.

This suggests that when the manipulation is too blatant it has a negative effect on audience's responses and further feeds into the distrust of agencies and their perceived manipulative intentions.

Words or images? The data suggest that words and images serve different functions and make distinctive impacts.

> *Marianne:* The photos are more instantly shocking. I think that gets your attention very instantly. I think the text, although it is shocking what you're reading, it takes that little bit longer, you've got to process it. I think you have to think about it more whereas something visual has an immediate impact and that takes your breath away.

Temporality is key here. Marianne spells out the differences between the processes involved in responses to imagery and text. Imagery evokes instantaneous response. It is important to note that it is expected that in order to do this the viewer has to be shocked. Marianne describes it as 'instantly shocking', making an 'immediate impact', and 'taking your breath away'. This further confirms that an arresting image manages to break through the tired response. Thus, if the desired effect of the appeal is immediate but short-term engagement for fundraising purposes, then images seem to yield the best results. On the other hand, writing seems to make a more lasting impression.

The response to text "takes a little longer" and requires processing. This is understandable cognitively as time is required to process and properly understand information. It also takes time to 'make sense' of information and to connect it to the reader's existing knowledge and meanings. This longer process can potentially enable cognitive integration and longer-term memory storage, but also longer lasting 'connectedness'.

Another factor that fosters deeper and longer-term engagement is when the information contained in the communication is reinforced by media or can be contextualised through other 'independent' information. Thus if NGOs' communications resonate and are consonant with information from other sources, in particular with documentaries and news, it enables audiences to recognise the appeal and inclines them to respond proactively. Nick, in making reference to the lasting effects of a 3-minute clip of a beneficiary's life, described graphically this phenomenon: ' visually seeing it which you could then remember (more) than things throughout the day, you can literally put that thing back in your head that you've seen on TV'.

Nicks seems to describe a mental reservoir of information that is subconsciously available and can be drawn on when seeing a relevant humanitarian communication.

Nick's reference to "literally put(ting) that thing back in your head" is a metonymy of reinforcement through memory retrieval. The important point Nick makes here is that knowing a personal story and seeing a short clip about someone's life prevents disconnection and desensitisation. This graphic rendition is also a helpful description of the operations of denial. Fatigue fosters denial by pushing knowledge to 'the back of people's minds', while good and 'successful' communication, in this case reinforced and contextualised through other mediated information, brings the knowledge to the fore and fosters acknowledgment. Reasoning, then, functions as a mechanism of grounding and anchoring of the information in a meaningful way.

Too much or too little information? Participants further elaborated on the qualities necessary to make a first impact on the viewer: the first page should be original and stand out from the many others, to intrigue the reader to look inside and continue reading it, rather than dismiss it as formulaic. Others said that the content should be "short and sweet" (Dennis), it should not be too verbose, but well worded, to the point, and punchy. This is because, as Lucy said: "when it (the content) is too much I think you just get bogged down in it". Francesca expressed a resistance to communications that have "too much information, to be honest. It's like a little book".

Of course, this kind of argumentation could simply be a 'Goldilocks' vocabulary of denial: some want more information, some less—how can NGOs get it right for all? It might then be more helpful to think in terms of what kind of demands, in this case in terms of time and attention, audiences perceive are made on them, an issue that many participants mentioned in various forms. Many agreed that if the appeal is too long, that is, if it demands prolonged attention from the reader, it discourages them from reading it. Lack of time and resources is one of the most frequently used vocabularies of denial (Seu, 2013) when justifying unresponsiveness. But it also illustrates how the length of the information provided can be a real turnoff for someone who is not already well informed or inclined towards humanitarian involvement. Hence, in terms of a dynamic equilibrium, length and a formulaic presentation can easily feed into operations of denial and tilt a 'hovering' reader towards disconnection.

Similarly, many participants in different groups made reference to the importance of the format. A small format was overwhelmingly preferred and it was suggested that it invites audiences to read the appeal (but not necessarily to act). For all these reasons, a short communication seems to work better, with the possibility of embedded links for those who welcome further information. In concluding this section I want to offer a long extract from Jonathan, because it provides a highly articulate description of the process of impact and reasoning of what seems a 'successful' communication.

> *Jonathan:* But this one, number 12, which is, I think, out of the lot, was the best one.... I saw that and I thought, I didn't particularly think that was an amazing picture, but obviously,

like, it's okay, and then I turned it over and saw the thing on the next thing, that artillery destroyer. At first I thought it was, like, fireworks or something, and then I read it and I was like, 'oh my God!!' That's, like, a cluster bomb attack or something, isn't it? And, then you re-alise these people are running for their lives, and that really hit home, and then that made me want to read all of this, and then what I realised is, as I was reading it, I didn't feel like when I read these things. I didn't feel like it was trying to get money out of me. I felt like it was trying to educate me, and so that made me want to read more. In fact, I didn't finish reading all of it, because I didn't have enough time, so... if you've got a spare one, I'll take it away.

It's worth following in detail Jonathan's complex engagement with the communi-cation. First, this communication shows that pictures and text together can make a powerful combination in fostering understanding and engagement. Following Jonathan's detailed account we can see how the moment of connection operates both cognitively (through the emergent understanding) and emotionally, as it is in the moment of understanding that the communication makes the real impact "that really hit home". Many things happen at that point, a very important one is that Jonathan experiences empathy, conveyed through his emotionally charged com-ment: "Oh my God... these people are running for their lives". That is, the com-munication enables Jonathan to imagine how it is to be someone else, to step inside their world and glimpse their concerns, cognitively and emotionally, as if from the other person's perspective (Cameron, 2011; Halpern & Weinstein, 2004). Also, at this point Jonathan recognises, through a careful monitoring of his feelings, that he could and would have switched off if he had experienced the cognitive-emo-tional impact of the communication to be manipulative or orchestrated to make him donate money. It is because Jonathan feels that the communication is trying to educate him that he does not resist its emotional impact. In fact, that emotional connection with the sufferer and the benign response to the communication make Jonathan eager to know more. That the combination of these elements fosters a lasting eagerness for deeper knowledge is demonstrated by Jonathan's request to me to take the communication away to read it fully. Implied here is also the po-tential opposite and negative reaction of disassociation which presents a challenge for fundraisers because of immediate negative responses to requests for donations, beyond emergency appeals. This raises the thorny issue of short-term engagement, which is sufficient for fundraising purposes, but might be at odds with attempts to foster a longer-term engagement with humanitarian issues and NGOs.[4]

2. Moral Principles Underpinning the Communication

While the previous section suggests that innovations in the *modality* of the commu-nication can be an effective way of getting through fatigue and break through de-nial, the public prefers established and traditional humanitarian *purposes* behind the communication and it expects NGOs to operate according to foundational moral principles (Seu, Flanagan & Orgad, 2015). Hence, humanitarian communications are expected to uphold and re-assert Other-centeredness, empathic altruism, and universalism. The next two extracts, from different groups, referring to a communication portraying a cheerful woman expressing good feelings for having helped, are a good illustration that when this doesn't happen, people respond negatively.

Jim: I thought she was nuts.

Lara: I saw it and just thought she was doing it for selfish reasons, as in, like, she was doing it to, like, kind of, get self-gratification for, like… make herself feel better as opposed to actually doing it for the actual purpose really.

Jim found the cheerfulness depicted in the communication annoying and inappropriate (to the point of implying insanity), while Laura's objection relates to the communication being centred on the (Western in this case) benefactor rather than on the beneficiary. These two different reactions hint at an implied expectation of what the emotional quality (traumatic and upsetting) and the motivation (altruistic, rather than self-gratification) should be in humanitarian communications.

Empathy and altruism. Empathic altruism was referred to by many participants and can be summarised as an expectation that humanitarian communications should make the reader consider doing helpful things and think about the suffering Other, that is, evoke empathy:

Francesca: And Action Aid, number five, I like the question that it posed, what you can do about poverty. I liked that question because it made me think a lot about, 'oh, what can I do', and it made me think about other people so when I started looking through it, yeah, it made me think about what people are going through because of the pictures and stuff, and I thought the list about what you actually could do was very good.

Francesca's words illustrate how the communication successfully enabled her to put herself into the sufferer's shoes without losing her own perspective. From there, she could think of what she could do to help the Other. At that point, when she is contemplating what life is like for the sufferers depicted, the list of what she can do is experienced as helpful and enabling.

Evoking empathy was also a sign of a successful communication when it engendered the kind of understanding that connects Self with the suffering Other, so nicely described by Jonathan earlier on and also referred to by Jerry who is reflecting on the effects of starvation on the body.

Jerry: Well, I was reading that (n.9) and it said about how the kidneys swell up, and I said, 'that's why they've got pot bellies'.

We can see here how a successful communication goes beyond making an emotional impact on the reader and engages them in thinking about the Other. In this case, empathy, rather than pity or sympathy, is evoked and exemplified by Jerry understanding something about the Other's suffering.

Seu and Cameron (2013) highlight the important function of empathy in reaching to the Other, across the many fundamental differences between the Self and Other, through a shared basis of humanity and vulnerability. Universalism expresses many of these principles, captured in Leanne's comment when explaining her choice of communication from the pack:

> *Leanne:* This is the one that I would donate to if I had to pick one, number seven.... I think it was the back part that first drew me to it and then it was the part where it... you know, it's got certain questions and then it says human at the bottom.... And when you read this you think, 'well, to tell you the truth, we... they are all human. Everyone needs the help'. And I think that's just what's drawn me to it. So that's the one that I would pick out of any of them

Similarly, Reba from a different group commented:

> *Reba:* I actually liked this one (n.7). I wrote down that it made me kind of think twice, because at the end of the day, it's just another human that some people say it's obvious, but you don't really think about that when you do see, like, kids in Africa, or that need help, and then, it's a horrible thing, but some people probably will think, 'oh, why should I help them', like... like that's obviously not what you want, but then you flip to the back and it's listing nationalities, what people are, and that's like another side to it, and it's like 'well, you wouldn't just leave a refugee to die', kind of thing, or you shouldn't. So it's like, 'they're just humans', if you looked at it that way, it kind of makes you want to not be so kind of narrow minded about it.

The comment that the communication made Reba "think twice" tells us that, in its way, it was arresting and captured Reba's attention. But, in the light of what she says later, it also implies that, even though the message was simple, it generated reflexivity and made her reconsider her own position: "it's obvious, but you don't really think about that". This is a good example of how a message can be simple, to the point of appearing obvious at first sight, but when it resonates with established moral norms, it can make a meaningful and lasting impact. Altruism as a moral imperative is expressed through the imperative: "you shouldn't (leave a refugee to die)", thus suggesting that, similarly to Singer's (2009) argument about the meaninglessness of distance when we can save a life, in the same way in which we wouldn't and shouldn't leave a refugee on our doorstep to die, neither should we let the kids in Africa die. This moral imperative is underpinned by the Universalist principle spelled out in the communication—"we should help kids of Africa... because they're just human". This extract thus makes clear that the communication is successful because it re-connects the viewer to well-established and accepted Universalist moral principles. It is also interesting to notice that, as a result, not only the Other changes through a reformulation of 'kids of Africa' to 'just human', the Self changes too. Reba claims that once the communication reconnects her to her foundational principles, her sense of Self also expands: "If you looked at it that way it kind of makes you want to not be so kind of narrow minded".

Act as you preach. Communications should also display everyday moral principles. It is important to realize members of the public expect these moral principles to apply not just to the communications but also to NGOs' conduct and their communications should make this explicit. People expect that moral leaders, in this case NGOs, should lead by example and act as they preach. Communications that convey this evoke respect for the agencies.

The importance of the communication in engendering respect and trust for the agency, and consequently enabling donations, is spelled out by Iris and Francesca:

> *Iris:* Because it's, the (MSF) are very well known… and you recognise them and I feel I've got a lot of respect for people who work for them.

> *Francesca:* I recognise the company so it's one I would donate to, it's one I feel confident and am able to trust.

But trust and respect have to work both ways. Below we can see the deleterious effect of communications that do not make the reader feel respected:

> *Orlando:* It's not worded in the sense that, can you help? It's more of a demand and that turns me off…. it's sort of the way they appeal to people, it's like they're talking down to you all the time. That's how it would feel with these, patronising, the way they deal with you.

Orlando highlights the value of communications that speak to the reader and don't patronise them. The perceived lack of a respectful approach produces antagonism and alienates the public by making people feel that the agencies are out of touch with them and are approaching them exclusively to demand money. We can see that, when the communication is not perceived as speaking to them, audiences lose interest and respect for the agency and feel insulted, irritated and infuriated. This acrimony can easily feed into denial and disconnection from humanitarian issue.

On the contrary, the next extracts illustrate the beneficial effects of communication that reaches the public by establishing a relationship between agencies and the public which is perceived to be respectful and reciprocal, rather than patronisingly demanding, and engages people in a dialogue. Additionally, signs that agencies are careful with resources (including natural resources, e.g., using recycled paper) were appreciated as agencies 'doing their bit'.

> *Florence:* I think from reading one of them, it said 100% recycled paper, which I really liked because it made me think that you should, they're doing their little bit, which would make me a little bit more likely to give, even though I wouldn't. It's nice to feel that they're doing something and they're not just telling me to do something and they're not doing something themselves.

Florence's words suggest that using recycled paper for the appeals is not simply something that she considers commendable in itself, it also engenders a more mutual relationship. This is particularly noteworthy here because Florence clearly states that she still wouldn't make a donation, thus suggesting that the issue she is addressing is not her response to the humanitarian appeal, which remains unchanged, but her relationship with the agency. The fact that "they are doing their little bit, not just asking from the public" hints at a discomfort with agencies for always approaching the public with demands, while in this case, agencies are perceived as ethical and in a reciprocal relationship with audiences. In other words, the communication is evidence itself that agencies are leading by example and applying moral principles audiences hold dear.

DISCUSSION AND CONCLUSIONS

Cohen's work on denial—what he called the 'twilight zone of knowing and not-knowing'—provided ground-breaking insights into public passivity in response to unpalatable knowledge. Cohen was primarily interested in the social mechanisms through which people avoid acknowledging and taking responsibility for the suffering of distant Others.

He used the term 'denial' to capture a series of complex psychosocial phenomena: blocking out and repressing the information, or registering the information but ignoring its implications. People's apathy, passivity, indifference, and unresponsiveness, together with convenient rationalisations to explain their passivity, are all aspects of denial. The opposite of denial—acknowledgment—also covers a range of responses: people respond to the information by getting upset, express sympathy or compassion and do something about it, they intervene, help, become committed (Cohen, 2001, p. x).

Through the conceptualisation of public passivity as a state of 'dynamic equilibrium' (Seu, 2013) the very notion of passivity is put under question and replaced with a reformulation of the manifested lack of action, ostensibly appearing as passivity, as the overt manifestation of a dynamic interplay of forces (Seu, 2013, p. 5). This captures the 'hovering' and unstable nature of action and inaction and fosters a fruitful engagement with the dynamism and complexity underpinning and leading to passivity. As a model of dynamic equilibrium describes a precarious stability which, by definition, is constantly under threat of disruption, it is possible to think of points of tension as potential openings for change and intervention (Seu, 2013, p. 5). Through the lens of dynamic equilibrium, the accounts discussed in this chapter identify characteristics in the communications that operate at points of tension and bifurcation, at which viewers can stay passive and unresponsive or engage with the communication and humanitarian issues.

In terms of content and style of the communications, participants highlighted the importance of first impressions in a climate of 'appeal fatigue'. This suggests that the first obstacle to be overcome by a successful communication is getting through the habituation. There was an overall consensus on the effectiveness of three factors: a non-formulaic presentation, a technically good and arresting picture, and a reader/viewer friendly format that is not too verbose or overwhelmingly demanding of the viewer's time and attention. Although these factors are deemed essential in engaging the viewer long enough to make them pay attention and read beyond the first page, they are not a guarantee against subsequent disconnection. The main danger following initial interest is presented by the "all they want is my money" response. The perception that this motivates the communication is one of the strongest factors triggering denial (see Seu, 2013, 2010) and suggests that we shouldn't confuse fatigue towards humanitarian issues with fatigue towards communications that are perceived as primarily instrumental and digitally enhanced to maximise donations. On the contrary, participants seemed eager to know more about the context of the humanitarian issues brought to them. They repeatedly suggested that they would like to be educated by the communication and indeed resented blatantly mechanistic communications aimed at shocking people into making a donation (Seu & Orgad, 2014; Seu, 2010). In line with a desire to be better informed about humanitarian issues, participants made reference to the reinforcing effect of having been informed by the media, particularly through documentaries, thus suggesting that communications from humanitarian agencies are better received when they resonate with pre-existing information.

This also draws attention to the link between emotions and cognition and the importance of bringing together emotional and cognitive responses in engendering a proactive response. For example, Loewenstein and Small (2007) recognise that, although the initial emotional impact plays an essential role, unless this emotion is then elaborated through cognition and connected to prosocial norms, it is likely to be short-lived. This is supported by participants' detailed and articulate accounts of the crucial role of 'thinking' through the communication. As pointed out earlier, temporality is terribly important here. Although pictures seem to be more effective in breaking through the fatigue at first impact, words make a more lasting impression. I want to conclude this section on communication with a brief observation about participants' overall response to the emotional upsetting quality of the information. I have discussed elsewhere (Seu, 2013) the intensely volatile and complex nature of emotional responses to humanitarian communications, in particular the backfiring of guilt, how shock tactics are counterproductive, and the intensity of public responses to feeling emotionally manipulated. All this notwithstanding, it is worth noting that participants *expected* the information to be shocking, to the point that communications that were perceived as 'cheerful', either in content or graphic presentation, provoked cognitive dissonance and confusion, as well as outrage in some cases. It appears that the public expects and accepts that the emotional register consonant with humanitarian communication is and should be troubling, even shocking. This suggests that it is not the shock in itself that is resisted and unwelcome (see Seu, 2014b, for further details) but the attributed reasons behind for having those emotions evoked.

Cognitive dissonance points to what seems to be canonical and expected in humanitarian communication. This was discussed in the second section of this chapter, looking at public expectations of what the appeal should do and achieve. Primarily, participants conveyed a strong sense that they would like humanitarian communications to go 'back to basics'. This was elaborated through the themes of wanting and expecting humanitarian communications (and humanitarian concerns in general) to be Other-centred, rather than self-centred, to evoke empathy for the suffering Other and to connect to members of the public's moral principles, in particular Universalism. Unsurprisingly, participants reacted negatively, but also with scorn and hilarity, to appeals making the Western reader and their well-being the focus of the communication. This suggests that altruism and Universalism are accepted and integrated canonical moral normative and are expected to guide humanitarian concerns and communications.

Equally expected, and welcome, was the evoking of empathy. Empathy refers to our understandings of and feelings toward other people (Cameron, 2011). At the core of the complex set of cognitive and affective/emotional processes of empathy is the activity of imagining how it is to be someone else, to step inside their world and glimpse their concerns, cognitively and emotionally, as if from the other person's perspective (Halpern & Weinstein, 2004, p. 581), and to imagine how it is for the Other in their world (Batson, Sager, Garst, Kang, Rubchinsky, & Dawson, 1997; Lamm, Batson, & Decety, 2007; Lamm, Meltzoff, & Decety, 2010).

Section 2 has given some examples of how evoking of empathy for the suffering Other is a welcome and, for some participants, an essential component of a 'successful' communication. In terms of dynamic equilibrium, empathy is antithetical to denial and can tip hovering people towards action. This doesn't exclude, of course, that also in operation are opposite processes pulling people the opposite way and interfering with the connectedness. A particularly powerful force counteracting empathy is a perception of agencies' manipulative intentions (Seu & Orgad, 2014; Seu, 2014a, b) and widespread distrust and suspicion towards agencies.

There is considerable empirical evidence that trust in the voluntary sector plays a central role in the development of donor, charity, and beneficiary relationships (Sargeant & Lee, 2002) and, within relationship marketing, in the fostering of long-term customer relationships (Morgan & Hunt, 1994), long-term commitment to an organisation and donor-giving behaviour (Sargeant & Lee, 2004).

Recent research into public responses (Seu, 2013, 2011a), further demonstrates how public perception and attitude towards the appeal makers play an important role in the neutralisation of the appeal and the resistance to collective action and participation. Particularly powerful is the passionate and antagonistic response from members of the public when they perceive appeal makers to have manipulative intentions in 'pulling at their heart strings' in order to get them to donate money (Seu, 2013, 2011a, 2010).

Similarly, Darnton and Kirk (2011) are critical of NGOs behaving as big businesses, with business models built around aggressive revenue targets and how this approach is reflected both in the content of communications and in the techniques used by NGOs. Research conducted by the sector has shown that the most effective messages for securing donations are those that pluck at the public's heartstrings (see Child Survival Attitudes, 2008). However, although the public might still respond in the immediate aftermath of receiving the information, data from the study's focus groups show that they build resistance and resentment. Messages of this kind are easily dismissed through the 'all they want is my money' script, which we have seen in these data and also discussed elsewhere (Seu, 2013, 2010). The negative reaction to appeals is bound to have a knock-on effect on the public engagement with humanitarian agencies because approaching the public in this instrumental fashion seems to introduce defensiveness right from the start, at the delicate point of the public hovering between disconnection or further connection with the information.

The counterproductive nature of this type of communication has also been identified by Darnton and Kirk (2011), who have argued that the practices of the development sector are strongly implicated in the state of public engagement. Increasing incomes have been gained by changing the nature of engagement by turning members into supporters and setting them at arm's length, but this might be feeding into the experience of agencies being out of touch with the public, as documented in this chapter. These concerns resonate with those expressed in recent work on the dangers of increased commercialisation of non-profit organisations' practices (Vestergaard, 2008) and their 'rebranding' in order to counteract the current 'crisis of pity' (Chouliaraki, 2008). If, as Vestergaard (2008) and Chouliaraki (2008) suggest, humanitarian agencies are being driven by fundraising pressures into moving away from a compassion-based type of campaigning towards a marketised ethical discourse, their efforts may be counterproductive. Such a move might actually increase audiences' moral detachment and, as Chouliaraki (2008) calls it, their 'narcissistic sensibility' by further strengthening the resistance of the 'savvy-consumer' bystander.

The focus-group data leave us in no doubt that the 'transactional frame', which reduces public participation to making donations, fosters a 'cheque-book' relationship with NGOs that the public intensely dislikes, but that is functional when wanting to distance themselves. In the long term it does not help NGOs either. An antagonistic relationship between NGOs and the public militates against further engagement with them and is likely to foster a logic of instrumental reason. The well-documented existence of a model of generalised decoding of their communications that affects all voluntary sectors' interactions with the public appears to contaminate longer-term and more complex engagement with humanitarian agencies, and also contributes greatly to a fraught relationship with NGOs. It might also partly explain why, as it has been illustrated in this chapter, members of the public experience agencies as being out of touch, patronising, and making unreasonable demands.

In conclusion, although the data analysis has identified several factors enabling communications to break through denial, these factors should not be taken as universally applicable formulas. They are contingent on several conditions, primarily the reader's original inclination and pre-existing knowledge, as well as whether the communication is set out to aim for short-term fundraising or fostering longer-terms engagement.

Bearing these variables in mind, the data suggest that in order for a communication to succeed in combating denial and fostering proactive engagement with humanitarian issues, it should contain manageable amounts of facts. This doesn't need to translate into superficial and functional information, mechanistically functioning as trigger to generate donations, which is ultimately counterproductive.

Overall, short communications seem to work better as they don't make too many demands on the public. In particular, the length of the information provided can be a real turnoff for someone who is not already well informed or inclined towards humanitarian involvement.

Communications should also foster better relationships between the public and humanitarian agencies. It follows that it would be counterproductive for the factors identified in this chapter to be applied mechanistically to generate more donations. Audiences are far too savvy for that. Instead the data suggest that the relationship with the public should be thought of more holistically.

A successful communication should speak to and activate the reader's foundational values and moral principles, in particular Other-centred Universalism and empathy. In the context of an empathic response, it is helpful when the communication offers practical, manageable, and effective actions and solutions to the problem depicted.

NOTES

1. I am grateful to the Leverhulme Trust for funding this 3-year project in collaboration with LSE (F/07 112/Y). For further information on the study, refer to the project website, http://www.bbk.ac.uk/psychosocial/our-research/research-projects-current/mediated-humanitarian-knowledge-audiences-responses-and-moral-actions.

2. For the sake of succinctness, in this chapter the term 'humanitarian' will be used to refer to both humanitarian issues and international development causes.
3. To see the exact communications used in the pack, please visit the project website, http://www.bbk.ac.uk/psychosocial/our-research/research-projects-current/mediated-humanitarian-knowledge-audiences-responses-and-moral-actions.
4. For further discussion of this issue see Seu and Orgad, 2014.

BIBLIOGRAPHY

Batson, C. D., Sager, K., Garst, E., Kang, M., Rubchinsky, K., & Dawson, K. (1997). Is empathy-induced helping due to self-other merging? *Journal of Personality and Social Psychology, 73*(3), 495–509.
Cameron, L. (2011). *Metaphor and reconciliation: The discourse dynamics of empathy in post-conflict conversations.* New York: Routledge.
Child survival attitudes. (2009, September). *Mango Research for Save the Children.*
Chouliaraki, L. (2008). Mediation as moral education in media. *Culture and Society, 30*(5), 831–847.
Cohen, S. (2001). *States of denial: Knowing about atrocities and suffering.* London: Polity.
Cohen, S., & Seu, B. (2002). Knowing enough not to feel too much: Emotional thinking about human rights appeals. In M. Bradley & P. Petro (Eds.), *Truth claims: Representation and human rights* (pp. 187–201). London: Rutgers University.
Darnton, A., & Kirk, K. (2011). *Finding frames: New ways to engage the UK public in global poverty.* London: Oxfam & DFID.
Harpern, J., and Weinstein, H. M. (2004). 'Rehumanizing the other: Empathy and reconciliation.' *Human Rights Quarterly, 26* (3), 561–583.
Lamm, C., Batson, C. D., & Decety, J. (2007). The neural substrate of human empathy: Effects of perspective-taking and cognitive appraisal. *Journal of Cognitive Neuroscience, 19*, 42–58.
Lamm, C., Meltzoff, A. N., & Decety, J. (2010). How do we empathize with someone who is not like us? A functional magnetic resonance imaging study. *Journal of Cognitive Neuroscience, 22*, 362–376.
Loewenstein, G., & Small, D. A. (2007). The Scarecrow and the Tin Man: The vicissitudes of human sympathy and caring. *Review of General Psychology, 11*(2), 112–126.
Morgan, R. M., & Hunt, S. D. (1994). The commitment-trust theory of relationship building. *Journal of Marketing, 58*, 20–38.
Sargeant, A., & Lee, S. (2002). Individual and contextual antecedents of donor trust in the voluntary sector. *Journal of Marketing Management, 18*, 779–802.
Sargeant, A., & Lee, S. (2004). Donor trust and relationship commitment in the UK charity sector; the impact on behaviour. *Nonprofit and Voluntary Sector Quarterly, 33*, 185.
Seu, I. B. (2010). 'Doing denial': Audiences' reactions to human rights appeals. *Discourse and Society, 21*(4), 438–457.
Seu, I. B. (2011). 'Shoot the messenger': Dynamics of positioning and denial in response to human rights appeals. *Journal of Human Rights Practice, 3*(2), 139–161.
Seu, I. B. (2013). *Passivity generation: Human rights and everyday morality.* London: Palgrave.
Seu, I. B. (2014a). *Public perceptions of NGOs and responses to individual communications.* Retrieved from http://www.bbk.ac.uk/psychosocial/our-research/research-projects-current/mediated-humanitarian-knowledge-audiences-responses-and-moral-actions.

Seu, I. B. (2014b). *Public knowledge, reactions and moral actions in response to humanitarian issues.* Retrieved from http://www.bbk.ac.uk/psychosocial/our-research/research-projects-current/mediated-humanitarian-knowledge-audiences-responses-and-moral-actions.

Seu, I. B., & Cameron, L. (2013). Empathic mutual positioning in conflict transformation and reconciliation. Peace and conflict. *Journal of Peace Psychology, 19*(3), 266–280.

Seu, I. B., & Orgad, S. (2014). *FINAL REPORT Mediated humanitarian knowledge: Audience responses and moral actions.* http://www.bbk.ac.uk/psychosocial/FinalReportBruna.pdf.

Seu, I.B., Flanagan, F. and Orgad S. (2015) The 'Good Samaritan' and the 'Marketer'; public perceptions of humanitarian and international development NGOs. *International Journal of Non-profit and voluntary sector marketing.* IDO: 10.1002/nvsm.1520

Singer, P. (2009). *The life you can save: Acting now to end world poverty.* London: Picador.

Supphellen, M., & Nelson, M. R. (2001). Developing, exploring, and validating a typology of private philanthropic decision making. *Journal of Economic Psychology, 22*(5), 573–603.

Vestergaard, A. (2008). Branding the humanitarian: The case of Amnesty International. *Journal of Language and Politics, 7*(3), 200–216.

Zagefka, H., & Brown, R. (2008). *Monetary donations following humanitarian disasters: Full research report.* ESRC End of Award Report. RES-000–22–1817.

CHAPTER THIRTEEN

NGO Communications in the New Media Ecology

How NGOs Became the 'New(s) Reporters'

KIMBERLY ABBOTT

If you've read an article recently about Syria, Central African Republic, or Chechnya, chances are an NGO working on the ground in that country was not only quoted but played a significant role in shaping the story. Sometimes, they wrote it.

When the journalism industry began its epic transformation at the onset of the internet age, foreign news was first to be hit: the high price of production and complexity of subject matter made it an easy target for cuts. Out of its ashes, and catalyzed by new technologies, a type of NGO communications has evolved that plays some of the roles journalism once did. As the Communications Director for North America at the International Crisis Group, a conflict prevention organization working on the ground in more than 50 countries, I was an eyewitness to and participant in this shift.

A decade ago, when I was a journalist, it was rare to find an NGO communications officer in the field. That role was an afterthought for many organizations and was left to overstretched field staff who were not trained in media parlance. Today, NGO communications experts are posted around the world, tweeting, photographing, producing video documentaries, creating mapping tools, blogging, and supplementing news coverage in parts of the world from which foreign reporters have retreated. NGOs have adapted to and become part of the new media ecology[1]—the technologies and codes of communication that together make up the environment for news production—by inventing and reinventing their communications strategies and making them an essential part of their mission—light years from where they started.

This evolution is not only because NGOs have stepped into the gulf left by a decimated foreign news corps, but also because technology and new social media platforms have allowed NGOs to communicate directly with their advocacy targets, donors, and the general public. Most organizations now understand that if they are not showcasing their work through these channels—delivering their products to people where they are and in the way they have become accustomed to receiving news—they will quickly become irrelevant.

The relationships between NGOs and journalists—and journalism—have blurred. Partnerships between news outlets and NGOs, once shunned, are now necessary and have been widely embraced. Rigid rules and practices have yielded to innovative models and new voices. The urgency to be objective at all costs has been superseded by a demand for transparency.

Of course, this trend is not without its critics. Journalism purists argue that all NGOs have an inherent bias or point of view, even if their information is grounded in facts. Their work, skeptics say, is ultimately shaped by an agenda and driven by fundraising.

This is a simplistic view of a very complex NGO industry. It also excludes the fact that NGOs are subject to scrutiny by donors, governments, and the public, and their reputations are staked in their ability to prove accountability and transparency. If the NGO is independent—meaning not beholden to a particular government, donor, or corporation—with a mission to save lives, feed people, help communities recover from a natural disaster, deliver medical care, prevent conflict, or uncover the truth, must there be an opposing mission to deem it fair or objective?

Changes in the NGO-journalism space have also opened more access to international news than at any time in the last decade. While at present the appetite for NGO-generated foreign reporting might be limited to specialized consumers, the increased availability of news from all corners of the world is a positive development. As NGOs become more accustomed to their role as content producers and mainstream media embrace their efforts, news consumers will have more opportunities to learn about the world.

BACKGROUND & EVOLUTION

The interdependence between journalists and NGO workers is longstanding. They rely on each other, one for access, the other for amplification. Consider the case of Katya Sokirianskaia, a longtime aid worker in the North Caucuses and current analyst for Crisis Group. In the early 2000s, she played an essential role in helping journalists access Chechnya and Ingushetia. Sokirianskaia regularly helped them across the border, dressing them in culturally appropriate clothes and coaching them on what to say to security guards.[2] "I would take off their Western tennis shoes, give them a sausage and tell them to pretend to be chewing or asleep in the back seat as we got near the border," she said. Once inside, she housed the journalists with friends and helped them with contacts. "We had quite a lot of influence over what the journalists wrote. Our contacts shaped the narrative. We offered them stories."

Her story is not unique. But today NGOs aren't just helping with the reporting, they are also doing it. It is an important change, and one that is informing critical foreign policy decisions and increasing the global information supply.

The crisis in Central African Republic provides a potent example. A simmering disaster for decades, it only became 'news' in late 2012 when the British government took a renewed interest, quickly followed by the BBC, the *Guardian*, and other British media outlets. The country is difficult to access, with impassable roads and harsh terrain. Still, humanitarian organizations have been working there for years, and news outlets have turned to them to guide coverage. In the case of the International Medical Corps, communications officer Laura Jepson "became a de facto content provider for Al Jazeera" (Jepson, 2013) said Global Communications Director Margaret Aguirre.[3] Jepson provided a steady stream of Instagram photos and information about what she saw on the ground in Bangui to news outlets unable to see for themselves. "I see her information retweeted throughout the universe by all sorts of entities—government agencies, UN agencies, media outlets." But it is a two-way street: IMC's reputation depends on the authenticity of the information. As it is verified and vetted, trust is secured or broken.

While accessing quick information is one reason media outlets use NGOs to supplement their reporting, another is to help them decipher complex situations. And because NGOs are on the ground and deeply involved in many of these countries, they understand context in a way others cannot. A recent *New York Times* article about the Syrian crisis detailed not only the difficulty in reporting in hostile terrain and accessing local populations but also in understanding the many layers of the conflict. It lauded a Human Rights Watch investigation that beat the UN's own reporting by a week. "Not for the first time, this kind of independent report made front-page news in the world's newspapers, which, for the most part, were unable to confirm the facts on the ground with their own reporting," the article stated.

The bottom line is today news outlets are more comfortable relying on trusted NGOs to report for them, and in being transparent about that trade-off. For a news organization, it is often a choice between not having any information about a crisis or being clear about how and where they got their information.

NGO reporting is not unlike that of a traditional foreign correspondent, and in many cases the role is occupied by former foreign reporters whose jobs no longer exist. For those who have straddled both sectors, the variance in the work is subtle but important.

Crisis Group's Turkey/Cyprus Project Director, Hugh Pope, who previously worked as the *Wall Street Journal's* Mideast correspondent, explained: "in a way, it's everything I wanted journalism to be but it never was... We're able to give a much fuller explanation of the basics of the situation than you can ever do in a journalistic narrative by the very nature of what newspaper journalism is... we can give a basic primer that is actually valid for two or three years after we write it, because it's so deeply reported that it stands the test of time" (2010). In Bishkek, Crisis Group analyst Deirdre Tynan, a former investigative reporter with EurasiaNet, finds information flows more easily now that she works for an NGO. "About one month after I joined, I started learning things that would have been gold dust if I had still had news stories to write," she said.[4]

JOURNALISM TRENDS: CAUSES AND ADVOCACY

When examining how NGOs fit into the news ecology, equally important is what is happening in the journalism sector. Some news organizations are bleeding into "advocacy journalism," beyond the familiar ideological bents of cable news or established worldviews of some newspapers, and openly adopting a point of view or advocating for a cause. In the process, they are blurring the line between NGOs and journalists even further.

The *Guardian* began publishing advocacy journalism as early as 2007. Its Global Development site (theguardian.com/global-development), with support from the Bill and Melinda Gates Foundation, reports on the Millennium Development Goals. The site grew out of the *Guardian's* Katine Project (theguardian.com/katine), which focused on the development work of two NGOs, African Medical and Research Foundation (amref.org/) and Farm-Africa (farmafrica.org/), in a small Ugandan village. The Project reported stories from the village, chronicled how NGO resources were used and even encouraged readers to donate.

Television networks are embracing causes and putting time, resources, and staff behind promoting them. CNN has embarked on a multi-year, multi-platform campaign, the Freedom Project (thecnnfreedomproject.blogs.cnn.com/), aimed at "shining a spotlight on the horrors of modern-day slavery, amplifying the voices of the victims, highlighting success stories and helping unravel the complicated tangle of criminal enterprises trading in human life." It is a worthy cause and an effort to be applauded, but it also demonstrates in stark relief how far television news has veered from its origins.

Al Jazeera, too, took on an activist role during the Arab Spring, facilitating the story for other media. The network became not only part of the story but also one of the reasons the Arab Spring received so much international attention, according to some media analysts. "Al Jazeera took the voice from these people and we amplified it," Wadah Khanfar, director general of the Al Jazeera network, told an audience at a TED conference (Khanfar, 2011). Al Jazeera was seen as a central player in the uprisings, even a liberator—Khanfar said he regularly heard pleas such as: "If you switch off the cameras tonight, there will be a genocide… You are protecting us by showing what is happening at Tahrir Square."

Individual journalists are lending their brands to causes as well. The *New York Times*'s Nicholas Kristof has elevated the art with high-profile reporting on human rights abuses around the globe. It shapes and colors his journalism, for which he is unapologetic. His work has spawned a bestselling book, *Half the Sky*, which has developed into a game, movie, advocacy initiative (womenandgirlslead.org), and foundation (halfthesky.org).

CNN's Anderson Cooper has long embraced advocacy journalism, abandoning the notion of objectivity by inserting himself in the story, whether it is carrying earthquake victims in Haiti to safety or admonishing public officials during Hurricane Katrina. "There are times when it's important to just be a person and help someone… being a human being first [and a reporter second]" (Wallace, 2013), Cooper has said in the face of criticism. His efforts have been rewarded by NGOs—Cooper is the first journalist to win Action Against Hunger's Humanitarian Award (Action Against Hunger, 2008) for his coverage of humanitarian issues—but they haven't been without risk. During coverage of Egypt's protests in Tahrir Square, he was attacked by a violent mob—an unfortunate incident that underscores just how much Cooper was seen to be part of the story.

For some startups, such experiential journalism is the preferred model and could foretell the future of news. VICE News, which caters to young viewers, claims its audience is tired of legacy news approaches. Producer and host Tim Pool told *Politico*, "It's not so much about trying to be omniscient, but to be a person there who's experiencing it and saying, 'what I'm telling you is one piece of the puzzle and here's what I experience.'"

In today's era of hands-on, carpe diem journalism, putting reporters at the center of a story and openly advocating for a public good could be a natural evolution. These trends also beg the questions: Is advocacy journalism simply a return to public interest journalism? Is experiential journalism inherently advocacy journalism, and vice versa? Is subjective journalism the new face of journalism, and if so, is it beneficial?

WHAT'S DIFFERENT: NGO TECHNIQUES

With growing opportunities to provide content and expertise, and a journalism industry ripe for new models, how are NGOs communicating today? Gone are the days of press conferences and telephone pitching. From interactive maps to photo documentaries, Storify to Tweet chats, NGOs have learned to deliver their messages, reports, and expertise to audiences on multiple platforms, and reach them when and where they are consuming their news.

"We can't make people come to us or make them absorb our information the way we want," said Oxfam press officer Vanessa Parra.[5] "We have to read and monitor how everyone is consuming the news and how they are getting their policy messages, and how they are working."

Social media have allowed NGOs to engage their varied audiences directly, and the growth of these platforms has created more space for NGO voices. A crucial part of any media strategy today, social media have both leveled the playing field and raised the bar: it is no longer enough to have the iconic image of a suffering child splashed on the pages of the *New York Times*; the image has to be on Instagram, Pinterest and Tumblr as well to make an impact on today's audiences.

Adapting to new tools is not only providing more opportunity to deliver messages but also to penetrate new audiences and build conversations around an issue. For example, on World Refugee Day, UNHCR asked people what they would take if they were forced to flee a situation, and invited them to upload pictures for the UNHCR Pinterest board (pinterest.com/refugees/the-most-important-thing). The campaign attracted more than 3,469 followers on Pinterest as of 13 November 2014—including celebrities—and raised awareness about the plight of refugees around the world. Or consider the charity WaterAid's campaign thebigdig.org which used the Instagram hashtag #thebigdig to chart the progress of a well as it was built in real time, enabling donors to witness how their money was being used and meet the people from affected villages through blog posts, videos, images—all with a mobile phone. NGOs are increasingly using Storify to amalgamate content across social media platforms and include community perspectives and audience voices. HRW uses it to curate their daily briefs (storify.com/hrw), regularly netting more than 5,000 views.

The social media shift has also changed the way NGO communicators interact with journalists. "The National Press Club system, if it ever existed, is now on Twitter," said Michael Boyce, a press and information officer for Refugees International. "We can engage directly, see what a journalist is working on and where it intersects with our issues."[6]

Parra said she increasingly provides official comment over Twitter rather than through a traditional press release. "The upside for us is we don't have to email it out, the press is already using the medium, policy makers monitor it," she said. "It gives us another option for getting the word out."

Not only have the delivery systems evolved, so too have NGO products. Media releases are now sophisticated news products. HRW is perhaps the best at unabashedly replicating a news style in media releases. "We consciously ape the style of media in our communication in order that what we produce looks more like journalism," Carroll Bogert, Deputy Executive Director for External Relations at Human Rights Watch, said in a Nieman Lab article. Their efforts yield regular stories in the *New York Times*, *Guardian*, and other major outlets, with copy virtually identical to HRW media releases. Websites have also evolved to look more "newsy". For example, Mercy Corps's website (mercycorps.org) features "top stories" from around the globe, reporting from Indonesia to CAR and information on what Mercy Corps is doing to help. Videos, photo essays, infographics, and maps are also used to provide more context.

More news savvy can also be found in NGO blogs, a staple for most groups today. They offer real-time field updates, "boots on the ground" narratives and eyewitness accounts. Some blogs are as simple as notes from a field mission; others employ writers to expertly craft dramatic, character-driven stories. For example, Oxfam America's blog is divided into first-person accounts (firstperson.oxfamamerica.org/), stories and news updates, including tutorials on food aid reform and emotional testimony from refugees. Save the Children CEO Carolyn Miles' blog, "Logging Miles" (savethechildren.org/loggingmiles), weaves moving narratives about the children she meets on her travels with facts about the crisis situations they live in, using photos, videos, and interactive—all of which draw the reader closer to the NGO's mission. Many NGOs, including Crisis Group, Amnesty International, and HRW, also republish posts from their blog on outside platforms like *Huffington Post* and AllAfrica with the aim of capturing a wider, more diverse readership.

Multimedia is perhaps the biggest adaptation in the NGO communications space. Compelling video documentaries and stunning photography are used to engage audiences and communicate their work to the world. CARE, Save the Children, The International Rescue Committee, and many others have used videos to introduce audiences to their beneficiaries, describe problems, demonstrate impact, and ask for support. Some, such as Mercy Corps, employ video editors to document their relief efforts in real time. Catholic Relief Services, MSF and many others, have in-house multimedia experts to produce video, photo slide shows, audio, and podcasts. Oxfam offers video press releases, with interviews and b-roll. Some NGOs and international organizations are moving toward their own in-house television channels: UNICEF has a dedicated television and radio site (unicef.org/videoaudio/) that offers free, professionally shot footage to broadcasters —a service started by a former journalist.

More complex interactive mapping projects are also proliferating. The Council on Foreign Relations (cfr.org/publication/interactives.html) has produced dozens of interactive projects on topics ranging from the Iranian nuclear crisis to the Darfur conflict to global climate change, which feature not only maps but also expert interviews, video, photography, and policy options. The Enough Project's Satellite Sentinel Project (satsentinel.org) is another savvy example, which uses satellite technology to track violence (with the aim of deterring further outbreaks) across Sudan. In 2013, after two years of using the tool to chronicle war crimes, the project presented its evidence to the UN and ICC. At Crisis Group, we found that when we created an interactive map of our most popular product, Crisis Watch (crisisgroup.be/maps/crisiswatch/index.html), it became one of the most viewed items on the website—ever—on its first day of publication. High-quality information was an essential prerequisite, but the packaging and delivery made a marked difference in attracting new consumers.

These multimedia projects are deeply reported and expertly produced. They are also free, and mainstream media have used them on their own pages. The *Los Angeles Times* crafted a piece around CFR's interactive "vaccine-preventable outbreaks" map (Hiltzik, 2014), which quickly went viral after publication; HRW's award-winning multimedia piece on Burma landed on the *New Yorker*'s website; IMC's photo essay on Syria was picked up by Time.com (Katz, 2014); and Crisis Group's podcasts have been featured in *Foreign Policy*, *Washington Post*, *Huffington Post*, and *USA Today*, among others.

The journalism community has also rewarded NGO multimedia with prestigious accolades. MSF, CFR, and HRW have been nominated for—and won— Emmy, Peabody, and Webby awards for their work on malnutrition, the Iranian nuclear crisis, and human rights violations in Colombia and Congo.

WORKING TOGETHER: PARTNERSHIPS

NGOs have mastered the art of communicating directly with their audiences by utilizing new technologies in lockstep with an evolving journalism industry. However, it is still clear that their reach is magnified through partnering with mainstream media outlets.

"You can spend tons of money producing a product, but if you don't have anyone helping you with the megaphone, it is pointless," said IMC's Aguirre, who recently orchestrated the project with conflict photo agency VII that was featured on Time.com and the *New Yorker*. On the flip side, "very few (journalism) leaders out there can do things on their own, whether it is CNN or NBC or the *New York Times*. You have got to have someone you are working with, either to get the information or spread the word."

The comfort level surrounding this model is rising, as is increased transparency. Oxfam's Parra said she has experienced a noticeable transition in the last five years. "I used to have editors say, 'I'm not comfortable with this yet' when we were talking about these efforts. But now, it makes it easier for them to take a blog from an organization if they make it transparent that it is not their content."

Indeed, official partnerships are proliferating at speeds unimagined just a short time ago. The French newspaper *Le Monde* has partnered with more than 10 think tanks including, EuropaNova, Fondation Res Publica, and Institute de L'entreprise, giving readers a better understanding of the complexity of both national and international news. Last fall, *The Nation* magazine teamed with Foreign Policy in Focus, a think tank dedicated to analysis of US foreign policy and international affairs, to deep-dive into topics that otherwise receive little attention, from Rwanda's post-genocide youth programs to presidential politics in Honduras. In January, the *Huffington Post* joined forces with the Berggruen Institute to create the *World Post*, which, according to Arianna Huffington, will be "a hub for everything from political and economic news to discussions of the cultural and artistic forces shaping and reshaping our increasingly global collective imagination" (Huffington, 2014). NBC's Stringwire, a user-generated live video service, has partnered with World Learning and other NGOs to capture footage from locations around the world.

The New America Foundation and Foreign Policy were among the early collaborators, creating the AfPak Channel (southasia.foreignpolicy.com) in 2009 for news dedicated to Afghanistan and Pakistan. FP has pursued similar partnerships with the Brookings Institution for news on global economics, the Legitium Institute for news on democracy transitions and the USIP for news about international conflict prevention and resolution.

Of course, the business of partnerships is tricky; just as journalists don't want to be seen as endorsing or advocating a point of view, NGOs—which are responsible to supporters, beneficiaries, and the public—must choose their partners carefully. The debate has shifted from one about objectivity and editorial control to one about transparency and trust.

The wrong journalistic partner can jeopardize NGO staff, beneficiaries, contacts, and reputation. RI's Boyce said the nature of his work is just too sensitive for partnering: "We are going to UN headquarters and asking probing questions about how the system is functioning. If we had a journalist along, we would never get the information we need." Crisis Group's Sokirianskaia agrees that it can compromise relationships with sources. When she helped an international television correspondent in town for the Sochi Olympics arrange an interview with a wrongfully jailed rights defender, the story took a negative turn and she was left to pick up the pieces: "The reporter leaves town, and then I face the consequences."

There are also the cases where choosing the wrong bedfellow simply backfires, such as with World Vision's project with the *Telegraph* newspaper and *Downton Abbey* star Elizabeth McGovern in Sierra Leone (Kozlowska, 2014). The celebrity's highly publicized gaffes were a huge embarrassment for the NGO and quickly became a shining example of everything not to do.

Notwithstanding the risks, the trajectory for partnerships writ large is positive. Both the media and NGOs are steeped in an era of doing more with less, and creative, innovative collaborations can be mutually beneficial. As new vetting tools come on the market, transparency is codified, and experience and trust are built, these non-traditional unions will become more commonplace and more widely accepted. While it is too early to tell, the result could be a resurgence in international news. The benefits of that—from a better-informed citizenry to a robust news media that supports democratic systems—are limitless.

TRENDS AND CAVEATS

The revolution in the way people consume news, increased content production from NGOs, and a newfound acceptance of new journalism models has yielded a new era of NGO communications. Creativity and innovation will further define its future.

Several trends are already emerging, and I predict:

- NGOs will become more expert at producing content, more comfortable moving beyond traditional mandates and more refined in their communication with specialized audiences.
- Their relationships with news outlets will continue to grow and evolve, and smart NGOs will understand that as they move deeper into the news space, their content must speak to a global audience to be truly useful to news organizations.
- The line between journalism and nonprofit media will likely become even more blurred and partnerships more firmly cemented. "Advocacy" will apply to both journalism and NGOs, openly.
- Transparency will outweigh any other journalism tenet and redefine how both NGOs and media outfits operate.
- Technological developments will continue to allow consumers, donors, and other interested parties to track the supply chain of information, and the truth.
- Ultimately, those organizations, journalists, and individuals—no matter what sector—that have proved their accuracy and transparency and earned the public trust will rise above the rest of the noise to become the new standard bearers of global information.

NOTES

1. "The study of media environments, the idea that technology and techniques, modes of information and codes of communication play a leading role in human affairs" (Media Ecology Association).
2. Sokirianskaia, Ekaterina, phone interview, 24 January 2014.
3. Aguirre, Margaret, phone interview, 7 January 2014.

4]4]4]4]4]4]4]4]4]4]4]4]4]4]4]4]4]4]4]4]4]4]4]4]4]4]4]4]4]4]4]4]4]4]4]4]4]4]4]4]4]4]4]4]4]4]4]4]4]4]4]4]4]4]4]4]4]4]4]4]4]4]4]4]4]4]4]4]

]4]4]4]4]4]4]4]4]4]4]4]4]4]4]4]4]4]4]4]4]4]4]4]4]4]4]4]4]4]4]4]4]4]4]4]4]4]4]4]4]4]4]4]4]4]4]4]4]4]4]4]4]4]4]4]4]4]4]4]4]4]4]4]4]4]4]4]4]4]4]4]4]4]4]4]

4. Tynan, Deirdre, phone interview, 2 February 2014.
5. Parra, Vanessa, personal interview, 21 February 2014.
6. Boyce, Michael, personal interview, 9 January 2014.

BIBLIOGRAPHY

Anderson Cooper Chosen for Action Against Hunger Humanitarian Award. (2008, 14 October). Action Against Hunger. Retrieved 13 November 2014, from http://www.actionagainsthunger.org/blog/anderson-cooper-chosen-action-against-hunger-humanitarian-award.

Bohen, C. (2013, 27 September). In Syria Advocates Step in to Sift for Truth. *New York Times.* Retrieved 13 November 2014, from http://www.nytimes.com/2013/09/28/world/middleeast/in-syria-advocates-step-in-to-sift-for-truth.html?smid=tw-share.

Byers, D. (2014, 26 February). Vice News, where video works. Politico.com. Retrieved 13 November 2014, from http://www.politico.com/blogs/media/2014/02/vice-news-where-video-works-184058.html.

Ellis, J. (2012, 12 September). How Human Rights Watch got into the Quasi-Journalism Business. Nieman Foundation. Retrieved 13 November 2014, from http://www.niemanlab.org/2012/09/how-human-rights-watch-got-into-the-quasi-journalism-business/.

Hiltzik, M. (2014, 20 January). The Toll of the Anti-vaccination Epidemic in One Devastating Graphic. *Los Angeles Times.* Retrieved 13 November 2014, from http://www.latimes.com/business/hiltzik/la-fi-mh-antivaccination-movement-20140120,0,5576371.story.

Huffington, A. (2014, 23 March). Covering the World: Introducing the WorldPost. *The Huffington Post.* Retrieved 13 November 2014, from http://www.huffingtonpost.com/arianna-huffington/covering-the-world-introducing-the-worldpost_b_4637990.html.

Jepson, L. (2013, 14 December). A look into the Central African Republic on Instagram. Al Jazeera. Retrieved 13 November 2014, from http://stream.aljazeera.com/story/201312140103-0023254.

Katz, A. (2014, 23 January). Syria's Lost Generation: Directors Give a Voice to War's Young Refugees. *Time.* Retrieved 13 November 2014, from http://lightbox.time.com/2014/01/23/ed-kashi-julie-winokur-meet-syrias-young-refugees/.

Khanfar, W. (2011, 1 March). A Historic Moment in the Arab World. TED. Retrieved 13 November 2014, from http://www.ted.com/talks/wadah_khanfar_a_historic_moment_in_the_arab_world/transcript?language=en.

Kozlowska, H. (2014, 23 January). Seven Times Lady Grantham Completely Embarrassed Herself in Sierra Leone. *Passport.* Retrieved 13 November 2014, from http://blog.foreignpolicy.com/posts/2014/01/23/seven_times_lady_grantham_completely_embarrassed_herself_in_sierra_leone.

Pope, H. (2010, 29 April) International Crisis Group Podcast, *Dining with Al-Qaeda, Part 2* http://www.crisisgroup.org/en/multimedia/podcasts/dining-with-al-qaeda-part-2.aspx.

Wallace, G. (2013, 29 October). Simon Benson Awards. *Portland State Vanguard.* Retrieved 13 November 2014, from http://psuvanguard.com/news/2013-simon-benson-awards/.

PART FIVE

Changing Communications and Communication Power

CHAPTER FOURTEEN

Visualizing Human Rights

The Video Advocacy of WITNESS

STUART ALLAN

On stage at the Rock and Roll Hall of Fame's induction ceremony in April 2014, British musician Peter Gabriel expressed his delight to be accepting the honour in recognition of his work as a solo artist (he left behind his role as lead singer in the progressive-rock band Genesis in 1975). In the course of sharing anecdotes about his experiences making music, he proceeded to elaborate a revealing point concerning its wider importance. 'Watch out for music. It should come with a health warning. It can be dangerous. It can make you feel so alive, so connected to the people around you, and connected to what you really are inside,' he maintained. 'And it can make you think that the world should, and could, be a much better place' (Gabriel, 2014). For many of those in the audience aware of his passionate commitment to wielding celebrity to help advance human rights causes over the years, this personal insight into how an ephemeral sense of musical connection can inspire political empowerment may well have created a lasting resonance.

It was almost three decades earlier when Gabriel realised that his 'part-time interest' in human rights—'mainly, it was something that happened to other people over there'—was slowly intensifying (2006). His acclaimed 1980 protest song 'Biko,' recounting the police killing of South African anti-apartheid activist Stephen Biko, prompted Bono of the Dublin-based rock band U2 to invite him to join a tour, A Conspiracy of Hope, on behalf of Amnesty International in the United States. The ensuing six benefit concerts held during June 1986, featuring fellow artists such as Sting, Bryan Adams, Lou Reed, Joan Baez, and the Neville Brothers, raised a reported $2.6 million and drew 40,000 new members to Amnesty. It was while on tour, Gabriel recollected, that for the first time he encountered former prisoners of conscience, and 'suddenly this world of human rights arrived in my world.' Deeply moved by their stories, it was all too apparent that he 'couldn't really walk away in quite the same way as before.' In the follow-up Human Rights Now! world tour, Gabriel played a lead role in its organisation, persuading Bruce Springsteen and the E Street Band, Sting, Tracy Chapman, and Youssou N'Dour, amongst others, to share the stage over six weeks in 1988. Altogether twenty concerts were held in fifteen countries across five continents, raising public awareness of Amnesty's activist interventions, as well as commemorating the Universal Declaration of Human Rights on its fortieth anniversary. 'Half the world is under the age of 25, and a great part can't read,' one of Amnesty's executive directors said at the time. 'With music, we can communicate to all people equally well in the rich and poor nations of the East and West, and demand that governments give human rights now' (cited in Trucco, 1988).

Later reflecting on what it meant to be hearing first-hand testimonies from survivors, Gabriel (2005) recounted his uncertainty regarding how best to respond to their requests for assistance. 'Some were living in fear, being regularly threatened and harassed, some had witnessed their family being murdered, and some had suffered terrible tortures,' while so often 'the perpetrators went unpunished.' Indeed, 'in many ways what most shocked me,' he recalled, 'was that many of these human rights abuses were being successfully denied, buried, ignored and forgotten, despite many written reports.' Equally apparent, however, was that 'in those cases where photographic film or video evidence existed, it was almost impossible for the oppressors to get away with it' (2005, p. x). It was on the basis of this understanding of 'the enormous power of the visual,' as he would later describe it, that Gabriel took the first steps to formulate an initiative to supply video cameras to activists (Gabriel, 2008). By 1992, WITNESS was launched, an international non-profit organisation that—in its website's words—'empowers human rights defenders to use video to fight injustice, and to transform personal stories of abuse into powerful tools that can pressure those in power or with power to act.' Its initial strategy, namely to provide 'people who chose to be in the wrong place at the right time' with cameras so as to help them document violations and abuses in the field, has evolved over the years to prioritise both activists' and ordinary citizens' engagement in personal reportage with a view to its evidential importance for the advancement of human rights causes. To date, WITNESS has partnered with more than 350 human rights groups in 87 countries, devoting particular effort to supporting the inclusion of video as a 'democratic tool' in campaigns seen by millions of people around the world.

In the course of tracing the contours of WITNESS's emergence and development over its first two decades, this chapter will offer an evaluative assessment of the challenges its members have faced in promoting this grassroots approach to 'seeding video advocacy.' The gradual consolidation of their present commitments to training, campaigning, and preservation will be shown to have been decisively shaped though a complex negotiation of exigent pressures and constraints, not least where harnessing the power of visual technologies in the service of digital storytelling is concerned. Differing perceptions of WITNESS's influence and humanitarian impact will be discussed throughout, particularly with regard to specific initiatives, such as its launch of 'the Hub,' the first dedicated website for human rights video created by activists for activists. In striving to bring to the fore certain ethical, journalistic, and strategic tensions at the heart of video advocacy, I will contend that WITNESS raises significant questions regarding how one of the most vital of human rights, the right to bear witness, has become a site of struggle amongst diverse communities of interest mobilising across globalising communicative networks.

'CAMERAS ARE MORE POWERFUL THAN GUNS'

'Let human-rights advocates around the world take heart. They will soon receive powerful new arms with which to wage their struggles against repression: hand-held video cameras, computers and fax machines,' Marvine Howe (1992) of *The New York Times* reported on March 20, 1992. Pointing to the launch of WITNESS set to take place the following Monday, she quoted Michael Posner of the New York–based Lawyers Committee for Human Rights (LCHR) stating: 'This program comes in response to requests from many local rights groups who say they need equipment to get their message out.' In the ensuing press coverage of the launch, Posner explained the rationale behind the intervention. 'Timely, accurate and impartial information is the most powerful weapon individuals and groups have to ensure that governments everywhere protect and promote the fundamental human rights of their citizens,' he declared. 'It's time for us, the human rights movement, to better use the communications revolution to expose abuses and galvanize public opinion to stop them' ("Witness, New Program Announced," 1992).

In the four years leading up to the announcement, LCHR had been working with the Reebok Foundation (sponsor of the Amnesty concert tours) and Peter Gabriel to put into place the necessary financial support for the initiative. A member of the Reebok Human Rights Award board of advisors, Gabriel had approached the Foundation to help him secure the means to supply video cameras to human rights workers.[1] It agreed to offer him a $150,000 (US) commitment to get the project started. 'It is much easier for those in power to get away with murder, torture, repression and the destruction of our environment,' Gabriel reasoned at the time of the launch, 'if their actions are not witnessed by the media and public' (cited in Howe, 1992). In many countries, 'cameras are more powerful than guns,' he pointed out. 'Technology transcends all borders. Information is power. We urgently need to get the technology in the right hands, the hands of those whose work for human and environmental rights can bring about real change' (Witness,1992; see also Trausch, 1993). Video imagery, in particular, was regarded as a vital factor to help generate television coverage of human rights stories otherwise more likely to be limited to newspaper reports. 'This is a weapon that activists can use,' Reebok's then-chief executive Paul Fireman maintained. 'Instead of just a few people watching, there will be millions of eyes that can witness abuses. This could be a powerful deterrent' (cited in Foltz, 1992). At the same time, WITNESS recognised its responsibility to provide the necessary training for the recipient rights groups, being all too aware—in Gabriel's words—that 'some governments might attempt to play "hardball" with those who use this hardware to expose human rights abuses' (Witness, 1992). The safety of activists, he and Posner stressed, would be a 'prime concern' for WITNESS in the days ahead.

Inspiration for the WITNESS project had come to Gabriel years earlier, but his plan had met with little enthusiasm when he proposed it to the Reebok Foundation upon his return from the second Amnesty tour, at least at first. Everything changed, however, in the immediate aftermath of a shocking incident involving the Los Angeles Police Department (LAPD) on the night of 3 March 1991. 'It was the Rodney King beating in L.A. last year that convinced people this was a viable idea,' Gabriel told a press conference in Toronto the following year (cited in Krewen, 1992). In an interview with *CBS This Morning* in the US a month later, he said that 'what is clear in this country since the Rodney King incident is that just a small strip of videotape can actually be an incredibly potent weapon for change' (CBS, 1992).

Here it is worth pausing to briefly summarise how a shaky, handheld 'amateur' video succeeded—in Gabriel's (2007) words—in 'galvanizing a global conversation.' George Holliday, a plumbing supply manager, was awoken in his Los Angeles apartment by the sound of sirens in the early hours of Sunday, 3 March 1991. Peering out at what he soon realised was some sort of disturbance involving the LAPD, he promptly picked up his new Sony Handycam and stepped onto his second-floor balcony. From this vantage point he shot eight minutes' worth of footage, bearing witness to several white police officers violently beating a black driver ordered from his car, Rodney King, aged twenty-five (it later emerged that King was on parole for a robbery conviction, and his car had been pulled over following what police alleged was a high-speed chase). In response to what officers claimed was King's resistance to arrest, they twice fired an electric Taser gun into his back before proceeding to kick and club him repeatedly as he lay on the ground, desperately pleading, 'Please stop! Please stop!' Several other officers arriving on the scene stood by and watched as King suffered more than fifty baton blows, leaving him with a fractured cheek and eye socket, a broken ankle, damaged kidneys, five teeth missing, and multiple bruises and lacerations. Holliday could not believe what he was witnessing. 'I was thinking, "What did the guy do to deserve this beating?",' he later recalled in an interview; 'I came from a different culture [in Argentina], where people would get disappeared with no due process. Police would pick people up on suspicion. I didn't expect this in the US' (cited in Goldstein, 2006; see also Allan, 2013).

In the morning, Holliday contacted the police department, asking for an explanation about what had transpired. He was rebuffed. He next telephoned CNN, but evidently no one would take his call, leading him to Los Angeles independent station KTLA-TV. In a handshake agreement, the station agreed to pay him $500 for first-run broadcast rights. Its affiliate agreement with CNN to share news footage enabled the latter to broadcast the video early Tuesday morning, followed later in the day by the three (ABC, CBS, and NBC) national networks. Allegations of police brutality, particularly from within Los Angeles's ethnic minority communities, seldom featured in news reporting for reasons typically to do with prejudice and discrimination (occasionally overt, but more typically inferential), but also because they simply occurred too frequently. Despite Police Chief Daryl Gates claiming the beating was 'an aberration,' and news reports describing it as 'shocking', several newspapers noted that civil rights leaders were pointing out that it was only the latest incident indicative of a wider pattern of police violence. King himself was quoted in some accounts shortly before his release from police custody three days later:

> I'm glad I'm not dead. I'm lucky they didn't kill me…. They handcuffed me and tied me and they shocked me with some kind of device they use… I was scared, I was scared for my life… The guns were pointed right at me… I wondered, 'Why are they drawing down on me like this?'… After they hit me with a shocker, they got a kick out of that… because how long they left it in me. It was like they had a little toy and wanted to see how it worked. ("Man Beaten by Police," 1991)

The same account noted several witnesses insisting that they had not seen King resist, flatly contradicting the LAPD's version of what happened.

Viewed in this context, Holliday's videotape could be credited with making an all-too-routine dimension of life in certain parts of the city—virtually invisible in newsworthy terms—visible in brutal detail, and thus into a news story of immediate national—and, soon after, international—significance. 'It's a picture medium,' Steve Friedman, Executive Producer of NBC's nightly news, told reporter Deborah Hastings (1991a). 'If you have a fire and you have no pictures of the fire and no one got killed, you don't mention it. If you have great pictures of flames leaping out, you use it.' CNN spokesperson Steve Haworth concurred: 'Even a verbal account does not carry the drama of a picture. It's hard to tell whether this story would have run without pictures' (see also Hastings, 1991b). The 'L.A. beating video worked because… just when you thought it was over, they started in on him again. It was ceaseless,' Peter Howe of *Life* added. 'One frame of that never would have worked by itself' (cited in Rubin, 1991).

In the months to follow, felony assault charges brought against four of the ten LAPD officers involved, together with deepening public pressure on Police Chief Gates to resign, ensured news reports returned time and again to Holliday's video footage. Tensions mounted as the court trial, relocated to Simi Valley, a conservative and predominantly white suburb, heard testimony from 5 March 1992. The repeated showing of Holliday's videotape having made it impossible for the police officers involved to deny the use of force, their attorneys concentrated on persuading the jury that it did not tell the whole story. Missing was the larger context, they argued, namely King's alleged act of defiance. Further, they proceeded to subject the videotape to a frame-by-frame analysis in order to demonstrate why the officers' actions constituted reasonable self-defence. Viewed in this way, it seemed, police actions could be made to fit a narrative whereby they were responsive to a threat posed by King, who was characterised as being in control of the situation (and therefore 'asking for it,' in the words of one juror quoted in the press). The jury, which did not include a black member, took seven days to find the officers innocent in a verdict announced on 29 April that stunned onlookers. 'Today, the jury told the world that what we all saw with our own eyes was not a crime,' the city's mayor, Tom Bradley (1992), declared at a press conference. Ted Koppel of ABC News stated: 'This is one of those cases in which the first reaction is one of slack-jawed amazement,' before posing the question that was already reverberating across the airwaves: 'How could that jury, if they looked at the same videotaped beating that we've all seen a dozen times or more on television, how could they look at that and then vote for acquittal?' (cited in Jacobs, 2000, p. 115).

The city erupted in flames within two hours of the verdict's announcement, with riots spreading through impoverished neighbourhoods, mainly in South Central Los Angeles, where racial divisions were bitterly entrenched. As the rioting continued to spiral out of control over subsequent days, the National Guard, and soon after the US Army, were mobilised to restore public order. King himself appealed for the violence to end, asking: 'Can we all just get along?' In the aftermath of the 'LA Riots,' as they were being called, it became apparent that more than 50 deaths were left in their wake, with hundreds of people injured, and over 1,000 buildings destroyed (estimated property costs were at the $1 billion mark). More than 7,000 people were arrested, the police making every effort—ironically, in the eyes of some—to secure photographs and videotapes from journalists and city residents alike to use as documentary evidence for mounting prosecutions.

'WEAPONS OF MASS COMMUNICATION'

Over the years, WITNESS has consistently acknowledged 'the impetus for its creation was the Rodney King, Jr. incident' in its promotional material, including on the Our Mission page of its website. This convergence of moral touchstone with technological affordance into an alternative visual politic underscored the incident's lasting symbolic value for efforts striving to elaborate a more egalitarian, decentralised ethos of video advocacy. 'Peter was really galvanized' by Holliday's amateur footage, former director of WITNESS, Gillian Caldwell, remembered years later. 'He had a fairly simple concept: give cameras to the world, and enable people to right the wrongs they see' (cited in Pollak, 1999). Gabriel himself has frequently recalled in press interviews how he had struggled to secure support for his proposal to set up WITNESS beforehand. 'It wasn't until the Rodney King incident that it started to be taken seriously,' he has maintained. 'That showed the world that the right tools in the right hands at the right time can have a major impact' (cited in Atwood, 1996).

Once strategic planning was agreed upon and WITNESS entered the public realm in March 1992, it quickly became apparent that the logistics involved would be more formidable than anticipated. By the six-month point in its first year of operation, only a small number of cameras had been sent to human rights organisations, principally due to the demands of processing some 2,700 applications. At the same time, negotiations with electronics manufacturers to supply equipment were underway, with some proving more open to persuasion than others. 'I should tell you that Polaroid walked right in and donated equipment and film,' Gabriel told one journalist. 'Because of their generosity, there are people documenting torture victims in Haiti. So the theories that information is as powerful a weapon as any are being proven at the moment' (cited in Krewen, 1992). More typical, however, were companies 'willing to pay us lip service,' Gabriel recalled (cited in Atwood, 1996). Choices to be made about technical matters were similarly complex, given the subversive nature of the protocols of visible evidence-gathering at stake. While the prospect of using miniature 'lipstick' cameras was deemed cost prohibitive, for example, experiments with new, more portable Sony camcorders were considered promising from the start (Lynch, 1992).

By 1995, WITNESS had distributed video equipment to more than sixty organisations. With the repercussions of the King moment still reverberating, videotaped documentation of police brutality in places such as Guatemala, Egypt, and Nigeria provided evidential support for victims' claims. Still, persuading the international media—such as the BBC or CNN—to use the material was frequently difficult, whether purposely shot by trained activists or by 'accidental observers,' or even to follow up on the story with their own correspondents. Compounding matters, as WITNESS director Sam Gregory (2008) pointed out in an interview discussing the early days, the news media often focused on 'episodic framing' emphasising 'individual actions, victims, and perpetrators,' being 'less interested in structural violence, systemic challenges, or the ongoing problems that characterize many of the most pernicious abuses, especially violations of economic, social, and cultural rights.' WITNESS Network spokeswoman Barbara Becker acknowledged in a press interview that the perceived credibility of the footage was key. Journalists were 'concerned with many things including timeliness, newsworthiness and authenticity,' she stated. 'We are working on these things, so hopefully the constant media attention we anticipated may come' (cited in Cobb, 1995). Equally encouraging, related positive outcomes were coming to light, including local activists' use of their videos as organising tools for meetings and public education workshops, as well as for fundraising initiatives for community projects. Repurposing camera equipment for training programmes similarly met with success, such as Becker's example of how the Centre for Victims of Torture in Nepal taped its psychology trainees counselling torture victims in order to assess their skills, and then passing along the footage to share good practice with others.

Indications of WITNESS's growing public profile during the first phase of its development included the television music channel VH1's tribute to the project with a star-studded concert broadcast live in the US (and subsequently on MTV) for its annual award ceremony in April 1996. By then WITNESS was being credited with numerous breakthroughs where its videotaped footage cast a spotlight on alleged violations eluding media attention, the visual impact of which helped to focus public pressure for change. 'It's hard for people to deny what is happening when they see it for themselves,' Gabriel insisted at the time. 'With text journalism, it is a lot easier to put off any emotional attachment. It's harder to explain away responsibility when it is in your face' (cited in Atwood, 1996). Moreover, as WITNESS coordinator Sukanya Pillay later pointed out, cameras in the right hands—by 'coincidence, luck or planning'—sometimes helped to reduce tensions, such as when WITNESS dispatched video monitors to Northern Ireland during its annual marching season in 1997. 'The kids were running up and throwing rocks and bottles at them, and they are going back and forth,' she told CNN the following year. 'And I felt strongly that our presence there stopped anything from happening beyond just this cat-and-mouse sort of game. And so it does show that a camera can be used as a deterrent' (CNN, 1998).

Further examples of video monitoring by organisations using cameras and training from WITNESS ranged from refugee camps in Rwanda (as well as recording the exhumation of genocide victims) to mental hospitals in the United States, to documenting the trafficking of women from the former Soviet Union forced to work as prostitutes, to massacres in Guatemala, military abduction in India, and the plight of children turned into soldiers in Sudan and northern Uganda. In pointing to these and related examples, Michael Pollak (1999) of the *New York Times* observed that it took a 'strong stomach' to watch the footage made available on the WITNESS website. 'Armed with light and sound in places where there may be no electric power or paved roads, the organizations, many of them impoverished and officially shunned, are documenting atrocities that would otherwise become dry reports to be dismissed by the authorities,' he wrote. In so doing, he added, they 'are turning them into riveting evidence of evil.' At the same time, some detractors were contending that WITNESS's forging of a 'new relation between aesthetics, commerce, and politics' was putting 'a "humane" corporate face on human rights issues' that contradicted 'the resistant identities of human rights victims,' thereby exacerbating the risk that suffering would turn into a 'web-surfer spectacle' (Schaffer & Smith, 2004, p. 39). New tactics continued to evolve, including with regard to how best to incorporate video footage of human rights cases into on-the-ground campaigns. The limits of documentation would have to stretch, in other words, to encompass possible solutions as well.

By the time it was marking its ten-year anniversary in 2002, WITNESS had evolved into a 'full service' organisation for its growing range of 'campaign partners.' In addition to distributing cameras—including in India, Romania, Gambia, the Philippines, and Palestinian communities of the West Bank, the Gaza Strip, and East Jerusalem that year alone—it was providing 'training and assistance in editing footage and in creating game plans for getting it seen, whether in a full-blown TV documentary or as streaming video on the Witness Web site' (Hornaday, 2002). The website was attracting hits from 37,000 visitors a month by then (helped, in part, by celebrity supporters introducing the videos, such as film stars Susan Sarandon and Tim Robbins or musicians like Lou Reed and Laurie Anderson), confirming expectations that cyberspace would prove to be a key component of new strategies to extend the reach of video advocacy. 'This kind of catalytic work that Witness is doing is really erasing a lot of the boundaries,' filmmaker Peter Wintonick observed, convinced that a paradigm shift in distribution was underway. 'Witness is at the forefront of this revolution of micro-documentaries, as I call them, or digi-documentaries,' he explained, which entailed 'putting documentaries up on the Net, so they're not only available to the North American community of activists, but in theory to anybody who wants to log on' (cited in Hornaday, 2002). Indeed, with the promise of broadband and wireless communications technology on the horizon, WITNESS was confident its partners in the field soon would be able to cut their own films using laptop editing systems (and relay them using proxy-servers to help protect their identity), rather than relying on the New York–based editors. Further training revolved around how to craft content to convey complex messages in a personal way for selected audiences ('smart narrowcasting' aimed at 'people who will act'), together with practical issues, such as handling mapping technology, the use of tools to blur or pixelate faces (or alter voices) to protect identities, archiving testimonies and related resources, as well as respecting privacy, copyright, and other intellectual-property rights, amongst other concerns.[2]

'Well, it's put cameras out in many countries all over the world, and armed human rights activists with a new tool,' Gabriel replied, when asked by ABC News to reflect on WITNESS's achievements in 2006. 'And I think both in changing laws, in getting their case heard around the world, in helping people not to feel isolated, desperate and forgotten, it's done a lot,' he continued (ABC News, 2006). Conceding that it was 'the tip of the iceberg,' with 'a huge amount that needs doing,' he nevertheless expressed his optimism that WITNESS was becoming ever-more effective in realising its aims. New, progressive opportunities were emerging to recast 'the original mission to get cameras out to the world,' not least by striving to make the most of camera technologies in cell or mobile telephones. The growing ubiquity of these relatively inexpensive devices meant that George Orwell's vision in the dystopian novel *1984*, where those in power control the population through observation, was set to 'flip... on its head,' Gabriel believed. 'If we get cameras out everywhere, perhaps through observation, the small guy, the little guy can keep an eye on those in power' (ABC News, 2006). The 'internet revolution' signalled 'a real point of transition,' in his view, opening up new ways to hold governments accountable for violations of human rights.

A case in point was the launch of a video-sharing site, simply called 'the Hub,' on Human Rights Day, 10 December 2007. As WITNESS's Meg McLagan (2007) wrote at the time, it was intended to foster participatory possibilities by 'acting as a facilitator in making, aggregating, organizing and disseminating human-rights videos,' and thereby help to summon into action 'a globally networked human-rights community' (p. 325). Envisioned as a 'central clearinghouse' for activists sharing visual material (raw footage as well as finished advocacy videos) and information resources, including anonymously when necessary for security reasons, the Hub was designed to be an open alternative to commercial video-sharing sites, such as YouTube. Material posted on the latter type of site sometimes encountered difficulties, the main concern being that it was difficult to find in the first place. Even then, it was 'often mischaracterized or mis-tagged and may even, at times, be the brunt of jokes,' Caldwell explained in a press interview, 'which is very disturbing to people who are placing their lives at risk to get it on there' (cited in Wallace, 2007; see also Caldwell & Federlein, 2008; Thijm, 2010). Furthermore, videos viewed without an adequate explanatory context risked promoting misconceptions—accidental and otherwise—as messages were actively shared, remixed or re-inscribed within alternative interpretive frameworks.

Refashioning what Caldwell and Federlein (2008) termed 'the vernacular language of human rights advocacy' in order to raise awareness and inspire action demanded fresh thinking about the strategic framing of harsh realities within the narrative conventions of digital storytelling. 'Obviously abuses being captured in the moment are incredibly powerful and can go a long way in changing a situation, but those moments are rare,' Jenni Wolfson of WITNESS pointed out where the Hub was concerned. 'A lot of the video that we work on with our partners are personal testimonies of people who have survived abuses. It's those personal stories that really help people to connect to the issues' (cited in Wallace, 2007). Her colleague Sam Gregory concurred. 'In a lot of cases (video documentation) can be the tipping point,' he told *The Gazette* in Montreal. 'The power... of someone speaking directly to you saying, "This is what is happening to me, this is what I want you to do"' was rapidly increasing, in his perception, as 'we move into a more video-literate culture' (cited in Valiante, 2008; see also Gregory, 2008).

By the time the Hub ceased accepting new contributions of footage (mainly witness documentation, though at times perpetrator-shot) in 2010, principally due to technical difficulties, it was one member of a rapidly growing Video for Change community of websites. Two years later WITNESS and Storyful announced they were joining forces to launch a Human Rights Channel on YouTube, the aim of the platform being 'to tell breaking stories through the lenses of citizen journalists that will change the way we view, share and engage human rights video' ("WITNESS and Storyful Launch New Global Channel," 2012). Storyful's expertise in corroborating video authenticity (using local sources, regional experts, and 'pioneering algorithms') has complemented WITNESS's proficiency in curating footage into compelling, evidence-driven narratives of direct interest to specific audiences. 'The greatest challenge for our work is scaling it up to properly educate the millions of people who now have cameras in their pockets and are willing to use them to document human rights abuses,' WITNESS's Chris Michael explained. 'This is creating enormous opportunities for video advocates to create, curate, and share stories that we may never have seen or heard previously' (cited in Romanelli, 2013). Moreover, to the extent citizen witnesses are empowered to foster a collective identity on these terms—as ad hoc members of 'witnessing publics' aligned with distributed network campaigns—human rights violations will be all the more difficult to perpetrate.

'SEE IT. FILM IT. CHANGE IT.'

Belief in the 'raw power of video' to instigate social change—'You may be able to question firsthand accounts,' Gabriel told CNN, 'but you can't say what you just saw didn't happen' (CNN, 1998)—has been a guiding principle of WITNESS's model of video advocacy from the outset. Despite its gradual evolution over the years in relation to the shifting imperatives of the wider mediascape, this conviction that once people see what is happening they will be moved to react accordingly has held firm. Equally apparent from the start, in the view of commentators such as sociologist Stanley Cohen (1996), has been the extent to which 'a very old-fashioned faith' in the 'power of knowledge' underpins this model. In his words:

> The human rights movement is one of the few survivors of the Enlightenment project. It not only upholds the ideal of universal values and standards, but also assumes that information about their violations will produce universal moral and emotional responses. The power of the camera just extends the power of the word. (p. 36)

For Cohen, it was not safe to presume that factual information in video images would necessarily engender the same response from everyone. This was so regardless of their visceral public impact, in his view, a point made clear by what he termed 'the Rodney King effect' where the truth-value of video footage was disavowed by the courtroom jury, leading to the acquittal of the police officers involved. 'The law allowed the obvious interpretation to be negotiated, reconstructed and eventually denied,' Cohen reasoned. 'The bystander had got it wrong: Mr King was perpetrator, not victim' (2001, p. 186).

This line of critique had become apparent to members of WITNESS itself, of course, being all too aware of what it meant in the hard, day-to-day grind to realise the mission's ideals. 'The vision of giving cameras to the world was beautiful and probably oversimplified,' Caldwell conceded in a retrospective about the project's origins. 'I think the Rodney King example perpetuated the early mythology that hand-held video footage is going to be plastered all over the world's television screens and revolutionize the debate,' she added. 'Unfortunately, because of television's appetite and the audience's limited attention span, most footage our partners are shooting, at least by television's standards, doesn't merit an international audience' (cited in Hornaday, 2002). Questions regarding how best to compel news organisations to cover human rights violations with sufficient depth and ethical integrity recurrently defy easy answers, but examples of WITNESS's achievements in prising open the visual boundaries of reportage have continued to proliferate over the years. 'I've been going to TV journalists for years about human rights stories, and the problem has always been the same,' Mary Daly, a consultant for the Lawyers Committee for Human Rights, told the *Los Angeles Times* shortly after WITNESS was launched in 1992. 'The human rights story is dramatic and compelling—but no pictures, no TV' (cited in Hall, 1992). Over two decades later, this problem has been further exacerbated by factors constitutive of the wider crisis in international journalism, yet there is scope for cautious optimism that Gabriel's initial vision—as strategic as it was 'simplistic'—is gaining a critical purchase in emergent participatory cultures of video advocacy occurring in unlikely places around the globe. While few would deny that the disconnect between visible evidence and social justice can be profound, WITNESS's citizen-centred ethos promises to continue to instantiate innovative forms of reportage to help narrow this gap in the years ahead. More often than not, citizen witnesses get it right.

NOTES

1. In an interview with *The Times* of London ten years later, Gabriel commented on WITNESS's partnership with Reebok, manufacturer of athletic footwear. 'The question is, are they just trying to buy credibility,' he shrugged; 'there is a dilemma there because for them to stay in competition

with Nike and Adidas they can't make their goods too expensive to produce. Their record (on Third World labour conditions) is not perfect, but I am convinced that they are moving in the right direction' (Dalton, 2002). Regarding his own celebrity status as an activist-musician, he told *Business Week*: 'Celebrities shouldn't take on causes in a trivial way.' Rather, they 'should find things that mean something to them and do their homework, so that they can speak as articulately as they are able, and then hand over to the people doing the real work' ("Capturing Human Rights Abuses," 2006; see also Chouliaraki (2013) on celebrities as 'expert performers' in 'the humanitarian imaginary').

2. In so doing, WITNESS 'does not call into question the category of human rights,' but rather 'aids with the work of issue formatting by bringing an issue into a human rights framework,' Margaret McLagan (2005) observed. 'For those struggling against injustice, the advantages of doing so can be significant, enabling them to initiate or engage with a set of rights-related mechanisms that in turn offer new platforms for action' (see also Cottle & Lester, 2011; Dencik, 2011; McCaughey & Ayers, 2013; Thorsen & Allan, 2014; van de Donk et al., 2004).

REFERENCES

ABC News. (2006, 30 January). Peter Gabriel talks about the documentary 'Witness'. Transcript, *The Charlie Rose Show*.

Allan, S. (2013). *Citizen witnessing: Revisioning journalism in times of crisis*. Cambridge: Polity.

Atwood, B. (1996, 12 March). 'VH1 Honors' to benefit Witness. *Billboard*.

Bradley, T. (1992, 30 April). Reaction. *The Los Angeles Times*.

Caldwell, G., & Federlein, S. (2008). Moving images: From vision to action, from action to transformation. *Innovations, 3*(2), 37–50.

Capturing human rights abuses. (2006, 1 February). *Business Week*.

CBS. (1992, 12 October). Peter Gabriel discusses his new album 'Us'. Transcript, *CBS This Morning*, M. McEwen, interviewer.

Chouliaraki, L. (2013). *The ironic spectator: Solidarity in the age of post-humanitarianism*. Cambridge, MA: Polity.

CNN. (1998, 18 May). Transcript, *CNN Newsroom Worldview*, Davin Hutchins interviewer.

Cobb, C. (1995, 25 February). New eye on the news. *The Ottawa Citizen*.

Cohen, S. (1996). Witnessing the truth. *Index on Censorship, 25*(1), 36–45.

Cohen, S. (2001). *States of denial: Knowing about atrocities and suffering*. Cambridge, MA: Polity.

Cottle, S., & Lester, L. (Eds.). (2011). *Transnational protests and the media*. New York: Peter Lang.

Dalton, S. (2002, 14 September). Camelot reborn. *The Times*.

Dencik, L. (2011). *Media and global civil society*. Basingstoke: Palgrave Macmillan.

Foltz, K. (1992, 5 April). Making a difference: Bearing witness for good deeds. *The New York Times*.

Gabriel, P. (2005). Foreword. In S. Gregory, G. Caldwell, R. Avni, & T. Harding (Eds.), *Video for Change* (pp. v–xi). London: Pluto.

Gabriel, P. (2006, February). Fight injustice with raw video. TED Talk. Retrieved from https://www.ted.com/talks/peter_gabriel_fights_injustice_with_video.

Gabriel, P. (2007). Global voices. In M. Benioff & C. Adler (Eds.), *The business of changing the world* (pp. 277–284). New York: McGraw-Hill.

Gabriel, P. (2008). Moving images: 'Beginnings.' *Innovations, 3* (2), 35–36.

Gabriel, P. (2014, 11 April). Peter Gabriel RNR HOF Speech 4–10–14 Rock and Roll Hall of Fame. Youtube, posted by D. Pastor. http://youtu.be/yZpTj9YT-IQ.

Goldstein, M. (2006, 19 February). The other beating. *The Los Angeles Times.*

Gregory, S. (2008, 31 March) Interview with H. Jenkins, From Rodney King to Burma: An interview with Witness's Sam Gregory (Part One), MIT Center for Civic Media Blog. http://henryjenkins.org/2008/03/from_rodney_king_to_burma_an_i.html.

Hall, J. (1992, 26 May). Electronic witness to rights abuses. *The Los Angeles Times.*

Hastings, D. (1991a, 6 March). Without videotape, TV officials say beating would not have stood out. Associated Press.

Hastings, D. (1991b, 27 March). Man who shot beating video trying to cope with national attention. Associated Press.

Hornaday, A. (2002, 21 November). A lens on the world. *The Washington Post.*

Howe, M. (1992, 20 March). Chronicle. *The New York Times.*

Jacobs, R. N. (2000). *Race, media, and the crisis of civil society: From Watts to Rodney King.* Cambridge: Cambridge University Press.

Krewen, N. (1992, 5 September). Gabriel the activist. *Hamilton Spectator.*

Lynch, C. (1992, 14 November). Recording repression. *The Globe and Mail.*

Man beaten by police gets released from jail. (1991, 7 March). Associated Press.

McCaughey, M., & Ayers, M. D. (2013). *Cyberactivism: Online activism in theory and practice.* New York: London.

McLagan, M. (2005). Circuits of suffering. *PoLAR: Political and Legal Anthropology Review, 28*(2), 223–239.

McLagan, M. (2007). The architecture of strategic communication. In M. Feher, G. Krikorian, & Y. McKee (Eds.), *Nongovernmental politics* (pp. 318–325). New York: Zone.

Pollak, M. (1999, 11 November). Screen grab: Vivid documents of human atrocities. *The New York Times.*

Romanelli, S. (2013, 20 May). Q&A: Video puts the human into human rights. Inter Press Service.

Rubin, S. (1991, 3 April). The home video news amateurs' tapes get on TV. *The San Francisco Chronicle.*

Schaffer, K., & Smith, S. (2004). *Human rights and narrated lives.* London: Palgrave.

Thijm, Y. A. (2010, 18 August). Update on The Hub and WITNESS' New Online Strategy. Bog.witness.org. http://blog.witness.org/2010/08/update-on-the-hub-and-witness-new-online-strategy/

Thorsen, E., & Allan, S. (2014), *Citizen journalism: Global perspectives, Vol. 2.* New York: Peter Lang.

Trausch, S. (1993, 10 March). Video vigilance. *Boston Globe.*

Trucco, T. (1988, 5 July). Rock's largest human rights tour. *The New York Times.*

Valiante, G. (2008, 20 July) Telling it like it shoots. *The Gazette* (Montreal).

van de Donk, W., Loader, B. D., Nixon, P., & Rucht, D. (2004). *Cyberprotest: New media, citizens and social movements.* London: Routledge.

Wallace, N. (2007). Calling the world as Witness. *The Chronicle of Philanthropy, 20*(3), 28.

WITNESS and Storyful launch new global channel for human rights video. (2012, 24 May). WITNESS news release. http://www3.witness.org/ar/node/3280.

Witness, new program announced to help the worldwide human rights movement join the communications revolution. (1992, 23 March). PR Newswire.

CHAPTER FIFTEEN

Big Data and Humanitarian Response

PATRICK MEIER

The overflow of information generated during disasters can be as paralyzing to humanitarian response as the absence of information. This overflow, "Big Data" (or Big Crisis Data), is driven by the massive volume of user-generated content publicly shared on social media platforms like Facebook, Twitter, Instagram, and YouTube. Recent empirical studies demonstrate that some of this content is directly relevant, informative, and even actionable for humanitarian response purposes. In other words, social media can accelerate the assessment of disaster damage and needs during disasters. The challenge, however, is that only a very small fraction of user-generated content presently adds to situational awareness. But this content could potentially be life-saving information. During Typhoon Yolanda in November 2013, for example, barely ~0.25% of the quarter-of-a-million tweets posted during the first 72 hours were informative and/or actionable. While this seems insignificant, 0.25% represents more than 600 geo-tagged tweets, or more than 60,000 words of relevant and timely information for disaster responders. Of the 5,000+ images posted to Twitter, only ~3.5% captured infrastructure damage cause by the Typhoon—but this still represents 180 individual geo-tagged pictures available in real-time. So identifying this content is like looking for the proverbial needle in the haystack—the growing stack of information generated during disasters.

Assuming that one person was tasked with reviewing each of the 250,000+ tweets, it would have taken that person well over 300 hours or 14 days to process all the content (at 5 seconds per tweet and image). And so, while social media content was available in real-time during Typhoon Yolanda, one would need half a month to make sense of it, which is hardly optimal. Indeed, time is a luxury that disaster-affected communities do not have during humanitarian crises. This explains why "microtasking" was used to make sense of the user-generated content posted in response to Typhoon Yolanda. Microtasking is the process of taking a large task—such as analyzing 250,000 crises tweets—and distributing this large task in the form of much smaller tasks. In the response to Yolanda, the microtasking platform was set up by the Qatar Computing Research Institute (QCRI) and the subsequent tasks were carried out by digital volunteers with the Digital Humanitarian Network. Thanks to microtasking, the 250,000+ tweets and 5,000+ images were filtered in near real-time and made available to humanitarian organizations over the course of 72 hours.

The purpose of this chapter is to highlight how microtasking—an example of human computing—can be used to make sense of Big Data during disasters. The first part of the chapter addresses the challenges around bias and reliability vis-à-vis Big Crisis Data. The second part uses the case study of Typhoon Yolanda to provide a real-world example of microtasking Big Crisis Data in action. The third part explains how machine computing (artificial intelligence) can support and indeed significantly accelerate the microtasking process. The conclusion addresses the need for enlightened policies and highlights the threat that Big Data poses to data privacy and security.

BIAS AND RELIABILITY

Perhaps the two most pressing criticisms around the use of crowdsourced user-generated content for disaster response is that content's bias and unverified nature. Traditional data sources and information collection methodologies, however, are far from perfect either. Take the November 2013 Multi-Cluster/Sector Initial Rapid Assessment (MIRA) report for Typhoon Yolanda in the Philippines. The report, which typically takes two weeks to produce, is simply a field-based survey of needs resulting from a disaster. The November 2013 report identified the following shortcomings vis-à-vis the methodology and data sources used: The data collected were not representative. The process of selecting interviewees was biased given that said selection was based on a convenience sample. Interviewees had to estimate (guesstimate?) the answer for several questions, thus introducing additional bias in the data. Since assessment teams were not trained to administrate the questionnaire, this also introduces the problem of assessment teams interpreting the questions differently, thus limits the ability to compare survey results. The data still need to be validated with secondary data. These shortcomings are not limited to MIRA reports, which explains why the UN recently stated the following in a high-profile official policy document: "The evidence suggests that new information sources are *no less representative or reliable* than more traditional sources, which are also imperfect in crisis settings" (OCHA, 2013).

As for reliability, the mainstream media also makes mistakes. Take the *New York Times*, for example. The NYT is considered by many to represent the best of Western journalism, the highest professional standards. Yet their journalists make more than 7,000 factual errors every year. The majority of crowdsourced phone calls made to emergency telephone services like 911 (US) and 999 (UK) are also not trustworthy. In New York City, for example, 911 operators receive more than 10 million false calls, hoaxes, or misdials every year. In the UK, only a quarter of calls made to 999 are legitimate. In sum, the vast majority of calls made to these crowdsourcing systems are unreliable. This doesn't mean that they should be abolished or abandoned. Instead, the US and the UK are actively developing new strategies to *manage* the challenge of false calls.

While many humanitarians still believe that social media cannot be verified, the BBC's User-Generated Content (UGC) Hub in London has been verifying social media since 2006. In addition, the company Storyful has also developed international expertise in verifying user-generated content during crises. In early 2014, the European Center for Journalism (ECJ) published a detailed *Verification Handbook* that draws on a wide range of best practices and strategies to verify social media. In other words, verifying Big Crisis Data is far from impossible. Moreover, recent research in Advanced Computing has shown that the credibility of tweets and pictures can be automatically computed.

HUMAN COMPUTING SOLUTIONS FOR BIG DATA

Typhoon Yolanda struck the Philippines in early November 2013. Yolanda was the most powerful typhoon to make landfall in recorded human history. The resulting devastation was total. Just hours before the typhoon hit the eastern coast of the Philippines, the United Nations Office for the Coordination of Humanitarian Affairs (OCHA) activated the Digital Humanitarian Network (DHN). Members of the DHN include groups like Humanitarian OpenStreetMap (HOT), GIS Corps, and the Standby Volunteer Task Force (SBTF). These groups comprise tech-savvy digital volunteers who offer their time and skills in support of humanitarian operations. The DHN thus serves as the official interface between established humanitarian organizations and global networks of digital volunteers.

As Typhoon Yolanda was about to make landfall, OCHA asked members of the Digital Humanitarian Network to collect all tweets posted during the next 72 hours and identify which tweets referred to urgent needs, displaced populations, and other issue areas. In addition, OCHA asked DHN members to collect all pictures posted on Twitter. More specifically, they wanted to know which pictures showed disaster damage and where in the Philippines those pictures had been taken. The Standby Volunteer Task Force (SBTF) accepted the request and partnered with the Qatar Computing Research Institute (QCRI) to deploy MicroMappers—a free and open source microtasking platform developed in partnership with OCHA. While MicroMappers was still under development at the time, OCHA and QCRI decided that deploying the platform early would still add value even if it had not been fully tested.

MicroMappers is a collection of apps—or Clickers as they are referred to by QCRI. The Tweet Clicker, for example, allows digital volunteers to quickly tag individual tweets with a simple click of the mouse. The Image Clicker invites volunteers to tag the level of damage they see in each picture, again with a simple click of the mouse. MicroMappers also includes Geo Clickers—the Tweet Geo Clicker and the Image Geo Clicker. These invite volunteers to geo-tag the tweets and images. The Geo Clickers display the original tweet/image along with a search box and a map. If the text of the tweet includes a reference to the name of a town or city, volunteers simply copy/paste the place name into the search box in order to geo-tag the tweet or image. Alternatively, they can use the map to zoom in to the location and add a marker there.

QCRI collected over a quarter of a million tweets within 72 hours of the typhoon making landfall. They used the AIDR platform (Artificial Intelligence for Disaster Response) to collect these tweets. Before uploading the tweets to the Tweet Clicker, they automatically filtered the tweets for unique tweets to weed out duplicates. They also used an algorithm to filter for general relevancy of the tweets. These two filters reduced the 250,000+ original tweets to approximately 55,000 tweets, which were uploaded to the Tweet Clicker. QCRI also used algorithms to automatically filter for images that were included in the 250,000+ tweets. This yielded just over 5,000 images, which were uploaded to the Image Clicker. The links to the Tweet and Image Clickers were then shared with members of the Digital Humanitarian Network and also publicly promoted via social media.

In order to ensure quality control, each single tweet (and image) was shown to at least 5 different volunteers. Only if there was complete consensus on the tagging did individual tweets/images get geo-tagged. In other words, if at least 3 out of 5 individual volunteers tagged a picture as showing "Severe Damage" that image was added to the Typhoon Yolanda Crisis Map, for example. This triangulation mechanism enables much higher data quality.

In total, just over 600 individual tweets were triangulated using the Tweet Clicker and about 180 pictures were triangulated with the Image Clicker. More than 400 volunteers contributed to these tagging efforts over the course of 72 hours. The greatest challenge to this digital humanitarian response was the geo-tagging of the triangulated tweets/images. This is because the Geo Clickers were not ready at the time. Based on the feedback received from volunteers, QCRI has also developed an iPhone and Android app for the Tweet and Image Clickers, which they expect will result in a much larger number of volunteer digital humanitarians during the next disaster.

While MicroMappers was initially developed to make sense of social media generated during disasters, another compelling use case is the tagging of Unmanned Ariel Vehicles (UAVs) imagery. Several UAVs were deployed following Typhoon Yolanda in order to assess infrastructure damage, search for survivors, and identify displaced populations, particularly in hard-to-access areas. Organizations like the Philippines Red Cross and the World Bank made use of this UAV imagery to inform their operations. As commercially available UAVs continue to drop in cost and become easier plus safer to use, it stands to reason that they will be increasingly used by many more organizations and private individuals to provide immediate situational awareness following disasters. This will inevitably result in a Big Data challenge. An Aerial Clicker is thus being developed for MicroMappers to rapidly microtask the tracing and tagging of aerial imagery during humanitarian disasters.

MACHINE COMPUTING SOLUTIONS FOR BIG DATA

The volume of user-generated content shared on social media during disasters is expected to continue accelerating for years to come. While "only" a quarter of a-million tweets were generated during Typhoon Yolanda, more than 20 million were posted during Hurricane Sandy in October 2012. In the immediate aftermath of the Japan earthquake and tsunami in March 2011, Twitter saw more than 5,500 tweets posted every second. In other words, it took less than a minute of tweets to generate more than 250,000 tweets. While MicroMappers will continue to grow its volunteer base, asking a million volunteers to tag tweets may not be the best use of human time—particularly if machines could carry out some of this work automatically.

This is where machine computing comes in. QCRI is developing a platform called Artificial Intelligence for Disaster Response (AIDR), which is integrated with the Tweet Clicker from MicroMappers. AIDR allows anyone to collect tweets during disasters based on keywords such as hashtags. Users can then download the resulting tweets at any time to analyze them with Excel, for example. But using keywords as filters is hardly effective. So users can use AIDR to create automated algorithms to automatically identify relevant tweets such as tweets related to urgent needs, for example. Since AIDR uses machine learning, the filtered tweets are far more relevant than those filtered using keywords alone. Another advantage of machine learning is that the algorithms are largely language independent, so users can create automated filters for a wide range of languages.

In order to create these machine computing filters, users simply classify tweets into the categories they are most interested in. One such category, for example, could be infrastructure damage during Typhoon Yolanda. Users simply use the Tweet Clicker to tag all incoming tweets that refer to infrastructure damage. They could also elect to crowdsource the tagging of these tweets. Once AIDR has enough examples to learn from, the algorithm for "infrastructure damage" automatically classifies all future incoming tweets and scores these based on how accurate each tweet classification is. For example, a tweet might be classified by AIDR with a confidence score of 80%. Automatic classifications for lower levels of confidence could be rerouted to MicroMappers for correct human tagging. In any event, the more data is classified, the greater the confidence scores for the automatic classification. At present, AIDR is producing automatic classifiers that range between 80% to 98% confidence. But these confidence scores can range widely from one hazard type or country to another.

This explains why AIDR will include a "Class Store" along the lines of an App Store whereby users share their classifiers for others to use. To this end, once a high-confidence classifier for infrastructure damage following a typhoon in the Philippines has been developed, this same classifier can be reused when future typhoons pass through the Philippines. QCRI is also exploring the possibility of uploading public Facebook status updates into MicroMappers and is collaborating with UNICEF to modify both AIDR and MicroMappers to work with text messages (SMS).

CONCLUSION

The application of Advanced Computing to address major information-based challenges in the humanitarian space is still a new field of exploration. Potential solutions to Big Crisis Data challenges are very much experimental and in their infancy. These challenges, however, are not only technical. Without enlightened leadership and policymaking, any technical solution will have limited impact. Take the needle in the haystack problem, for example. While sophisticated technical solutions can be developed, these alone are insufficient. Humanitarian organizations are not actively or explicitly creating demand for high quality, relevant user-generated content during disasters. So why assume that supply will follow? If the 911 emergency number were never advertised, then would anyone call? If 911 were simply a voicemail inbox with no instructions, would callers know what type of actionable information to relay after the beep?

Perhaps the single biggest challenge, however, is Big Data's threat to data privacy and security. While the International Committee of the Red Cross (ICRC) and the Global Association of Mobile Operators (GSMA) have recently developed new data protection guidelines to manage user-generated content, these are difficult to enforce. Even those who are familiar with these codes of conduct often ignore them as witnessed in early 2014 when the conflict in South Sudan escalated. The principles of informed consent and do no harm are more important than ever in the era of Big Data. Whether these principles can ever be enforced, however, remains to be seen.

REFERENCES

Meier, P. (2014). iRevolution blog. http://www.iRevolution.net.

Meier, P. (forthcoming). *Digital humanitarians: How big data is changing the face of humanitarian response*. Oxford: Taylor & Francis.

OCHA. (2013). Humanitarianism in the network age. http://www.unocha.org/hina.

CHAPTER SIXTEEN

'Power in my Pocket'

How Mobile Citizen Reporting Challenges Digital Elitism

ALICE KLEIN

News of emergencies, conflict, and major international events has traditionally been reported by foreign correspondents, based abroad where the action happens. Reports back—originally via telegram, then phone and now email—have seen British journalists based in bureau in the Americas, Asia, and Africa for decades (Sambrook, 2010).

As Sambrook explains in his paper *Are Foreign Correspondents Redundant?* (2010), 'The model of a foreign correspondent, working from a fixed overseas bureau, is well established across all forms of international newsgathering—newspapers, wire agencies, broadcasters.'

But this has changed dramatically over the past 10–20 years. The World Wide Web now allows news to travel from all over the world at high speeds. Meanwhile newspaper budgets have been cut back, due to falling advertising revenue, making it harder to justify sending reporters overseas or paying for correspondents based abroad.

Where (few) foreign correspondents do remain, they are often based in regional 'hubs'—the capital cities of key countries such as Nairobi in Kenya, Rio De Janeiro in Brazil, and Bangkok in Thailand.

This results in an urban bias, with events unfolding in these cities taking precedent over far-flung, rural, or less accessible areas of the respective country or region. Reporters are predominantly male and have had the opportunity and privilege of quality education (Kuypers, 2002).

Arguably, these factors mean foreign correspondence at best lacks diversity and at worst is fundamentally skewed and biased.

In the UK and US, the lack of gender diversity in media is such a big issue it has spawned campaigns and advocacy groups such as Women in Media & News (WIMN). WIMN (About WIMN, 2014) says 'women of colour, low-income women, lesbians, youth and older women' are especially excluded in the US. In December 2011, Kira Cochrane reported in the *Guardian* that around 80% of newspaper articles are produced by men in an average month in the UK (Cochrane, 2011). And attempts to redress the issue in countries across the developing world appear to be lagging behind Western efforts.

There is also bias in the issues and interviewees journalists choose to report on. Traditionally, they have not sought the views of those on the margins of society—such as people with disabilities, people living with HIV, women and girls, slum dwellers, and the rural poor living in remote and offline areas—often referred to as 'last mile' communities.

'CITIZEN JOURNALISM'... OFFERING AN ALTERNATIVE?

Citizen journalism—which is widely accepted as non-professional journalists bearing witness to events—has gone some way to counter this, by offering alternative views irrespective of age, gender, and location. And mobile technology is now offering the ability to effectively 'shrink' space and, accordingly, offer an antidote to otherwise unrepresentative and biased media coverage (Bartlett, 2010).

Photos and video used to illustrate the Arab Spring cemented citizen journalism as a new form of media production in the mid-2000s, though these outputs have their own issues—for example they are not always verifiable.

But the rise of citizen journalism has widely been welcomed as making news production more democratic, especially as citizens can use simple technology, such as their mobile phones, to get involved. In *The New Foreign Correspondence* (2003), Maxwell Hamilton and Jenner say, 'Although not yet well understood, technology-driven changes are reshaping international news flows by lowering the economic barriers of entry to publishing and broadcasting and encouraging the proliferation of non-traditional international news sources'. And while opinions on the value of citizen journalism vary widely, most mainstream media editors and experts agree that citizen journalism needs to be at least incorporated into mainstream news packages of breaking events, even if only to complement or bolster traditionally gathered foreign news.

This has meant agencies like Reuters and AP have created new posts and teams to deal with user-generated content (UGC). Some outlets have even created dedicated online spaces where members of the public are encouraged to upload their own photos and videos such as CNN's iReport, Guardian Witness and Al Jazeera's Sharek portal (MacMillan, 2013).

And whole organisations have been formed to curate and verify social media such as Storyful. Mark Little, Storyful's founder, explains the idea behind it: 'I watched the Arab Spring unfold on YouTube and saw an authenticity I had rarely seen on TV news. I realized the potential to get closer to the story, faster. I was inspired by the collaborative spirit of social networks. I saw all the things that had inspired me to be a journalist in the first place. This is what Storyful is all about. Social media hasn't killed journalism. It has given it a new lease of life' (Lee, 2014).

Storyful uses a combination of human and technological verification procedures to check the authenticity of UGC. Others have created websites and apps which editors can run photos through to check they haven't been used online before, such as TinEye, JPEGSnoop and Findexif.com (Silverman, 2014). Meanwhile websites like Emergent.info and AfricaCheck.org track and verify online rumours about a photo's source in real time.

However, definitions of 'affordable' and 'accessible' tools used in the production of citizen journalism vary widely. The cost of cameras and camera phones needed to produce photos, video, and audio clips remains a barrier for many of the world's poorest people.

Moreover, citizen journalists need access to the internet in order to share stories and materials. But accessing information still remains a challenge in many countries. While the world has never been more connected—with millions of emails sent and received every day—most of the world's population is not yet online. In rural India, for example, only 2 per cent of the population has access to the internet (Vaidyanathan, 2012).

A LOW-TECH SOLUTION

In response to both the need to address bias in mainstream foreign news reporting by opening it up to citizens, and the fact that not all people have access to computers and the internet, a British citizen journalism start-up named Radar was launched to train citizens to report via their mobile phones.

Radar was set up in 2011 by a team of passionate journalists and development professionals with the aim of training and mentoring networks of citizen reporters from some of the world's most marginalised communities, and empowering them to bring their news and perspectives into the public dialogue. Radar set out to do this by focusing reporting around one of the most affordable communication tools available: basic mobile phones.

In practice, for a few pence, a news alert sent via SMS from a village in India can be received in London, analysed and verified, and shared online with influential audiences within minutes.

Radar offers new citizen journalists pro-bono editorial support. In addition, alongside telling stories in their own way, they can be linked with professional reporters around big events, often acting as fixers. And when linked with digital storytellers, mappers, and bloggers they can help to produce collaborative multimedia reports covering neglected news and fresh perspectives.

Like many tech start-ups, Radar was originally seed-funded by philanthropists. Radar then set up a third sector communications consultancy offering solutions to communication challenges, primarily in the developing world. Radar's training framework and web app can be easily adapted for a range of external organisations or situations including emergencies.

Within its first year, Radar had covered two African elections and supported 250 reporters to share more than 2,000 SMS news alerts from their communities, producing media that has been seen by more than half a million people across social media sites. Work from Radar reporters has appeared in the *Guardian*, *New Internationalist*, and the *Ecologist*, along with contributions to the BBC World Service and international television features.

In addition to articles, many Radar journalists have exposed issues that have been picked up by campaigners, advocacy organisations, and policy networks, including EU election observation teams in Africa.

Most of the communities Radar continues to work with live off grid, in slums or rural villages. More than half are women and girls, and over a third have a physical or sensory disability.

RADAR'S TRAINING AT A GLANCE

Radar starts by identifying low-resource countries where citizen journalism has not featured strongly until now so as to add value. This is often where partner organisations are already working and have identified need but they are also influenced by upcoming major events such as elections. Radar identifies potential trainees via trusted civil society organisations who are asked to put forward a few members each, and we ask that these candidates have a genuine interest in reporting.

Many are already engaged with an issue/issues within their communities. Through intensive face-to-face training workshops, Radar gets to find out who the trainees are and vice versa—which builds trust and decreases the risk of plagiarism. The fundamentals of journalism are taught including the importance of reporting accurately and avoiding hate speech or hearsay. Teaching materials are adapted from material made available by trusted sources and teachings including the BBC and UK's National Council for the Training of Journalists.

Rather than training citizen journalists how to write 400-word articles, the training focuses on 'micro-reporting' via SMS. For the price of a local text, news alerts of just 140 characters can be sent using any phone—from a green screen Nokia to the latest iPhone. Radar headquarters in London acts as a central hub, receiving the SMS reports, verifying and editing them where possible, and sharing them online via Twitter—so they can be read by internet users around the world alongside international journalists and editors.

This allows the reporting of events in real time, as experienced in Sierra Leone and Kenya with national elections, and also during small-scale disasters including disease outbreaks, and localised conflicts and crime. Reporters can also seek guidance on whether an event in their community is newsworthy enough to pursue.

Stories that need extra research, or are strong enough to be pitched to external media as features, are developed by Radar staff. This 'mentoring' approach builds reporters' capacity and means their work can reach beyond social media channels and can, occasionally, even generate income for the reporter. This simple model means people can share news and opinions from wherever they are in the world—from Kenya's Masai Mara or Sierra Leone's Freetown slums to the Himalayan foothills in rural northern India.

CASE STUDY: SIERRA LEONE

Seray Bangura is a disability rights activist working with Leonard Cheshire Disability International and was trained by Radar in 2012. Shortly after, he heard rumours that a tactile balloting system in Sierra Leone for people with visual impairment, funded by the UK and US governments, was going to be scrapped. He sent a news alert via SMS and the story was pitched by Radar to UK editors. The *Guardian*'s Global Development hub commissioned the story and Radar mentored and supported Seray to write an article on the issue (Bangura, 2012).

Radar tweeted the *Guardian* link and the story was picked up by the EU Observation Mission, who raised it as a concern in their official report on the election. Seray was paid for his article and his confidence swelled, inspiring him to write other stories for other outlets.

LOCAL REPORTERS—PROS AND CONS

The advantages of hyper-local reporters are that, when combined with the ease and inconspicuousness of mobile phones and mobile reporting, they can get news and information out of their communities swiftly. They are in the thick of the action, understand the local context, including local dialects, and have good connections with interviewees and spokespeople in their communities.

They can provide news alerts from areas the urban-centric correspondents miss, through being located in smaller towns and cities, slums and villages.

But their reports can also present problems.

Radar attempts to train accurate reporting and the importance of avoiding bias in its workshops but these are often only a few days long. In addition, the lack of face-to-face time with the citizen journalists means they are often open to bias. Some have only ever attended one initial training so if they are new to writing and journalism, they do not necessarily grasp fundamental concepts like neutrality.

This is especially true during elections or political crises, when personal opinions on candidates and parties are rife in the everyday lives of reporters—from discussions with family and friends to mainstream media to electioneering. Unfortunately, this is exactly the time when citizen journalists' reports could become of particular use to mainstream or international media.

And the most active reporters—considering none get paid (unless their stories are sold or commissioned by outlets to be expanded)—are those who are already engaged as community activists. They are therefore most likely to have their own agendas.

As we have seen in other political crises, activists can infiltrate social media and spread misinformation. This is why during crises, like that in Crimea in 2014, citizen journalists' updates must be treated with caution and treated as one of many sources rather than the basis for whole stories (Hauser, 2014).

Accordingly, when Radar's reporters sent stories about the Kenyan election of 2013, many had to be treated with caution to ensure online channels did not become the vessel through which reporters spread misinformation or hate speech, and subsequently exacerbate tension. Tainted by still-vivid memories of the post-election violence that led to the death of more than 1,000 people in 2007–2008, reports on electioneering and ties between political parties were discouraged (Klein, 2013).

Radar found a handful of community activists, who often had access to other training and resources, swiftly became the most prolific reporters. Their visibility perpetuated their success, and they were frequently relied upon, again and again, to provide stories and comment. Radar inadvertently re-created the power structure of a few speaking for many that it was attempting to challenge.

DEMOCRATISING NEWS: AT WHAT COST?

Citizen journalists cannot only put others in danger, they can also put themselves in danger by virtue of exposing wrongdoing. Fragile states—whether undergoing political repression or conflict—are especially high risk for both professional and citizen journalists (Holmes, 2013). Intelligence agencies, informants, and secret police can follow reporters in person while mobile and online surveillance can see and hear what they are communicating electronically (Morozov, 2011).

In his book *The Net Delusion* (2011), Morozov is skeptical that the internet is in fact helping to democratise authoritarian regimes and argues it is conversely a powerful tool for engaging in mass surveillance, political repression, and spreading nationalist and extremist propaganda. Citizen journalists leave leaders and politicians with what De Saulles and Horner (2011) describe as 'nowhere to hide'. But if there are not strong enough institutions to hold corrupt individuals or institutions to account, then the citizen journalists or whistleblowers responsible are at risk of intimidation, violence, and repression. Accordingly, citizen journalism organisations like Radar need to put robust safety mechanisms in place to protect citizen journalists at every stage of the media production process.

Radar's reporters can be anonymised and, as the organisation is registered in the UK, the information it receives remains in this jurisdiction. However, there is no time during initial training for adequate sensitization about the risks posed to the reporters on the ground. There is also no safety mechanism in place to deal with the legal repercussions if and when things do go wrong—such as intimidation, violence and repression, or lawsuits.

EMPOWERING, OR NOT

When dealing with more general non-political news, and despite challenges with verification, citizen journalism is generally viewed as empowering for opening up and 'democratising' media production. Using a low-tech mobile model like that developed by Radar means many everyday citizens come to realise they have power in their pocket with their phones, allowing them to communicate from anywhere about anything—all for the price of an SMS.

Girls and women, who are frequently excluded from news production, are encouraged to share their news and opinions, which can seem especially significant considering they are not always listened to in many of the society's where we train (Kenya, Sierra Leone).

It is widely accepted that women's engagement in politics is lacking, including in developing countries. The following was written by Liberian President Ellen Johnson Sirleaf in the 2008–2009 *State of the World's Women Report*:

> The Universal Declaration of Human Rights states that 'the authority of government is grounded in the will of the people'. Half, even more than half, of 'the people' are women. Yet for far too long, women's will, women's voices, women's interests, priorities, and needs have not been heard, have not been heard, have not determined who governs, have not guided how they govern, and to what ends. Since women are amongst the least powerful of citizens, with the fewest social and economic resources on which to build political power, special efforts are often needed to elicit and amplify their voice. (UNIFEM, 2008)

UNICEF was later merged into UN Women in 2011 but many see a continued lack of female voice in politics over the past five years. That's why Radar piloted an approach to ensure *at least* 50 per cent of participants in its training workshops were female, starting in Kenya in February 2013—in advance of national elections. Radar trained more than 120 new citizen journalists at eight workshops in Nairobi including Kibera Slum, Kajiado, Kisumu, and Mombasa. Of these, more than 60 were female. And yet on election day, an overwhelming majority of unprompted reports were from males. Radar's editorial hub in London had to proactively prompt female reporters via SMS, to check if they were safe, why they were not reporting, and to encourage them to report.

Whether it is a lack of confidence, social conditioning, or economic issues (such as a lack of access to household mobile phones or the money needed to top up credit), many women repeatedly went quiet once training was over and the reporting was to begin. Further research into why women engage with training but later disengage with reporting is needed.

As Spivak notes (1988), the labeling of groups in terms of their marginalisation is problematic anyway. Labeling women as 'marginalised' by Western NGOs, such as Radar, runs the risk of romanticising identity and national origins. This rewards those who are already privileged and upwardly mobile at the expense of those they proclaim to benefit—further disempowering the 'third world'.

The same could be said for multiple groups of people Radar aimed to benefit including people living with disability, slum dwellers, and the rural poor.

EXTRACTING NEWS

Many journalists thrive on seeing their work published and are keen to observe how the public receives it. Alongside being a matter of pride, especially after a challenging story which has taken time and effort to develop, feedback can help them improve. Unfortunately, feeding back is one of the greatest challenges when working with offline communities such as Radar's and thus increases the risk of 'extracting' news from communities, with little benefit for them.

In lieu of the reporter having an internet connection, feedback usually comprises an initial short message via SMS to acknowledge the report and then another to explain how it has been used and where. Occasionally, the second messages will outline next steps—such as questions for verification or instructions on how to develop the story.

For example, messages may simply say 'thank you for your story, it has now been published on Twitter' or 'congratulations, 10 people have liked your story on Facebook'. Because most feedback takes place on a case-by-case basis rather than via an automated system, there is space to tailor each message. This ensures each reporter feels they are being listened to. However, the downside is the amount of time it takes the editors in Radar's London hub to analyse each story and send each acknowledgement message. In time, the initial feedback message will be automated and then messages classified based on the type of next step they warrant—from 'good to go' to 'needs verification' to 'high risk' or 'worth saving for in-depth investigation' (such as a feature piece or film).

Of course, when reporters do have access to the Internet, links to their work are shared so they can see the final versions of their stories for themselves.

CONCLUSION

As citizen journalism is rarely remunerated, the people who engage are motivated enough to want to share their news. This means a number of citizen journalists are already activists, including political or those trained in campaigns and by NGOs, who lobby for their communities or on certain issues. It cannot be claimed, then, that these 'citizen journalists' are completely marginalized nor truly free from the bias of mainstream media journalists.

So while mobile technology can be an enabler for many people who are not engaged in traditional newsgathering, it is not a magic bullet that will solve all the challenges of modern-day newsgathering nor can it make up for decades of inequality in developing countries. However, it can facilitate participation and, in so doing, flip the power dynamic so that citizens become active creators and curators of news, not merely consumers or passive subjects in a correspondence that is carried out around them.

REFERENCES

About WIMN. (2014). Women in Media and News. Retrieved 14 February 2014, from http://wimnonline.org/about/.

Bangura, S. (2012). Sierra Leone scraps tactile voting system for elections. *The Guardian*. Retrieved 14 February 2014, from http://www.theguardian.com/global-development/2012/nov/16/sierra-leone-tactile-voting-elections.

Bartlett, R. (2010). Podcast: CNN mobile journalism event at the Frontline Club. journalism.co.uk. Retrieved 14 February 2014, from http://blogs.journalism.co.uk/2010/08/12/video-cnn-mobile-event-the-frontline-club/.

Cochrane, K. (2011). Why is British public life dominated by men? *The Guardian*. Retrieved 14 February 2014, from http://www.theguardian.com/lifeandstyle/2011/dec/04/why-british-public-life-dominated-men.

De Saulles, M., & Horner, D. (2011). The portable panopticon: Morality and mobile technologies. *Journal of Information, Communication and Ethics in Society, 9*(3), 206–216.

Hauser, J. (2014). A place for professional journalism in the age of the citizen journalist. Storyful Blog. Retrieved 14 February 2014, from http://blog.storyful.com/2014/03/30/a-place-for-professional-journalism-in-the-age-of-the-citizen-journalist/#.U0GR9K1dWRg.

Holmes, O. (2013). Running toward danger, Syria's citizens become journalists. Committee to Protect Journalists. Retrieved from 14 February 2014, from http://www.cpj.org/2013/02/attacks-on-the-press-on-syrias-citizen-journalists.php.

Klein, A. (2013). Citizen journalists report for the price of a text. BBC News. Retrieved 14 February 2014, from http://www.bbc.co.uk/blogs/blogcollegeofjournalism/posts/Citizen-journalists-report-for-the-price-of-a-text.

Kuypers, J. (2002). Press bias and politics. Westport, CT: Praeger.

Lee, E. (2013). News Corp. Acquires Video Startup Storyful for $25 Million. Bloomberg. Retrieved 14 May 2014, from http://www.bloomberg.com/news/2013–12–20/news-corp-buys-social-media-startup-storyful-for-25-million.html.

MacMillan, G. (2013). Guardian launches citizen journalism platform GuardianWitness. MediaWeek. Retrieved 14 February 2014, from http://www.mediaweek.co.uk/article/1178494/guardian-launches-citizen-journalism-platform-guardianwitness.

Maxwell Hamilton, J., & Jenner, E. (2003, September–October). The New Foreign Correspondence. Foreign Affairs. http://www.foreignaffairs.com/articles/59194/john-maxwell-hamilton-eric-jenner/the-new-foreign-correspondence.

Morozov, E. (2011). The net delusion: The dark side of internet freedom. New York: PublicAffairs.

Sambrook, R. (2010). Are foreign correspondents redundant? Reuters Institute for the Study of Journalism.

Silverman, C. (2014). Verification handbook. Verificationhandbook.com. Retrieved 14 February 2014, from http://verificationhandbook.com/book/chapter10.php.

Spivak, G. (1988). Can the subaltern speak? In C. Nelson & L Grossberg (Eds.), Marxism and the interpretation of culture (pp. 271–313). Urbana: University of Illinois Press.

UN Development Fund for Women (UNIFEM). (2008, September). Progress of the World's Women 2008/2009: Who Answers to Women? Gender & Accountability. Retrieved 14 February 2014, from http://www.refworld.org/docid/4a09773a2.html.

Vaidyanathan, R. (2012). Indian internet seeks the masses. BBC News. Retrieved 14 February 2014, from http://www.bbc.co.uk/news/business-16354076.

CHAPTER SEVENTEEN

New Approaches to Aggregation and Verification in Humanitarian Newsgathering and Coverage

CLAIRE WARDLE[1]

Social media have changed the way charities, NGOs, and humanitarian organisations communicate. Successful organisations were always good at nurturing their own 'audiences', reaching their supporters and volunteers via newsletters and other direct forms of communication. They also had the opportunity to reach wider audiences via the traditional news media who might cover their work—if they were able to get their attention! However, with the advent of social media these types of organisations are now able to connect with a range of different audiences quickly, easily, and, significantly, more clearly.

YouTube, Twitter, and Facebook all allow organisations to post frequent updates, including pictures from the field, updated statistics, inspiring quotes, and full-blown policy discussions via blog posts. These platforms also permit hyper-targeted messaging, from a fast-paced video on YouTube aimed at 'millennials'[2], to an Instagram 'takeover' by a 'mummy blogger' sent out to the field to witness for herself the work being done by an organisation, to a LinkedIn article aimed at potential donors, or to a blog post aimed at academics working on a specific issue. As a consequence of these opportunities now afforded to organisations, these platforms, in turn, have forced a much higher degree of transparency by organisations about their daily work, and the impact of that work on the communities they are attempting to help.

Social media were designed for peer-to-peer communication. Brands and organisations quickly recognised the power of these networks, but in almost all cases, individual users on social networks see more engagement and activity than 'corporate' accounts. Accounts of individual staff often draw large numbers of followers and interest, and play a different, but complementary, role to 'corporate' accounts. This recognition has also led organisations who wish to be successful in maximizing their presence in social media to highlight the activities of their individual staff. In so doing, even the most institutionalised organisations have become far more human.

Crucially, the networked element of all these platforms means that these organisations can reach new audiences. Previously, newsletters were sent to people who had already expressed an interest in the work of the organisation. Now an individual, having never even heard of the organisation or its work, can be so moved by a post on Facebook or Twitter that they share information with their own networks, who then share with their own and so on, allowing messages to travel at speed, reaching and, potentially impacting, many different audiences.

However, while the ability of organisations to connect directly with audiences via social media represents a fascinating shift, it has not replaced the role mainstream media plays in amplifying the work and key messages of a particular organisation. The mass media still has an incredibly important agenda-setting role, shaping the conversations and priorities of the political and cultural elite. Press officers at humanitarian organisations, as anywhere else, still crave column inches, airtime, and opportunities for spokespeople to be interviewed.

But it is not a case of social media versus mainstream media. In this chapter, I will be focusing on the increasingly important role social media plays, both in terms of connecting organisations with mainstream media, as well as allowing content created by NGOs to be used by the media. Journalists and media organisations are now just one of the many audiences organisations are targeting with social media. But unlike the targeted messaging used for other groups, the way social media is used within mainstream media is much more subtle and, ultimately, interesting.

TWITTER AS THE LITTLE BLACK BOOK

Back in 2011, Neal Mann, when working as the Digital News Editor at Sky News, tweeted this picture:

Credit: https://twitter.com/fieldproducer/status/147010379833282560

Mann is considered a pioneer of using social media for newsgathering. Maybe four screens could be considered excessive, but this picture shows the reality faced by many journalists today. They use multiple screens to monitor internal content management systems, the news wires, and social media feeds. Journalists are starting to look more like financial traders than journalists.

Although, for some, email still plays an important role, in this world of information overload, inboxes are increasingly groaning with press releases. More journalists have turned to Twitter to build relationships with press officers, and to listen out for announcements or discover story opportunities.

Journalists were some of the earliest to adopt social media for professional purposes. From January 2009, the moment the plane landed in the Hudson River and an eyewitness posted the infamous picture on Twitter (http://twitpic.com/135xa), those in the media profession started joining the social network. Journalists realised that news was increasingly starting to break on Twitter, and the first pictures and videos from a breaking news event were emerging on social networks. With journalists setting up camp here, the more savvy press officers realised they needed to be there too.

More advanced humanitarian organisations have invested in social media training for their press teams. Not just how to open a Twitter or Facebook account, but how to use accounts in a professional capacity, how to remain open and authentic, and not simply be a corporate mouthpiece. Team members have been taught to live-tweet from events and how to write speeches for senior management that include 'tweetable' sound bites no longer than 140 characters[3]. They have been taught how to take photos from the field, instantly tweet them and share them on Instagram and Facebook. They are able to curate social media content on Storify to share with the press as background and context. And they have been shown how to bring a situation to life using video via their mobile phones in the field. They have also been taught how to turn statistics into engaging infographics that will get picked up by the media.

One of the greatest strengths of these tools, particularly Twitter, is the way they have helped press officers build relationships with individual journalists, who otherwise would not have come into contact with each other. In Geneva, the press corps mingle with press officers for the major humanitarian organisations on a regular basis, but it is much harder to find ways to connect face to face with the photo editor at the *Wall Street Journal* in New York, or the online news editor at the *Guardian* in London. Twitter has enabled journalists and press officers to connect and build trusted relationships.

Rather than hiding behind 'corporate' social accounts, the most successful organisations have realised that the power of social media lies with individuals. A spokesperson can say things on Twitter that would not be appropriate on their 'corporate' account, for example, congratulating a journalist on the birth of her son or the fact that their favourite football team won an important match. The type of relationships that press officers have always had with journalists can be mimicked online. And those that have understood this have seen real benefits.

Here is an example of how these relationships can benefit both sides, which is played out on a very regular basis. Early morning a spokesperson tweets a statistic that is about to be included in a press briefing later in the morning. A journalist they have connected with on Twitter sends them a private message saying, 'This sounds interesting, can you send me more details as I'm looking for something to write for my column this afternoon?'. Alternatively, a journalist tweets that they are writing about a particular subject and a press officer who understands the power of listening on social media responds with a quote or additional information.

In the increasingly competitive environment in which many of these organisations work, being the one providing the main quote on a subject, or explaining the situation from their own perspective, is crucially important.

IMPACT OF SMARTPHONES IN THE FIELD

The smartphone has had just as much impact on the work of humanitarian organisations, in terms of communicating their messages, as social media. Indeed, the impact of each is inter-related with the other.

Many field officers now have some form of smartphone which allows them to 'make content out of process'. They have been trained to document their work, such as live-tweeting a day of providing vaccinations in a remote village, taking a time lapse video of a new field tent being constructed, or posting beautiful photos to Instagram.

A UNHCR Protection office in the field in Iraq took this set of photos in mid-August 2013. She happened to have a camera with her and, as she saw people swarming across the bridge, she took out her camera and started shooting. The photos were sent back to Geneva Headquarters on a Saturday and uploaded to Flickr and tweeted from the main @refugees account very quickly afterwards.

Credit: http://www.flickr.com/photos/unhcr/sets/72157635098748544/

By that afternoon, the photos were gaining traction with mainstream journalists, and over the next few days, the photos were seen in photo galleries on the BBC, Al Jazeera, and other locations, credited to UNHCR.

Credit: http://www.bbc.co.uk/news/world-middle-east-23745201

At that point there were no press photographers in the area. Everyone was caught off guard by the sudden influx of refugees over this border crossing. A private conversation I had with a BBC journalist confirmed that they would not have run with this story without pictures, and these photographs gave the story 'legs' which it would not have had otherwise, despite the agreed upon importance of the story.

Other staff, such as Andrew Harper (@And_Harper), who live-tweeted from the middle of the night as Syrian refugees crossed the border into Jordan, or Kathryn Mahoney (@nineteenfiftyone), whose stunning photos from a South Sudan refugee camp gained her more than 35,000 followers on Instagram, provide further good examples of how powerful content can resonate with general audiences, as well as demonstrating how it can pique the interest of journalists and editors.

Staff in the field are creating incredible content which they are sharing with their own, often small networks, and then these messages are being amplified by larger accounts within the same organisation, normally coordinated by a social media manager. And this content is playing a crucial role in connecting with the different types of audiences described above. Beautiful Instagram photos, for example, allow many new types of people to come into contact with the work being done by a particular organisation, while videos posted on Facebook can get 'liked' and shared'. Significantly, some of the most powerful visual content ends up also being used by the mainstream media.

SOCIAL MEDIA NEWS AGENCIES

An additional element to the relationship between organisations and the media are news agencies. Good press officers should always have strong relationships with editors at Reuters, AP, and AFP. But in this 'new' world there are companies such as Storyful, Demotix, and Newsflare, who are playing an increasingly interesting, and different, role. They are social media news agencies. Their sole job is to discover and verify social media content so that newsrooms can use that content with confidence.

These types of companies began to spring up around 2010 when it was evident that more and more breaking news content was appearing on the social web, but newsrooms were still too wary of using this type of content as they did not know how to verify the content or secure the rights. They act in a very similar way to the traditional agencies: they source content and newsrooms pay a monthly subscription to access this content.

The reason these organisations are interesting within this particular analysis is because organisations such as these know that NGOs and humanitarian organisations are creating content and placing it directly on social media channels such as YouTube or Twitter. In many cases, aid organisations have access to locations that journalists simply cannot get to. Films uploaded to YouTube or photos posted to Instagram by humanitarian organisations are, therefore, treated in the same way as pictures posted to Twitter by an eyewitness to a breaking news event. Knowing this, journalists at these agencies have alerts set up on certain accounts, such as an organisational YouTube account or a Twitter account of a field officer on the Syrian border. When new content is posted, these agencies look to see whether the content might have news value. If so, they run verification checks, knowing already that the content is very likely to be exactly as described, as it has been posted on a trusted account. Once it has been verified it is placed on the internal dashboards used by news clients to access the content, along with contact details attached, in case a newsroom wants to talk to the person who shot the footage.

This is an interesting model, as it requires NGOs and humanitarian organisations to think about these social media platforms as a conduit for getting content out to newsrooms. It prevents organisations having to reach out to separate newsrooms individually, and it also means content is more likely to reach newsrooms, who themselves do not have time or the inclination to set up alerts for all possible social accounts.

These social news agencies have also played a role in flagging up the types of content that aid organisations have that news organisations want. With ever-decreasing foreign budgets, aid organisations can no longer rely on news organisations sending a news crew out to the field. They are starting to learn the importance of creating their own content, which newsrooms can then use themselves.

What is arguably even more interesting, however, is the organisations, themselves, having to learn what media organisations want in terms of content. News websites want something different to TV news; radio editors want something different to the social media editor. Online editors want photo galleries where the photos are beautifully shot or show a news event not covered by anyone else. Television news editors want B-roll—the type of background footage that accompanies a voice-over during a news package. They want to hear from people directly affected by a situation, not a two-way interview. They want to hear the voices of the people who have been directly impacted. A newsroom, however, does not want a fully packaged piece with a professional voice over, but rather 'atoms'—bits of content they can drop into their own packages.

This has been a learning curve for many organisations who felt happier 'controlling' the message, and hoping it would get picked up by a wider audience. But what organisations are learning, particularly with YouTube, is that millennials want shorter, snappier video that they can share with their social networks, while live bloggers, as another example, want short videos and photos they can drop into their rolling coverage. As a result, the more sophisticated organisations are thinking more creatively about their YouTube presence to maximise the chances of effectively reaching different audiences.

THE HUMAN RIGHTS CHANNEL

A useful case study for examining the ways humanitarian organisations are having their content disseminated is the Human Rights Channel on YouTube managed by the organisation Witness (http://www.youtube.com/user/humanrights). It describes itself as "curating verified human rights video from citizens and activists around the world." They talk about citizen videos, but the channels include videos from activists as well as large organisations like UNHCR, MSF, or WFP.

The channel is curated by Storyful, one of the new social media agencies mentioned above. Storyful is responsible for adding videos to the playlist that they have found from activists and organisations around the world. The Storyful journalists have alerts set up for known accounts, and every time new footage is uploaded to YouTube they watch it, make an editorial decision about whether it fits the description of the Human Rights Channel, verify the video, and add it to the playlist.

It is an interesting model of work because some videos are so compelling they will also be added to the Storyful dashboard for paying clients to see. Even if there is no contemporary news value, they will be added to this Human Rights channel, which has its own audience of people who care about the topic. The 2013 Year in Review compilation video already had almost 100,000 views by the end of January 2014, a number helped by a mention on Upworthy, a site that shares items concerned with social good, and has a very significant online audience. (http://www. youtube.com/watch?v=Mil3zPB_S-4).

CONCLUSION

Social media have significantly changed the way humanitarian organisations interact with their audiences. Different platforms can be used to target different types of audiences, and the metric tools can provide very granular insights into the demographics of the people who click and share content.

Social media have, to a certain extent, levelled the playing field between different charities, NGOs, and humanitarian organisations. A striking, emotive piece of content will travel across the social web whether it was created by Amnesty International or a small charity in West Wales. Social media allow new audiences to see different types of content by different types of humanitarian organisations every day.

But what is perhaps most interesting is the way that social media have impacted upon the relationship between press officers and journalists. Successful press officers understand the importance of Twitter, in terms of listening out for opportunities to contribute to a story, suggesting story ideas, and, most important, in strengthening relationships with key journalists.

Taking Syria as an example, UNHCR currently has a large number of staff working inside Syria, as well as hundreds more working directly with Syrian refugees in Lebanon, Jordan, Turkey, Iraq, and Egypt, all of whom have stories to share. There have been many examples of organisations such as UNHCR, MSF, UNICEF, and WFP creating content within communities that has been picked up directly by the mainstream media and used in a variety of ways. This allows these organisations to be included and quoted in the mainstream media, thereby reaching large mass audiences, as well as using the same content to connect with their own audiences on their own social media platforms.

To be blunt, with overseas reporting budgets being slashed, although they may feel uncomfortable about this, newsrooms need humanitarian organisations more than ever, in terms of access and content. The smartest organisations recognize this and are actively training field staff to create the type of content that newsrooms want, using smartphones and lightweight digital technology.

Many people will look back at this period and see it as a time when 'viral' YouTube videos gave humanitarian organisations the ability to connect with new audiences in incredible ways. While there have been some powerful examples of this, for me, however, this period is about a far more subtle shift, when the combination of smartphones and social media, along with the simultaneous cuts in foreign reporting budgets, meant journalists and press officers started working together far more closely, using the informal mechanisms of social media to support one another's needs.

There are many other interesting questions that arise from this shift, in terms of the challenge to impartial reporting, the continued influence of primary definers drowning out other voices, and the persistent power of news values shaping what humanitarian organisations create in order to guarantee coverage. But it is still too early to study these as yet. These shifts are evolving every day, as more and more people are trained and case studies convince more people that they should be 'doing what that organisation is doing'. Let's wait and see how this plays out.

NOTES

1. Since 2009 the author has trained journalists and communications professionals at the BBC and UNHCR, as well as staff at other news organisations and NGOs to use social media to support their professional goals. Between 2012 and 2013, Claire also worked for the social media news agency Storyful. She is now the Senior Social Media Officer at UNHCR.
2. The term 'millennials' is used to describe the generation of people who reached adulthood around the year 2000.
3. Tweets can be no longer than 140 characters.

CHAPTER EIGHTEEN

Mobile Emergencies, Mobile Phones

The Hidden Revolution

IMOGEN WALL AND KYLA REID

When local news journalist Erel Cabatbat arrived in Tacloban in the central Philippines, hours after Typhoon Haiyan in November 2013, he was expecting to report on one of the biggest disasters ever to hit his country for his company, GMA. Instead, he found himself running an ad hoc family reunification service. Erel, who, as a reporter, had a working phone, found himself surrounded by survivors desperate to get a messages to loved ones. 'I have pages full of the numbers of people who begged me to text their families and let them know they were OK', he says. In particular, he remembers one doctor, covered in mud, who had walked the five miles to the airport in the hope of finding someone who could contact his children. 'I managed to send them text messages and posted on my Twitter account and they called me back and told me that they were coming to Tacloban to take him to safety.' As the BBC also reported, other journalists returned from reporting trips with hundreds of scraps of paper, on which were scrawled the numbers of relatives.

Anyone who visited Tacloban in the early days of the Typhoon Haiyan disaster can be in no doubt as to the crucial importance of mobile phones for those survivors. From the desperate pleas with outsiders to use their phones to text loved ones, to the use of generators everywhere to power phone-charging systems, and the massive popularity (once the network returned) of free SMS services, connectivity was clearly an overwhelming priority.

The importance of phones and connectivity for survivors in disasters is a phenomenon whose rapid growth is a corollary to the exploding demand for mobile services in the developing world. This has been extraordinary: according to the GSMA, the global trade association of the mobile industry, in Africa and South Asia the numbers of people owning a phone have grown 20% year-on-year. More people in developing countries now have access to a mobile phone than to basic sanitation or reliable electricity. And it is still accelerating: 130 million people in the developing world will become mobile service users every single year until at least 2017.

CONNECTIVITY AND DISASTERS: A GROWING NEED

A mobile phone is now seen as a daily necessity for millions of people. In a crisis, however, it is increasingly becoming a lifesaving service. Statistics around the demand for mobile phone services in disasters are scarce, but remarkably consistent. A study of call patterns around the 7.2 Oaxaca earthquake in Mexico in 2012, which caused severe shaking in four major cities, reveals that not only was there a large spike in use immediately after the quake, but also that the spike increased in proportion to closeness to the epicentre, implying that the more affected people were, the more they wanted to communicate. The researchers also found that highly connected users tended to reach out to people with whom they were not normally in contact, thus also increasing the number of calls.

In addition to such studies, the anecdotal experience is remarkable. In 2013, for example, a team from Vodafone travelled to areas in Mindanao devastated by Typhoon Bopha, a category 5 storm that killed more than 1,000 people and caused widespread damage including to the mobile network infrastructure. Their Instant Network re-established mobile capacity for a radius of 5 kilometres. The update of the service once established was immediate, and Vodafone reported that more than 1,000 SMS per minute were being carried by the system, which was operating at maximum capacity from the very start. Vodafone reported that when the team returned to the Philippines in 2013 to support the response to Typhoon Haiyan, the local community felt the network was so important they siphoned fuel out of surviving cars to keep the generator powering the system running.

The demand for mobile phone services by disaster-affected communities should not be a surprise. Increasingly, mobile technology is the fastest, cheapest way to convey basic information: I'm alive, I'm trapped, we need water. SMS and social media platforms are the most efficient way to share information to many people simultaneously so they are also very effective More profoundly, mobile phones are also increasingly central to a survivor's capacity to self-organise: to access the information that will drive their decision making and the help they need to survive, whether that be help locating a loved one, organising a rescue, receiving financial support from a relative overseas, or finding out which services (hospitals) are available to them. As the Red Cross noted in their 2013 *World Disasters Report*, the reason phones really matter is because they are changing the ways that communities are able to prepare for, survive, and respond to crises. Mobiles matter because they facilitate community organisation and connect survivors to sources of help across the world, increasing their ability to be the architects of their own recovery.

This is vitally important as it has long been known that, in disasters, most first response work is done not by professionals (local or international) but by the survivors themselves. From earthquake survivors dug from the rubble by friends to flood victims pulled from the waters by neighbours, an estimated 90% of lives at risk in disasters are saved by the local population. Increasing their capacity to connect, therefore, is increasing their capacity to save lives.

Those who understand best what value mobiles have in disasters, and how to use their services most effectively, are almost always local. During the devastating 2010 earthquake in Haiti, local DJ Carel Pedre, whose station, Radio 1, was the only one undamaged by the quake, began broadcasting within hours of the disaster. Pedre, already a sophisticated user of social media, was quickly inundated with requests from Haitians inside and outside of the country for his help in locating loved ones. These requests came predominantly via Twitter, Facebook, SMS, and phone calls, and through survivors coming in person to the station. He and his team developed an ad hoc system of collecting requests, investigating, and then sharing every evening what they had found, via Facebook, Twitter, and radio broadcast, helping thousands find out what had happened to people they loved. Without access to functioning phones and internet connections, none of this work would have been possible. A further lesson for humanitarians lies in the sophistication, complexity, and context-specific nature of Carel's model: much of the innovation in this sector is coming not from Silicon Valley or the West but from local communicators and companies whom communities already trust, and who understand how local communications networks function.

In addition to SMS and calls, mobile phones are increasingly the portal through which disaster survivors connect to the information services available on the internet, including social media. In recent years, platforms such as Facebook and Twitter have emerged as crucial to the way in which those affected by disaster ask for help, and find out if loved ones are still alive and where they are. So important are these platforms to disaster management in the Philippines, for example, that the government has designated official hashtags to be used by tweeters—#rescueph—for those in need of immediate assistance.

Building on this, specialist online tools to meet specific needs such as survivor location and reunification have been developed, for example, Google Person Finder. This is a simple online platform that allows those looking for loved ones to register a missing person profile and search an existing database, and those with news (including survivors themselves) to upload status information. All of these activities can be undertaken via SMS. Google Person Finder was developed as part of the response to the Haiti earthquake and is now available in 40 languages. Google Person Finder was launched in Japan within two hours of the 2011 tsunami and earthquake; 90 days later, more than 610,000 profiles of survivors and missing individuals had been uploaded. An additional feature was added in Japan when developers realised how much survivor information was actually being shared via public lists in evacuation centres. Using mass media, Google asked those in the centres to take photos of the lists with their phones and upload them to the site—10,000 pictures came in and the data was uploaded by volunteers.

CONNECTIVITY AND DISASTERS:
THINKING BEYOND COMMUNICATION

Humanitarians tend to think of mobile phones primarily as tools of communication. Evidence from developing countries, however suggests that this is too narrow a view. The most obvious example of this is the dramatic increase of mobile money, and the use of phones as a way of accessing and managing cash, especially in the developing world. Of the 219 mobile money services available in 84 countries at the end of 2013 (a year-on-year increase of 22%), 52% were in sub-Saharan African. Increasingly, services that can be paid for using mobile money include basic humanitarian resources such as water, electricity, and transport, as well as the capacity to transfer money from user to user. Services are becoming increasingly interoperable, meaning that money can be sent from one service provider to another seamlessly. Moving towards mobile-based cash transfers may also lead to improved security and efficiency within the humanitarian system, whilst empowering those affected to make their own financial decisions and buy goods within their communities, thus supporting local economic recovery. This area is still in its infancy but is growing quickly: for example, in December 2013, United Nations Development Programme (UNDP) entered into a partnership with local mobile operator Smart Communications to roll out mobile-based cash for work programming, with plans to scale to 50,000 participants in affected areas. Mobile vouchers and cash transfers are being increasingly used for food assistance, with the World Food Programme (WFP) aiming to have a third of its assistance delivered digitally by 2015. New partnerships between the mobile industry and humanitarian organisations will be required in order to scale these kinds of initiatives.

Mobile money services will also have increasing ramifications for the role of diasporas in disaster response, as the capacity to transfer money across borders becomes greater. In February 2014, two mobile money operators in Rwanda and Tanzania (Tigo Cash and Tigo Pesa, both owned by Millicom International Cellular) launched the first cross-border mobile money services. This follows the partnership in 2011 of Vodafone and Western Union, also in Tanzania, to allow customers to transfer and receive money from overseas. According to one study in Tanzania, carried out by InterMedia for the Bill and Melinda Gates Foundation, sending and receiving remittances is the most popular application of mobile money services in the country (the second is saving, an important consideration in resilience and the capacity of families to cope with sudden emergencies). Similar services are also already in operation in Asia. Given that remittances already outstrip official overseas aid in every country in Africa (in Somalia remittances are worth $2 billion annually, compared to the $1 billion entering the country as aid), the importance of international mobile banking transfers (often cheaper and faster than traditional remittance channels) to disaster response will only increase. In addition, Bodomo's research carried out in 2012 found that remittance money is faster, more flexible, and more likely to reach the end user than official development assistance (ODA).

There are also likely to be many other ways in which mobile services and data are important to those surviving and responding to disasters, about which there is insufficient research. Among Syrian refugees, for example, there is also anecdotal evidence that phones are used as a way of collecting and carrying photos of home: a critically important psychological function for those who have been displaced. In Bangladesh, when the Rana Plaza clothing factory collapsed in 2013 killing more than 1,000, the numbers of the mobile phones found on the bodies were used to identify those dead without ID cards. Additionally, the opportunities presented by mobile "big data"—for example, anonymised call detail records (CDR) to determine displacement patterns around a disaster epicentre—could add significantly to the ability of humanitarian responders to predict where displaced populations are going and better allocate assistance accordingly. These opportunities are being explored by academic institutions, humanitarian organisations, and mobile network operators alike, with a growing body of supporting evidence, as demonstrated by the Orange Data for Development Challenge and the work of the Flowminder Foundation, who specialise in analysis of telecoms data for humanitarian purposes, in Haiti.

As mobile-based services become integral to the daily business of living, the connectivity that underpins telecommunications is becoming increasingly important to all aspects of a response. In the Philippines, for example, disease surveillance and health monitoring is heavily dependent on SMS. During the response to Typhoon Haiyan in 2013, health responders found that the lack of mobile services after the disaster (mobile infrastructure was very badly damaged) was seriously inhibiting their ability to identify and respond to outbreaks of disease.

MEETING THE NEED: CHALLENGES FOR RESPONDERS

When a disaster like a typhoon hits, mobile operators face formidable challenges: attending to the needs of staff caught up in the aftermath, restoring networks—which can include considerable logistical challenges—and coping with the massive demand for mobile services. As Typhoon Haiyan showed when it hit the Philippines in November 2013, even the most prepared countries and mobile companies can be overwhelmed. To meet the telecoms' needs of the affected community in future emergencies, mobile phone companies and humanitarians will need to build strong working partnerships, starting well in advance of a catastrophe.

Preparation, and the application of humanitarian thinking to mobile industry growth also means considering those social groups who can't access phones. A key challenge at present even before a disaster is the fact that not everyone in a crisis zone has access to a phone even in normal circumstances. Some may be in an area out of network coverage, some may be unable to afford a phone, others may be constrained by illiteracy. Other barriers are more complex: 74% of married women without phones told GSMA researchers in 2012 that they couldn't have one because their husbands would not allow it. That this finding derives from research including more than 2,500 women from a wide range of developing countries (Egypt, India, Papua New Guinea, and Uganda) suggests this is not necessarily a culturally limited phenomenon.

Supporting mobile operators and the wider eco-system to tackle the digital divide is of critical importance to ensuring that the next billion have access to connectivity and the services and potentially life-saving information it provides.

The challenges faced in conflict environments and disasters generated through war are profoundly different and will require serious consideration. In some contexts, phone companies are owned by parties to conflict and used for political ends. From the alleged use of SMS to incite violence in Kenya during the 2008 elections to the Ethiopian government's shutting down SMS service to inhibit the organisational capacity of the opposition, parties to conflict have understood and exploited the power of telecoms for many years. State interference with the mobile networks was well documented during the Arab Spring, serving as a reminder that while mobile technology can have a profound social and economic impact, it can also be manipulated for more nefarious purposes. Such efforts have become ever more sophisticated, most notably in Syria where concerns around the use of government telecoms services to track and target opposition members led the US government to impose sanctions against the state-owned Syriatel mobile service provider in 2012. In some conflict environments, such as South Sudan, mobile network equipment itself has been targeted because of its perceived value as critical infrastructure.

Even without such manipulation of the service, research has recently demonstrated that simply the presence of a functioning mobile network can increase incidents of conflict. A paper published in 2013 by two Cambridge academics found that availability of cell phone coverage 'significantly and substantially' increases the probability of violent conflict, as it allows the groups involved to overcome collective action and coordination challenges. This is perhaps unsurprising—that phones increase the capacity of communities to coordinate does not imply that that coordination is necessarily for positive ends—but such research raises ethical considerations for mobile and technology companies and humanitarians alike as they consider the impacts of improved access.

Issues around data protection and risk mitigation also become particularly acute in conflict contexts. Any projects involving tracking movement of populations via mobile data, creation of inadvertent mobile number databases (e.g., as a result of collecting this data when registering refugees), or projects that ask for information to be submitted via SMS will need to think carefully about security, protection, and risk management.

WHAT NEEDS TO HAPPEN?

The changes outlined in this chapter are profound and ongoing. Their implications are not yet fully understood, either by the mobile industry or by humanitarians. However, what is becoming increasingly recognised by a multitude of actors is that restoration of telecommunication services needs to be recognised as a humanitarian priority. This will require an increased investment in preparedness and partnerships on the part of MNOs and humanitarian actors, with government support and involvement to ensure that when required, these networks and partnerships are resilient, dependable, and effective. There are strong examples of the benefits of humanitarians working closely with the private telecommunications sector before a disaster hits. In Turkey, local MNO Turkcell has been working closely with UNDP and other local and national response agencies on expanding their portfolio of disaster response services following the 2011 Van Earthquake, and holding drills and simulations to test network restoration plans and partnerships. Prior to the 2013 Typhoon Haiyan response, Filipino MNOs and their humanitarian and government counterparts were brought together in a series of workshops and forums to share response strategies and learn about respective capacity, roles, and operating principles. The impact of bringing these parties together ahead of a disaster was demonstrated in new collaborations and improved information sharing between local carriers, the GSMA, United Nations Office for the Coordination of Humanitarian Affairs (UNOCHA), WFP, the Emergency Telecommunications Cluster, and others.

For their part, mobile operators will need to evaluate what a changing climate and vulnerability to disaster means not only to their infrastructure but also to the types of services they offer to support their customers and responders. They will also need to build the organisational capacity required to meet the challenges ahead, for example, preparing network engineers to cope psychologically with the demands of working in a disaster zone. Preparing for and responding to a disaster is a matter for governments as well as mobile service providers: regulators may have a key role in leading the sector. In Japan, the government is funding a project focussed on building a resilient and reliable communications infrastructure following the 2011 earthquake and tsunami. International cooperation is also important: the Japan project includes studying and learning from similar efforts in Taiwan.

Humanitarian actors will need to adapt to the fundamental changes that growing connectivity has on the way those affected by disasters communicate and access information during crises and work to understand how this reality impacts their activities and partnerships both locally and globally. Fundamentally, learning how to apply humanitarian principles in this emerging sector, especially the importance of meeting the needs of the most marginalised (in this instance those with no or limited access to services), is critical for mobile phone companies and humanitarians alike. As mobile phones become central to the daily life of the majority of human beings, so their services will increasingly become in crisis situations a matter of life and death. This is a reality to which humanitarians, mobile phone companies, governments, and media now have no choice but to adjust.

BIBLIOGRAPHY

#RescuePH: Tweeting in the flood. (2013, 20 August). Al Jazeera.

Appleby, L. (2012). Connecting the last mile: The role of communications in the great Japan Earthquake. *Internews*.

Bodomo, A. (2013, December). African diaspora remittances are better than foreign aid funds. *World Economics, 14*(4).

Cash and Vouchers for Food. (2012, April). Organisational brochure, World Food Programme.

Dissanayake, S. (2013, 11 November). Scrawling messages of survival from Tacloban. BBC News.

Frias-Martinez, E., Frias-Martinez, V., & Moumni, B. (2013). Characterising social response to urban earthquakes using cellphone network data. UbiComp Adjunct Proceedings of the 2103 ACM Conference on Pervasive and Ubiquitous Computing. Adjunct Publication, pp. 1199–1208.

Gardside, J. (2014, 24 October). Vodafone foundation creating instant mobile networks for disaster areas. *The Guardian*.

Hollenbach, F., & Pierskalla, J. (2013, May). Technology and collective action: The effect of cell phone coverage on political violence in Africa. *American Political Science Review, 107*(2), 207–224.

Manicad, J. (2013, 10 November). 'Buhi Kami Tanan': Yolanda survivors send messages to loved ones. GMA News.

Millicom launches world's first international mobile money service with currency conversion. (2014, 24 February). Business Wire.

Mobile cash system goes live in Tacloban. (2013, 23 December). Press release, UNDP.

Mobile Money in Tanzania: Use, Barriers and Opportunities. (2013, February). Intermedia and the Bill and Melinda Gates Foundation.

Mobile Technologies in Emergencies. (2012). Vodafone Foundation and Save the Children.

Obama unveils tech sanctions against Iran and Syria. (2012, 23 April). BBC News.

Quist-Arcton, O. (2008, 20 February). Text message used to incite violence in Kenya. NPR.

SMS ban lifted in Ethiopia after two years. (n.d). *Balancing Act Africa, 374.*

Torres, I. (2013, 13 February). Japan to learn from Taiwan in disaster proofing telecoms. Japan Daily Press.

Wall, I. (2013, March). *Still Left in the Dark?* Policy paper #6, BBC Media. Action Humanitarianism in the Network Age.

World Disasters Report 2013. (2013). International Federation of the Red Cross.

Conclusion

CHAPTER NINETEEN

Humanitarianism, Communications, and Change

Final Reflections

GLENDA COOPER AND SIMON COTTLE

When Michael Buerk revealed to the world the extent of famine in Korem, Ethiopia, in 1984, his startling report became perhaps the biggest story that the BBC did in the 1980s until the fall of the Berlin Wall (Simpson, 1998). His seven-minute report contained only his own voice and that of a white doctor (Cooper, 2007); the video rushes were carried back to London, as Buerk wrote and rewrote his script on the night flight from Kenya. The result however was astonishing. As Franks writes: "In an era before satellite, social media and YouTube, the BBC report went viral—being transmitted by more than 400 television stations worldwide" (Franks, 2013).

The iconic imagery of the Buerk report still overshadows humanitarian reporting today. But the world in which one man told an amazing story, able to keep it as an exclusive as he travelled back across the world, has changed. Today, as this collection shows there are many more channels for such stories to be told through, and many different types of storytellers. Journalists and aid agencies are no longer the sole gatekeepers to such information.

Instead we have seen how citizens have taken on the role of witness, how NGOs have transformed themselves into storytellers, and how journalists such as CNN's Anderson Cooper have abandoned traditional approaches of objectivity in order to intervene themselves. Edited highlights of Cooper's career on YouTube (https://www.youtube.com/watch?v=aosNAGt3AxQ) show him rescuing a small boy from a mob in Haiti, taking on a US senator during Hurricane Katrina, and being attacked on the streets in Egypt; Cooper himself wrote in a blog about his actions in Haiti of stepping outside the journalist role: "No one else seemed to be helping him [the boy]" (http://ac360.blogs.cnn.com/2010/01/18, anderson-in-the-midst-of-looting-chaos/).

These arguments are nothing new: the debate about journalists as objective onlookers (or not) was discussed at the time of Buerk, and reach back to Frederick Forsyth's coverage of Biafra in the 1960s. User-generated content—that most current of media obsessions—can be traced back to events such as the Kennedy assassination or even letters to the editor.

But what differs today is the volume and the speed of information that can be relayed to a globalized audience. How does that affect the kind of story told—and crucial for humanitarian issues, how does that affect help given or donations made to those in the most desperate of conditions?

The increased use of innovation and innovative partnerships between technology companies and humanitarians offers a real chance to reveal to the rest of the world who needs relief and when. So the widespread cover up of the Bengal famine of 1943–1944, in which 10 million are believed to have died is almost unthinkable in an interconnected world like today's—although not quite.

Many of the chapters in this collection focus on the breakthroughs that such technology has achieved. In this new media ecology, significant new players have been introduced. Some of the most exciting developments, analysis of tweets, and other social media information help accelerate the assessment of disaster damage and needs during real time (Meier, chapter 15), while a simple mobile phone message can be a fast, cheap, effective way to convey the most vital of basic information (Wall and Reid, chapter 18).

For those whose role is to help tell the stories of those caught up in humanitarian crises, the consequence of such changes in the NGO-journalist space have opened potential access to international news (Sambrook, chapter 3; Conneally chapter 4; Abbott, chapter 13); the use of wide-ranging tools such as Pinterest, Instagram, and Storify have helped explain to more diverse audiences the issues at stake (Wardle, chapter 17). Start-ups such as Radar (Klein, chapter 16) have made real efforts to put the power of storytelling in the hands of citizens rather than 'fireman' reporters or even NGOs with their own agendas, empowering ordinary people to describe what is important to them. At the other end of the scale WITNESS, with its celebrity backers such as Peter Gabriel and VH1, and YouTube channel can challenge social injustice on a worldwide stage (Allan, chapter 14).

Yet it would be wrong to write off traditional journalism, which has evolved and adapted to this new media ecology. Journalists, too, have learned to use social media to their advantage; like NGOs, smartphones and Twitter are increasingly used in the field to send back instantaneous reports, while more sophisticated verification methods and use of social media news agencies have given journalists access to more material that they can use as part of their role to explain and set information in context (Wardle, chapter 17). For many NGOs and citizen ournalists, using social media to make a traditional media outlet take notice of their campaign has been vital.

Despite these new developments, there are still old tensions. The internal NGO opposition between fundraising and development remains as acute as it was back in 1977 when Lissner first described it (Cooper, chapter 5)—if anything 'Consumer Aid' appears to be on the rise. The work that Dogra, Orgad, and Seu (chapters 8, 9, 12) describe in this volume shows that NGOs often still depend on traditional images of suffering to 'sell' stories—and we as the public still respond to them, although only in the short term (Franks, chapter 11). And an increasingly competitive marketplace, in a world suffering an economic downturn, means that twenty years after the Red Cross Code was first implemented to ensure dignity in portrayal of the suffering, we still see advertisements today from multinational, reputable NGOs which are transgressing, if not the letter of the code, certainly the spirit. And wider cultural shifts in how we, the public, respond to such images in a 'post-humanitarian age' also diminish our capacity to empathise and respond in ethical, in contrast to self-focused, ways (Chouliaraki, chapter 10).

So what can we take from this collection of chapters which cover academic, practitioner, and journalistic outlooks? What do they suggest that we need to consider about the future of humanitarian communications?

1. HUMANITARIANISM IN GLOBAL CONTEXT IS CHANGING

Humanitarianism in the twenty-first century has become an increasingly contested terrain. Its ideals, ethos, and practices now encompass differing positions of principle and a growing myriad of organisational aims and perspectives (Cottle, chapter 1; Kent, chapter 2). Humanitarianism also overlaps but sometimes exists in some tension with human rights advocacy and the wider analysis of human security in a globalising world. The mega-trends of globalisation, including economic interdependency and market meltdowns, environmental despoliation and climate change, as well as late modern forms of conflict such as 'new wars' in failed and failing states, transnational terrorism and Western interventionism all contribute to or cause humanitarian crises and catastrophes. These violent conflicts, further, have positioned humanitarians (as well as journalists) at increased risk and deliberately in targeted harm's way.

Today's global challenges converge in many current humanitarian crises, exacerbating the abuse of human rights and contributing to the contemporary condition of human insecurity around the globe (Duffield, 2001, 2007; Kaldor, 2007; Beck, 2009). It is also essential, we think, to keep the multidimensional and mutating character of humanitarian crises and catastrophes clearly in view if we are to avoid dissimulating the complex local-global interconnections and inequalities involved. We are thereby in a stronger position to recognise and respond to the different roles and responsibilities of different media within humanitarian crises as they spill across borders and unfold over time. These and other processes converging in new humanitarian crises will become exacerbated if remedial actions are not forthcoming in the global future (Kent, chapter 2).

It is also important to properly ground and theorise the current deployment and future potential of humanitarian communications within today's global context if we are not to fall into the unthinking trap of technological (communications) determinism —proffering simple technological fixes to deep-seated and complex world problems. New technologies of communication are deployed and shaped in humanitarian practice and they can be directed at different ends for diverse political reasons. They are put to work and conditioned by, for example, professional practices, organisational logics, and available resources. Their increased centrality and exciting capabilities have yet to be fully recognised and leveraged across global-local contexts and in respect of the often complex dynamics of humanitarian crises' reactions and responses.

2. COMMUNICATIONS ENTER INTO HUMANITARIAN DISASTERS THROUGH AN INCREASINGLY COMPLEX AND OVERLAPPING GLOBAL MEDIA ECOLOGY

Whether produced by poverty, climate change, food and water shortages, population movements, virulent pandemics, or new wars and terrorism, humanitarian crises today become signalled in (and variously shaped by) their representations in today's complex media and communications ecology—an ecology that is itself increasingly globalised and encompassing (Cottle, 2009, 2011). Satellites in space can monitor acts of inhumanity and atrocity around the globe, as can social media on the ground in interaction with telephony, the Internet, and 24/7 news broadcasters. This global communication ecology can thereby play its part in the international community's 'responsibility to protect' (R2P), alerting the UN and the world's nations to their obligation to safeguard populations from war crimes, genocide, ethnic cleansing, and crimes against humanity.

But contemporary media and communications can also perform a less progressive or benevolent part in communicating humanitarian crises (Cottle, chapter 1). They can, for example, shape the "new Western way of war," (Shaw, 2005) in which democratic governments, sensitive to Western public opinion and images of their maimed or dead military in national news media, seek to transfer risks (e.g., via high-altitude bombing) and thereby increase civilian casualties and deaths—so-called collateral damage. The media's 'silent moral scream' also unwittingly facilitates the deliberate killing of civilians under the blanket of news media invisibility in hidden wars and conflict-based humanitarian crises. And so too can today's interconnected global communication networks be put to morally repugnant ends when deployed in image wars deliberately enacting atrocious acts against humanitarian hostages.

Today's media and communications ecology we also contend is not usefully interrogated through an anachronistic dualism of 'old' and 'new' media because both are now intimately interconnected in and through today's new communication networks. If we are to better appraise communication performance and capacity and leverage their future potential in respect of humanitarian crises (anticipating, signalling, coordinating, mobilizing, responding, mitigating, rebuilding) we need to understand these interconnected capabilities and also to innovate when useful new communication tools—as was demonstrated, for example, in the Haitian earthquake disaster response (Nelson, Sigal, & Zambrano, 2011; Crowley & Chan, 2011). This is no time, then, for unhelpful position taking or dualistic thinking (Cottle, 2013), whether in respect of 'old' and 'new media', or indeed a bifurcated politics that remains unremittingly critical of 'mainstream' media representations on the one hand, and uncritically celebratory of 'alternative' communications and their enhanced capacity for connectivity, on the other. Both the complexity of today's global communication ecology and the complexity of contemporary humanitarian crises played out at a global-level demand that we fully appraise communications in their interrelated and fast-moving capabilities.

3. NEW TECHNOLOGY WILL HELP DELIVER AID— BUT THERE ARE LIMITATIONS

The growing connectivity via mobile phone networks and the use of new technologies such as the Micromappers' microtasking platform during Typhoon Yolanda/Haiyan (Meier, chapter 15) undoubtedly means that user-generated content and new technologies can help NGOs to pinpoint where aid is needed and the type of relief may be increased.

Meier points out that traditional means of gathering data in crisis situations often have inherent biases, inaccuracies, and misinformation in them—so suspicion of user-generated content as unreliable in comparison may be misguided. Using the case study of Typhoon Yolanda, even if 0.25% of tweets were useful and accurate and 3.5% of images posted to Twitter, that still represented 600 geotagged tweets and 180 geotagged images.

Volunteers helped to map these tweets and images in real time, leading to better information being deployed more rapidly. Meanwhile people are helping themselves as Wall and Reid illustrate in chapter 18: turning to their phones to try to contact friends, families, and authorities in emergencies, to access official sources of information and also—important—using the devices to send money to where it is needed quickly.

But many of these computer models are still very much in their infancy technically speaking. The best of models will not work without strong leadership and enlightened policymaking. Meier talks of the issue of finding a 'needle in a haystack' when sifting through tweets and social media updates; as more people use social media, more sophisticated algorithms will be needed.

Issues around privacy and security remain unresolved for those who do wish to tweet or SMS information about their situation during disasters—although one of the biggest problems may simply be encouraging the public of the need to provide user-generated content when a disaster happens. At present many of these tools are simply not well known enough to have the required impact.

It is also easy to forget in a developed world that while the use of phones, particularly smartphones, has increased dramatically in recent years, there is still a sizeable population who do not have access to phones. While using phones to communicate messages quickly is something that should be encouraged, it will not be able to reach everyone, and those without telephonic access should not be discriminated against.

4. MORE DIVERSE VOICES WILL BE HEARD—BUT THAT DOES NOT MEAN MORE DIVERSE STORIES

Tom Glocer of Reuters admitted after the 2004 tsunami that none of Reuters' correspondents or stringers were on the beach when the wave hit—they were dependent on the stills and videos of ordinary people for eyewitness accounts of the event (Glocer, 2006).

Nearly a decade on, the photograph-sharing app Instagram logged nearly 1.3 million pictures of Hurricane Sandy either tagged #sandy, #hurricanesandy, or #Frankenstorm (Taylor, 2012). It's been argued there's been a massive paradigm shift "in which once the media was the center of the universe and now the user is the center of the universe" (Robinson & De Shano, 2011, p. 977).

The use of Twitterfeeds by mainstream media, replication of blogs by newspaper websites, and use of tweets both in newspapers and broadcast media means that the eyewitness role once taken as a right by journalists is no longer necessarily the case. The success of start-ups like Radar (Klein, chapter 16) and the combination of NGOs and beneficiaries to tell stories (Scarff, chapter 7) has led many to believe that we are increasingly hearing from more diverse voices.

Undoubtedly in many cases this is true; Buerk's Korem piece speaking only to an MSF doctor is unthinkable these days. As Robinson (2009) details in her work on Hurricane Katrina, and Russell (2007) in her work on the 2005 French riots, citizen journalists and bloggers have acted as a corrective to mainstream media coverage of disasters and crises. The use of channels such as WITNESS's YouTube channel has encouraged abuses of human rights to be aired in ways that they simply could not have been done before (Allan, chapter 14).

Yet social media has its drawbacks too. For journalists the benefits of using such material are often clear: it is usually donated for free. The problem is that the sheer volume can leave them overwhelmed as to where to turn to in order to access the most useful material. As Malachy Browne of the social media news agency Storyful sums up the problem: "[It] is like being Superman, you can hear everyone's voices, but you need to know which ones to listen to" (Hanska-Ahy, 2013, p. 436).

For journalists under time pressure and with limited verification resources the result can be that the voices that they tend to listen are those who already occupy a privileged position. A recent paper by Lin, Keegan, Margolin, and Lazer, who looked at tweets around the US election, concluded despite the potential for social media to create larger public squares with more diverse voices speaking, "occasions for large-scale shared attention appear to undermine this deliberative potential by replacing existing interpersonal social dynamics with increased collective attention to existing 'stars'" (2014).

Added to that the kinds of disasters that are privileged by the use of social media tend to be the rapid-onset disasters: exactly the ones that NGOs have complained for years that journalists spend too much time on already. Twitter, Facebook, Instagram, and Flickr lend themselves to the dramatic over the chronic; the earthquake over the long-term famine—it is not an accident that the disasters we have seen framed through the lens of user-generated content and social media are Typhoon Haiyan/Yolanda and the Haitian earthquake rather than the East Africa famine.

NGOs are aware of this. For example, the Save the Children UK campaign #hiddencrisis tried to counter this by setting up a Twitter event for the West African hunger crisis with the then–Sky News digital media editor Neal Mann and Storyful, to plot Mann and Save's journey across Burkina Faso, while Oxfam GB authorised a "Twitter takeover" of their feed in March 2013 by Hasan, who had taken refuge in the Zaatari camp in order to focus attention on the longtime plight of displaced people in the Syrian conflict (Cooper, 2013).

But the fact remains that 'famine' tweets are rare—and user-generated content in long-running conflict, which does not relate to a sudden event does not get into the mainstream media (apart from rare projects such as the Guardian Witness project). The very technology which can bring hidden disasters to a connected world may militate against such disasters being heard in the maelstrom of online traffic.

5. RAISING MONEY IS EASIER—BUT THE CONTINUING RISE OF CONSUMER AID RAISES WORRYING QUESTIONS

Back in the 1960s, charities had a rather diffident attitude to fundraising. It's hard to imagine it now, but Oxfam used to send out only two mailings a year to its circulation list, one at Christmas and it was considered impolite to ask for money in the same letter as saying thank you (interview with Elizabeth Stamp, cited in Benthall, 1993, p. 57).

Compare the situation now where donations can be made by PayPal or send-ing an SMS in seconds. According to one Twitter-tracking service, 2.3 million tweets included the words 'Haiti' or 'Red Cross' between 12 and 14 January 2010 The Twitter account for the Red Cross, which had been adding 50–100 followers a day before the quake, added 10,000 within three days and during that time, donations to the Red Cross had exceeded $8 million (Evans, 2010). It wasn't just Twitter. Oxfam America's Facebook fan base jumped from 35,000 to 250,000 during Haiti. This resulted in $1.5 million raised within 48 hours (Byrne, 2010).

The Disasters Emergency Committee put out a press release during their 2013 Syria appeal stating that for the first time more than half of donations had come via digital sources (http://www.dec.org.uk/appeals/syria-crisis-appeal/press-release/record-digital-gifts-to-dec-syria-crisis-appeal). Although this is likely to reflect the fact that it was early in the appeal, it makes clear the importance of PayPal—the ease with which donations can be made without reaching for a wallet.

The growth of online does not mean conventional means of donation should not be overlooked, however; the final figures for the DEC Philippines appeal later that year showed 25% of donations coming via the DEC website, 9% via PayPal and only 3% via SMS (personal communication, 2014).

While the mode of giving may be more diverse than ever, selling a solution as an actual physical product is a new one. The closer relationship between charity and consumerism has led to some uncomfortable situations for some agencies, whether Save the Children UK defending itself against too cosy a relationship with its sponsors, or the relative taste of Product RED objects (an iPod Air case, a red skateboard, a Galaxy bar) or even whether Make Poverty History wristbands were made in factories with poor labour records (McCormack, 2005).

If charities become just another product to sell, not only do they become com-petitive with each other (which charity is fashionable to support), the communi-tarian ethos is diluted.

6. IMAGERY REMAINS A PROBLEM

In 2013, the DEC appeal for the Philippines centred on a single boy, "Joshua", alone, bearing scars from the typhoon, and with a scene of devastation in the background. Brendan Paddy of the DEC had said he felt uncomfortable about the use of such an image but that "Joshua", when approached by a journalist, had felt empowered by the use of such an image (Kageura, 2013).

As Paddy Coulter (chapter 6) makes clear, from many years ago the imagery and approach of NGO advertising was often patriarchal and based on shock fac-tor, after the intervention of Cecil Jackson-Cole and Harold Sumption. These two imported commercial business practices into fundraising and the result was often crass, without due respect for the dignity of those involved. The emphasis was on striking images and punchy copy.

Coulter goes on to describe how increasing concern over the approach to fundraising and the need for public education post-Ethiopia culminated in the writing of the Red Cross Code in 1992.

But what has improved since then? Coulter is concerned that contemporary advertisements for some of the best-known agencies are falling into old habits—that intervention is risk-free, with easy solutions which do not point out the important contribution that partners on the ground make. This is echoed in Dogra's content analysis (chapter 8) which found many agencies in the year 2005–2006 relied on pictures of children (an infantilisation of the majority world experience) and gave the impression that the developed world held the answer to the problems the survivors of such disasters faced. Is that so far different from Sumption's adverts of the 1950s and 1960s?

Seu's research (chapter 12) found that while audiences were initially arrested by striking and dramatic images—and might very well donate—without educative information as well, this could lead very quickly to a disconnect and a feeling that all the charity/charities were after were donations, particularly if the fundraising materials were thought to be manipulative to evoke an emotional response. Advertisements that could induce empathy in viewers were far more likely to be successful, as opposed to those which offered solutions and actions.

Many NGOs are unhappy about the complexities and there are ongoing tensions, contradictions, and lack of coherence in their communications with the public, as Orgad points out (chapter 9). Reassurance and comfort take precedence over disruption of the social order with the result that there is often a lack of clarity and truthfulness about the very factors that may lead a humanitarian crisis to come about.

7. THE USE OF SOCIAL MEDIA HAS BEEN HARNESSED DESTRUCTIVELY AS WELL AS CONSTRUCTIVELY IN HUMANITARIAN CRISES

Wide use of mobile phones has fuelled normative expectations of communication in a crisis. In many situations this has beneficial effects as outlined by Meier and Wall and Reid (chapters 15 and 18).

But these new technologies have also been widely used in humanitarian crises to promulgate violence and fear. This phenomenon was documented widely at the time of the 2007–2008 Kenyan elections in which SMS and blogs in particular were used to spread inter-tribal hate speech. The crowd-sourced website Ushahidi (Swahili for *witness*) was set up in response to this in order to collate eyewitness accounts of post-election violence.

Coverage of the Arab Spring and then of the Syrian conflict was often heavily reliant on user-generated content because journalists had limited access to the areas where the news was happening. Verification processes had to be quickly professionalised to deal with the sheer volume of content, and at times the propaganda element of such content was not fully appreciated by journalists. Activists also learned how to manipulate the story for their own benefit; an arresting 2012 report by Channel 4 News from Homs about the video activist Omar Talawi revealed how the veejays were embellishing a report by burning a tyre behind them (http://www.channel4.com/news/syrias-video-journalists-battle-to-tell-the-truth).

But the growth of social networking and smartphones with high-quality video has altered the way that those with a message of terror to spread now have increasing ways to do so.

In the early days after 9/11, "martyrdom" videos were seen as a key part of the process of preparing an act of terror and making sure its effect spread. There was widespread debate—and often condemnation—if broadcasters such as Al Jazeera transmitted those messages.

Twitter, text, and video changed this. Here in the UK, after the murder of Lee Rigby in Woolwich in 2013, one of the killers, Michael Adebolajo, handed out a pre-prepared written statement at the scene and also made remarks filmed on a mobile phone by a bystander in the hopes that this would go viral via social networks such as YouTube and Twitter, as well as being scooped up by the mainstream media. Instead of engaging journalists, they engaged passersby and got them to do their work for them.

The media regulator Ofcom later warned the major broadcasters to learn lessons after "looping" mobile phone footage, showing one of the killers (Sweney, 2014). But the perpetrators had achieved what they set out to do: this was a murder committed in the public eye to be spread via social networks.

It has often been said that when the mainstream news media is absent from a field of conflict, the most inhumane acts can pass unnoticed. However, recent coverage by news media is not a guarantee that dreadful acts will not happen again. What has been particularly concerning is the use of social media in order to ensure mainstream media cover the most grim of stories—in particular the deliberate targeting of humanitarian workers and journalists.

At the time of writing (September 2014), Islamic State, also known as ISIS and ISIL, has released three professionally edited videos purporting to show the beheading of two American journalists, James Foley and Steven Sotloff, and David Haines, a British aid worker—while using another hostage, freelancer John Cantlie to seemingly present videos espousing their cause.

Unlike previous videos emanating from militants of hostage killings of humanitarian workers, journalists and civilians—such as Margaret Hassan, Daniel Pearl, and Ken Bigley—the Islamic State videos are increasingly slick with high production values. The videos of Foley, Sotloff, and Haines use multiple cameras, professional microphones and sophisticated editing techniques, interspersing the unfolding events with footage of leaders such as David Cameron and Barack Obama. The captives are all dressed in the orange jumpsuits identified with Guantanamo Bay.

The earlier hostage videos were so gruesome that sharing was limited and were narrated in Arabic rather than English. But the most recent films appear to be designed to have wider coverage in the West. And if that is the intention, Islamic State have succeeded, with front pages dominated (at the time of writing) every time a video is released.

After the announcement of Sotloff's death, Al Jazeera PR put out the following tweet:

> We respect Steven Sotloff and won't air images of his death, or him in a jumpsuit. We suggest all media do the same. #ISISmediaBlackout (Al Jazeera PR (@AlJazeera) September 2, 2014).

The same calls were heard after the death of Haines. And while some newspapers did focus on the kind of images that the Sotloff and Haines family would prefer, most of the mainstream media found the imagery too compelling—and indeed often compared them with Foley's appearance, handing IS the result that they wanted.

This becomes, as Cottle puts it in chapter 1, "image wars": when the use of such media techniques becomes implicated in the acts of violence. The fears that non-reporting of conflict in the past allowed inhumane acts to occur has now become disturbingly twisted as the presence of media—social media, then re-mediated by mainstream media—fuels such barbarous acts.

CONCLUSION

In September 1943, famine engulfed Calcutta in what Ian Stephens, then editor of the Indian publication the *Statesman* described as "slow dispirited noiseless apathy" 1966, p. 184). When he started to comprehend the suffering that was happening, he found official denials and cover-ups all around him. Cables leaving Bengal were watched carefully, and all "such meaningful words as famine, corpse, starvation were methodically struck out" by (India's) central government (p. 187) and the Bengal government stopped putting out mortality statistics. For two months the *Statesman* waged a campaign to allow the truth about the famine to get out. Yet even so, estimates are that between 7 and 10 million people died of starvation, malnutrition, and disease out of a population of 60 million, during 1943–1944.

On 12 January 2010, an earthquake measuring 7.3 on the Richter scale hit Haiti at 16.53 local time. At 17.00 Haitian Fredo Dupoux posted one of the first recorded tweets: "Oh shiet [sic] heavy earthquake right now! In Haiti", along with tweeter @FutureHaiti who said "Earthquake 7 Richter scale just happening #Haiti" (Macleod, 2010).

On the surface the difference between the cover-up of the Bengal Famine nearly seventy years earlier and the extensive coverage of the Haiti earthquake could not appear more stark: one characterised by no information or disinformation; the other by "ordinary" people getting volumes of material out about the trauma.

The communication of humanitarian issues has undergone profound changes in recent years, and the introduction of new technologies has aided this. But it would be naïve not to realise that, alongside the opportunities, there are grave problems exposed.

For journalists, many working in increasingly squeezed financially situations, the temptation in crisis stories to rely increasingly on social media accounts and film/photos provided by either onlookers or humanitarians—at least initially—is huge. But there are dangers here. While much of social media rumour is quickly self-corrected, alongside the deluge of genuine pictures of 2012's Hurricane Sandy, an analysis of the top 100 most-tweeted picture stories for the *Guardian* datablog showed that 15% were fakes (Burgess, Vis, & Bruns, 2012). And following the Boston Marathon bombings, social media tried to crowdsource the identifying of the perpetrators with a terrifying lack of success (Shih, 2013.) While the growth of agencies like Storyful and the aftermath of stories such as Boston have meant that journalists are increasingly cautious about the use of such material, there is still much unverified material used. Journalists need to continue to be transparent about the material they use and give the credit to citizen journalists if they reproduce such material.

For humanitarians, the attraction of the idea that Big Data could rapidly transform the dispersal of aid is huge; but while there are many exciting steps forward in this area, the best use of such computer models will only come about with clear leadership and protocols to ensure it is deployed most successfully. Technology alone is no substitute for experience.

To make sure that the connection between donor and agency and beneficiary remains strong, aid agencies need to challenge themselves about the fundraising images they use. While most would agree past tasteless and patriarchal imagery, promulgating the idea of a dependent majority world 'saved' by rich white Westerners, is recognised as unacceptable, many of those involved in this book warned that agencies were still using imagery and text that portrayed a majority world in an infantalised and simplistic way—combined with an approach which consumerises the very act of giving.

Finally, journalists and aid agencies have worked together for years to try to bring to public attention those stories that the public should hear: often those in the most obscure part of the world. While criticisms have been made of the symbiotic relationship these two groups have had, at its most positive it is clear that by working together, journalists and NGOs have brought some of the most important humanitarian stories to the public domain. What is worrying is that in the determination to share these stories, journalists and aid workers have themselves become not just storytellers but an integral image of the story. The increased targeting of both by groups such as Islamic State raises questions of the safety of both aid workers and journalists and the ability for both to do their jobs. But most of all it shows the sad fact that one of the key changes in humanitarian communication is the fact that they are now seen as valid targets.

BIBLIOGRAPHY

Beck, U. (2009). *World at risk*. Cambridge, MA: Polity.

Benthall, J. (1993). *Disasters, relief and the media*. London: I. B. Tauris.

Burgess, J., Vis, F., & Bruns, A. (2012, 6 November). Hurricane Sandy: The most tweeted pictures. *The Guardian*. Retrieved 14 September 2014, from http://www.guardian.co.uk/news/datablog/gallery/2012/nov/06/hurricane-sandy-tweeted-pictures.

Byrne, K. (2010). Social media plays growing role in aid world. Thomson Reuters Foundation. Retrieved 4 July 2013, from http://www.trust.org/item/?map=social-media-plays-growing-role-in-aid-world.

Cooper, G. (2007). *Anyone here survived a wave, speak English and got a mobile? Aid agencies, the media and reporting disasters since the tsunami*. Oxford: Nuffield College.

Cooper, G. (2013). *Heading for a Disaster? Ethical and Legal Questions Raised when Mainstream Media Use User-Generated Content to report Humanitarian Crises*. Conference Paper, International Association for Media and Communication Research, Dublin, Ireland.

Cottle, S. (2009). *Global crisis reporting: Journalism in the global age*. Berkshire, UK: Open University.

Cottle, S. (2011). Taking global crises in the news seriously: Notes from the dark side of globalization. *Global Media and Communication, 7*(2), 77–95.

Cottle, S. (2013). Environmental conflict in a global, media age: Beyond dualisms. In L. Lester & B. Hutchins (Eds.), *Environmental conflict and the media* (pp. 13–28). New York: Peter Lang.

Crowley, J., & Chan, J. (2011). *Disasters Relief 2.0. Information Sharing in Humanitarian Emergencies*. United Nations Foundation. Retrieved from http://hhi.harvard.edu/sites/default/files/publications/publications%20-%20crisis%20mapping%20-%20disaster%202.0.pdf.

Duffield, M. (2001). *Global governance and the new wars*. London: Zed.

Duffield, M. (2007). *Development, security and unending war*. Cambridge, MA: Polity.

Evans, M. (2010, 15 January). Haitian earthquake dominates Twitter. Sysomos. Retrieved from http://blog.sysomos.com/2010/01/15/haitian-earthquake-dominates-twitter/.

Franks, S. (2013, 11 October). Why Michael Buerk's 1984 famine report from Ethiopia entered media history. BBC. Retrieved 11 September 2014, from http://www.bbc.co.uk/blogs/blogcollegeofjournalism/posts/Why-Michael-Buerks-1984-famine-report-from-Ethiopia-entered-media-history.

Glocer, T. (2006). We Media Speech. Tom Glocer's Blog. Retrieved 20 May 2012, from http://tomglocer.com/blogs/sample_weblog/archive/2006/10/11/98.aspx.

Hanska-Ahy, M. (2013). Social media & journalism: Reporting the world through user generated content. *Participations: Journal of Audience and Reception Studies, 10*(1), 436–439.

Kageura, A. (2013, 15 January). Pictures of suffering—do we have to choose between impact and dignity? LSE. Retrieved from http://blogs.lse.ac.uk/polis/2013/12/05/pictures-of-suffering-do-we-have-to-choose-between-impact-and-dignity/.

Kaldor, M. (2007). *Human security.* Cambridge, MA: Polity.

Lin, Y., Keegan, B., Margolin, D., & Lazer, D. (2014). Rising tides or rising stars?: Dynamics of shared attention on Twitter during media events. *PLoS ONE, 9*(5), e94093. doi:10.1371/journal. pone.0094093.

Macleod, L. (2010, 22 January). New media vital in breaking Haiti earthquake. BBC. Retrieved 16 May, 2012, from http://www.bbc.co.uk/worldservice/worldagenda/2010/01/100122_worldagenda_haiti_monitoring.shtml.

McCormack, H. (2005, 30 May). Anti-poverty bands made with forced labour, Oxfam says. *The Independent.* Retrieved 25 February 2014, from http://www.independent.co.uk/news/uk/politics/antipoverty-bands-made-with-forced-labour-oxfam-says-6145147.html.

Nelson, A., Sigal, L., & Zambrano, D. (2011). *Media information systems and communities: Lessons from Haiti.* Miami, FL: Knight Foundation.

Robinson, S. (2009). "If you had been with us": Mainstream press and citizen journalists jockey for authority over the collective memory of Hurricane Katrina. *New Media and Society, 11*(5), 795–814.

Robinson, S., & De Shano, C. (2011). "Anyone can know": Citizen journalism and the interpretive community of the mainstream press. *Journalism: Theory, Practice, Criticism, 12*(3), 963–982.

Russell, A. (2007). Digital communication networks and the journalistic field: The 2005 French riots. *Critical Studies in Media Communication, 24*(4), 285–302.

Shaw, M. (2005). *The new Western way of war: Risk-transfer war and its crisis in Iraq.* Cambridge, MA: Polity.

Shih, G. (2013, 20 April). Boston Marathon bombings: How Twitter and Reddit got it wrong. *The Independent.* Retrieved 14 September 2014, from http://www.independent.co.uk/news/world/americas/boston-marathon-bombings-how-twitter-and-reddit-got-it-wrong-8581167.html.

Simpson, J. (1998). *Strange places, questionable people.* London: Pan Macmillan.

Smith, R. (2014, 1 September). The science behind the success of the ALS ice bucket challenge. Forbes. Retrieved 14 September, 2014, from http://www.forbes.com/sites/ricksmith/2014/09/01/the-science-behind-the-success-of-the-ice-bucket-challenge.

Stephens, I. (1966). *Monsoon morning.* London: Ernest Benn.

Sweney, M. (2014, 6 January). ITV and BBC told to learn lessons from Lee Rigby coverage. *The Guardian.* Retrieved from http://www.theguardian.com/media/2014/jan/06/itv-bbc-lee-rigby-murder-coverage.

Taylor, C. (2012) Sandy Really Was Instagram's Moment: 1.3m Pics Posted Mashable Retrieved 12 May 2015 from http://mashable.com/2012/11/05/sandy-instagram-record/'

Contributors

Kimberly Abbott is the Vice President of Communications at World Learning, a nonprofit organization advancing leadership through education, development, and exchange in more than 60 countries. She was previously Communications Director for North America at the International Crisis Group and a journalist at CNN. She may be contacted @kimberlymabbott.

Stuart Allan is Professor of Journalism and Communication, as well as Deputy Head of School (Academic), in the School of Journalism, Media and Cultural Studies (JOMEC) at Cardiff University, UK. Stuart's books include *Citizen Witnessing: Revisioning Journalism in Times of Crisis*, as well as the edited *The Routledge Companion to News and Journalism*, and *Citizen Journalism: Global Perspectives, Volume 2*. He is currently engaged in research examining citizens' uses of digital imagery in news reporting, while also writing a historiography of war photography. Stuart's contact information is AllanS@cardiff.ac.uk.

Lilie Chouliaraki is Professor of Media and Communications at the London School of Economics. Her research focuses on human vulnerability as a problem of communication and she has written extensively on war and conflict reporting, disaster news, humanitarian and human rights campaigns, as well as on digital media and citizen journalism. She is the author or editor of, among others, of *Discourse in Late Modernity*, with Norman Fairclough; *The Spectatorship of Suffering*; *The Soft Power of War*; *Self-mediation: New Media, Citizen-*

ship and Civic Selves; The Ironic Spectator. Solidarity in the Age of Post-human itarianism.

Paul Conneally, Head of Corporate Communications ITU—Internationa Telecommunication Union (UN's specialized agency for information an communication technology). Paul is a former journalist who moved to the International Red Cross in 1995 where he remained for 16 years, working in media and communications as well as partnerships, development, and operations During this time he worked with the telecommunications sector to develop two-way communications systems during disasters with a specific emphasis on leveraging high mobile penetration rates and engaging disaster-affected communities.

Glenda Cooper is a lecturer in journalism at City University London and a PhD researcher at the university's Centre for Law, Justice and Journalism. Before that she was a journalist working at the national level for over a decade at organisations, including the BBC, the *Independent, Daily Mail, Washington Post*, and the *Daily Telegraph*. She is the editor of *The Future of Humanitarian Reporting.* You may contact her at Glenda.cooper.1@city.ac.uk.

Simon Cottle is Professor of Media and Communications, Head of School and Director of the Mediatized Conflict Research Group in the School of Journalism, Media and Cultural Studies (JOMEC), Cardiff University. His latest books are *Disasters and the Media* (co-author), *Transnational Protests and the Media* (co-editor), and *Global Crisis Reporting: Journalism in the Global Age.* He is currently writing with colleagues *Reporting Dangerously: Journalist Killings, Intimidation and Security* and researching the history of violence and communications. He may be contacted at CottleS@cardiff.ac.uk.

Paddy Coulter is a specialist in media and development, currently working as Communications Director for the Oxford Poverty & Human Development Initiative (OPHI) in the Oxford Department of International Development. He was previously Director of Studies at the Reuters Institute for the Study of Journalism (2001–2007), Director of the International Broadcasting Trust (1990–2001; Deputy Director, 1987–1990) and Head of Media for Oxfam (1982–1987). Paddy is an Associate Fellow of Green Templeton College at the University of Oxford, Visiting Fellow at the University of Bournemouth Media School, and co-author with Cathy Baldwin of 'Digital Deprivation: New Media, Civil Society and Sustainability', in *Civil Society in the Age of Monitory Democracy.* He may be contacted at paddy.coulter@gtc.ox.ac.uk.

Nandita Dogra, a freelance academic, is the author of *Representations of Global Poverty: Aid, Development and International NGOs.* An experienced practitioner in development and communications, she has taught in the Departments of Media & Communications and Social Policy at the London School of Economics (LSE), UK. She has also been an ESRC postdoctoral fellow at Goldsmiths, University of London. She holds an MA in Economics from Bhopal, India, and an MSc in NGO Management, and a PhD in Social Policy from the LSE. Her email is nanditadogra@hotmail.com.

Suzanne Franks is a former BBC TV journalist who worked on programmes such as *Newsnight* and *Panorama*. She later founded an independent production company for which she made several films about Africa. She is now Professor of Journalism at City University, London, and she also teaches a course on Humanitarian Communication. She has published widely on international news coverage and her latest book is *Reporting Disasters: Famine, Aid, Politics and the Media*.

Randolph Kent (PhD) was a senior UN official responsible for humanitarian coordination in Ethiopia, Kosovo, Rwanda Somalia, and Sudan from 1987 to 2003. He joined King's College, London, in 2003, where he founded and directed the Humanitarian Futures Programme in 2005, and subsequently became Director at King's College, London, of the Planning from the Futures project, with the Overseas Development Institute and Tufts University.

Alice Klein began her career in journalism in local newspapers before moving to the *Daily Telegraph*. She later freelanced for a range of international media outlets from Eastern and Southern Africa. With an MSc in Globalisation and International Development, she has worked for various NGOs including Médecins Sans Frontières, UNICEF, and Save the Children. She co-founded Radar in 2012.

Patrick Meier (PhD) is an internationally recognized thought leader on humanitarian technology and innovation. He is the author of the book *Digital Humanitarians: How Big Data is Changing the Face of Humanitarian Response* and he also writes the influential blog iRevolutions, which has received more than 1.5 million hits. Follow him on Twitter at @PatrickMeier.

Shani Orgad is Associate Professor at the Department of Media and Communications, LSE. Her areas of interest include representation and globalization, suffering, war and conflict in the media, gender and the media and health communication. She explores these issues in her books *Media Representation and the Global Imagination* and *Storytelling Online: Talking Breast Cancer on the Internet*, a research project on humanitarian communication which she has co-directed, and various journal articles. You may contact her at s.s.orgad@lse.ac.uk

Kyla Reid is the Head of the Disaster Response Programme at GSMA Mobile for Development and a Research Associate at the Justice Peace and Security Research Programme at the London School of Economics. Kyla's professional and research interests include communication ecologies, partnerships and technologies in humanitarian emergencies, and post-conflict justice. She has led fieldwork and projects in East Africa, Asia, and the Middle East. Her latest article (co-authored with Tim Allen) is "Justice at the Margins: Witches Poisoners, and Social Accountability in Northern Uganda" in *Medical Anthropology*. Email: k.reid@lse.ac.uk.

Richard Sambrook is Professor of Journalism and Director of the Centre for Journalism in the School of Journalism, Media and Cultural Studies at Cardiff University. Previously, he was a journalist at the BBC for 30 years, producing and editing many national radio and TV programmes, and he was on the board of the BBC for a decade as Director of Sport, Director of News, and finally Director of Global News and the World Service. He is also Chair of INSIUK—the International News Safety Institute—which supports the safety of journalists reporting around the world and is currently writing with colleagues *Reporting Dangerously: Journalist Killings, Intimidation and Security*. You may contact him at sambrookrj@cardiff.ac.uk.

Liz Scarff is Director of Fieldcraft Studios—an agency working on the intersection of social media, technology, media and social change. A former national journalist she has produced pioneering projects for the world's leading charities and organisations including Save the Children, UNESCO, Marie Curie Cancer Care and Sightsavers. Her work has won awards from the Guardian Digital Innovation Awards and SOcial Buzz Awards, and has been featured in the *Guardian*, Mashable, TEDX and the *Telegraph* among others. Find Liz on Twitter: @LizScarff.

Bruna Seu is Reader in the Dept. of Psychosocial Studies at Birbeck, University of London, and a practicing psychoanalytic psychotherapist. Her main research interests are social responsibility and prosocial behaviour in the context of human rights violations and humanitarian crises. Her latest book, *Passivity Generation: Human Rights and Everyday Morality*, proposes a psychosocial reformulation of public (un)responsiveness to the knowledge of human rights violations. For the last four years, in collaboration with Shani Orgad (LSE), she has investigated audiences' responses to humanitarian communication through a research grant from the Leverhulme Trust.

Imogen Wall is a freelance communications consultant who focusses on policy, advocacy, and use of communications technology in disaster response. A former

BBC journalist, she specialises in the theory and practice of communication as a form of assistance for affected people and has designed and implemented projects to this end in a number of subsequent emergencies including Haiti, Sudan, East Timor, and the Philippines. She is currently advising the DfID response to Ebola. She is the author of a number of policy papers, and has worked for organisations including UNOCHA, UNDP, Save the Children, BBC Media Action, the World Bank, and DfID. She is based in London.

Claire Wardle until very recently was the Senior Social Media Officer for UNHCR. She is now the Research Director at the Tow Center for Digital Journalism at Columbia University. Previously she was a Tow Fellow at Columbia Journalism School where she led a research project on the integration of UGC by global news organisations (usergeneratednews.towcenter.org). She is an expert on UGC and verification, and co-founded the Eyewitness Media Hub, a research and outreach initiative aimed at improving how publishers work with socially sourced content. In a past life she was a lecturer at the Cardiff School of Journalism, Media and Cultural Studies.

Index

Simon Cottle, *General Editor*

From climate change to the war on terror, financial meltdowns to forced migrations, pandemics to world poverty, and humanitarian disasters to the denial of human rights, these and other crises represent the dark side of our globalized planet. They are endemic to the contemporary global world and so too are they highly dependent on the world's media.

Each of the specially commissioned books in the *Global Crises and the Media* series examines the media's role, representation, and responsibility in covering major global crises. They show how the media can enter into their constitution, enacting them on the public stage and thereby helping to shape their future trajectory around the world. Each book provides a sophisticated and empirically engaged understanding of the topic in order to invigorate the wider academic study and public debate about the most pressing and historically unprecedented global crises of our time.

For further information about the series and submitting manuscripts, please contact:

Dr. Simon Cottle
Cardiff School of Journalism
Cardiff University, Room 1.28
The Bute Building, King Edward VII Ave.
Cardiff CF10 3NB
United Kingdom
CottleS@cardiff.ac.uk

To order other books in this series, please contact our Customer Service Department at:

(800) 770-LANG (within the U.S.)
(212) 647-7706 (outside the U.S.)
(212) 647-7707 FAX

Or browse online by series at:

www.peterlang.com